CLASSICAL
LITERARY CRITICISM

CLASSICAL

LITERARY CRITICISM

Translations and Interpretations

EDITED BY

ALEX PREMINGER

LEON GOLDEN

O. B. HARDISON, JR.

KEVIN KERRANE

FREDERICK UNGAR PUBLISHING CO.

NEW YORK

Library of Congress Cataloging in Publication Data
Main entry under title:

Classical literary criticism.

Abridged ed. of: Classical and medieval literary
criticism. 1974.
Bibliography: p.
Includes index.
1. Criticism—History. I. Preminger, Alex.
II. Classical and medieval literary criticism.
PN86.C57   1984   801'.95   83-24196
ISBN 0-8044-6664-5 (pbk.)

ACKNOWLEDGMENTS

Acknowledgment is gratefully made to the following who have granted permission to use copyrighted material.

Clarendon Press, for "Ion" and selections from "Gorgias," "Laws," "Phaedrus," "Republic," and "Symposium" from *The Dialogues of Plato*, tr. by B. Jowett, 4th ed. (Oxford 1953); and for *"Longinus" on Sublimity*, tr. by D. A. Russell, copyright 1965 by Oxford University Press.

Mrs. Norman J. DeWitt, for translation of Horace's *Ars Poetica* by Norman J. DeWitt.

Drama Survey, for translation of Horace's *Ars Poetica* by Norman J. DeWitt in the October 1961 issue, by permission of John D. Hurrell on behalf of *Drama Survey*.

Faber and Faber Ltd., for passages from Plotinus: *The Enneads*, 4th ed., copyright 1969 Faber and Faber Ltd. and copyright 1969 Random House, reprinted by permission of Faber and Faber Ltd.

Harvard University Press, for selections from Book X of Quintilian, *Institutio Oratoria*, tr. H. E. Butler and reprinted by permission of the publisher and The Loeb Classical Library.

Richmond Lattimore, for translation from Aristophanes, *The Frogs*.

Macmillan & Co., Ltd., for chapters X-XIII of Dionysius of Halicarnassus, *On Literary Composition*, tr. by W. Rhys Roberts and reprinted by permission of the publisher.

Prentice-Hall, Inc., for the translation of the *Poetics* from Leon Golden and O. B. Hardison, Jr., *Aristotle's Poetics: A Translation and Commentary for Students of Literature*, copyright 1968. By permission of Prentice-Hall, Inc., Englewood Cliffs, New Jersey.

Random House, Inc., for passages from *The Enneads*, 4th ed., by Plotinus, copyright 1969 Faber and Faber Ltd. and copyright 1969 Random House (Pantheon Books, a Division of Random House, Inc.). All rights reserved.

University of Michigan Press, for an extract from Aristophanes, *The Frogs*, tr. by Richmond Lattimore, copyright 1962 by William Arrowsmith.

University of Toronto Press, for selection from *A Greek Critic: Demetrius on Style*, by G.M.A. Grube, by permission of University of Toronto Press. Copyright, Canada, 1961 by University of Toronto Press.

CONTENTS

PREFACE

One of the controlling premises of this anthology is that the truest history of literary theory is a history of major documents. The opening sentence of our general introduction—"Classical criticism was born of classical philosophy"—reflects our belief that the most significant critical works embody sustained analysis and argumentative rigor, and that the methods a critic uses to arrive at his conclusions can be as important as the conclusions themselves. Consequently, we have tried to avoid relying on short or truncated selections. We have focused on influential texts, reprinting whole chapters and even complete works whenever possible. In addition to works which are significant in themselves and seminal in the history of poetics, we have included texts which, though generally neglected, are historically important and are genuine contributions to critical thought.

It was our aim to provide accurate and readable translations. For Plato, we have used Jowett's translation, still unsurpassed for its fluid and easy style. On the other hand, Leon Golden's translation of Aristotle's *Poetics* is a new one, based on a review of all the important Greek texts from Bywater to Kassel.

Our major aim has been to provide interpretation in depth. Thus a considerable part of this volume has been given over to general and individual introductions, notes, an annotated bibliography, to a glossary of proper names, and an index.

The selection from each critic is prefaced by an introductory essay, prepared by Leon Golden, which places the critic's work in the context of its time, summarizes its substance and method, assesses its influences on later poetics, and points out significant problems. We have also provided a "General Introduction," emphasizing larger historical movements in criticism, and commenting on critics and texts not represented in this collection.

The result is, we hope, something substantially more than a conventional anthology. While one of its functions is to make available important texts, another is to provide the framework of an interpretation of the history of classical criticism.

We are grateful for advice, concrete suggestions, and criticism received from Professors Gerald F. Else, the late Procope S. Costas, and Roy Arthur

Swanson. We also wish to thank Professor Antoinette Ciolli for her contribution, Frances McConney for typing the manuscript, and Calliope Scumas, formerly of Frederick Ungar Publishing Co., for her invaluable assistance. Finally, we would like to acknowledge with appreciation a grant from The City University of New York Faculty Research Award Program, which helped to expedite this work.

THE EDITORS

CLASSICAL
LITERARY CRITICISM

Leon Golden

GENERAL INTRODUCTION

Classical literary criticism was born of classical philosophy. In the fourth century B.C., through systematic investigations by Plato and Aristotle into the nature of artistic imitation and specific poetic techniques, Western literary criticism first emerged as a distinct and rigorous inquiry. Much of the enduring influence of classical criticism derives from this philosophical orientation—a comprehensiveness and complexity in practical analysis, and a vocabulary and perspective for discussing the value of literature itself among the manifold activities of man.

But the liveliness and force of classical criticism are also embodied in the writings of numerous poets, scholars, and rhetoricians who—without benefit of a clear critical terminology or an explicit theory of literature—offered opinions on matters of style, pronounced judgment on particular poems, and struggled to articulate some larger questions about literary art. This vitality is clearly evident in the stage of "proto-criticism" that preceded the work of Plato and Aristotle. The poets themselves, from Homer to Aristophanes, in exploring issues relating to their own art, dealt with topics that were to preoccupy the later theorists. Although this early criticism was generally intuitive and unsystematic, and can only be pieced together from scattered references in literary works, it is a key to understanding many of the premises and themes of the whole classical tradition in criticism.

GREEK PROTO-CRITICISM

The earliest classical criticism focuses on the social role of the poet. He is viewed as a moral teacher, and as thus in need of occasional censorship. But most often he is simply venerated—usually through the claim that he is protected and inspired by a divine muse, who enables him to please his audience through stories and words that convey a unique kind of knowledge. This claim, suggesting man's early identification of the poet's role with that of priest and prophet, is close in spirit to the modern romantic image of the artist—and it may reflect the basic aesthetic insight that the workings of imagination are mysterious, irreducible to sheer logical explanation. At any rate, when this theme found its fullest classical expression in Plato's dialogue *Ion,* it must al-

3

ready have been a commonplace of critical thinking, for it appears explicitly in the writings of Homer, Hesiod, and Pindar.

Homer (ca. 8th century B.C.) addresses the muse in his own poetic invocations, but his most striking references to inspiration appear in his characterizations of two poets in the *Odyssey*. In Book VIII Homer describes the banquet which King Alcinous holds in honor of Odysseus. Here the bard Demodocus is presented as a man cherished by the muse: although she took away his sight, she granted him the sweet gift of song. Homer later says that all men owe honor to the poets, for they are dear to the muse, who puts upon their lips the ways of life. In Book XXII (344–49) Phemios the minstrel, pleading for his life amid the slaughter of the suitors, tells Odysseus that a god shaped the songs which it is his gift to sing.

Similarly, Hesiod (8th or 7th century B.C.) claims in the invocation to his *Theogony* that the muses, daughters of Zeus, taught him his lovely songs. He credits them with having given him a divine voice to sing of the future and the past, and he asserts that inspired poetry can give a pleasure so great as to charm away the melancholy of any man. Hesiod's own poetry is far more didactic than Homer's, dealing less with heroic legends than with theology (stories of the gods) and practical instruction. Thus he seems led to express an ethical concern that the poet can relate falsehoods in the form of truths. This concern, which later assumed great importance in the Platonic approach to art, is also reflected in the writings of such early classical moralists as Solon and Xenophanes (6th century B.C.). Xenophanes, for example, scorns the anthropomorphic gods of the epics, objecting to the presentation of theft, lying, and adultery as divine attributes (Fragment II).

Pindar (518–438 B.C.) also expresses moral criticism of certain episodes in the epics, claiming that Homer's vast artistic skill makes some of his poetry all the more capable of leading men astray (*Nemean* VII.22). "Inspiration," he says, must be tempered by "accuracy" (*Pythian* IV.279). Usually, however, Pindar discusses the poet's role in much more positive terms. In *Pythian* (I.41–42) he asserts that the gods provide the means for achieving every excellence, and he includes here wisdom, might of hand, and skill of speech. Elsewhere he indicates his agreement with Hesiod's view of poetry as a healing agent (*Olympian* II.14–15; *Pythian* I.6–14; *Nemean* IV.1–5). He suggests that the poet serves as a mediator between men and the gods who are so often indifferent to them, and as the agent who makes eternal the glory won by men in athletic contests.

Aristophanes (ca. 450–385 B.C.) was much more concerned with the social and political aspects of poetry than with the question of its divine origin. Eleven of his plays have survived, and nearly all of them investigate with brilliant and often sardonic humor the disintegration of the quality of Athenian life in the latter decades of the fifth century B.C. Aristophanes' stance is that of a social and political conservative who looks back to a "golden age": the austere, salubrious morality of a predominantly rural Greek culture. This conservatism guides Aristophanes' caricatures of sophistic and militaristic mentalities, and also leads him to use his satire for the purpose of literary criticism. Aristophanes often focuses on contemporary poetry, attacking literary trends which, in his opinion, were operating together with the sophistic movement and political demogoguery to subvert the integrity of society.

One of Aristophanes' consistent targets was Euripides. In the *Acharnians* (393–489) Euripides is presented as a destructive realist, lowering tragedy from an ideal to an ordinary level. In *Peace* Aristophanes begins by ridiculing Euripides for excessive experimentation in stage spectacle. But the *Frogs*, written shortly after Euripides' death, offers a more balanced assessment: Euripides, although ultimately judged as inferior to Aeschylus, is clearly perceived as a great poet. The plot of the *Frogs* involves nothing less than a venture in practical literary criticism, for it turns upon a contest for the Chair of Tragedy in the Underworld: Dionysus, god of tragedy, attempts to judge between the idealism and grand style of Aeschylus and the realism and novelty of Euripides. This play is the high point of Greek proto-criticism. It abounds in critical insights and sharply focuses on one of the most important and persistent problems in the evaluation of literature as it portrays the conflicting views of Aeschylus and Euripides. For Aeschylus represents the position, favored by Aristophanes himself, that poets are ethical teachers and that art has a moral purpose to fulfil. By contrast, Euripides represents the view that the essential goal of art is the illumination of reality without regard to moral or ethical consideration.

PLATO AND ARISTOTLE

Aristophanes' concern with art as a social influence anticipates much of the work of Plato (ca. 429–347 B.C.). But Plato's writings on poetry constitute the emergence of proto-criticism into true literary criticism. His position is far more sophisticated than Aristophanes': his preoccupation with the moral force of literature cannot be isolated from a larger, more "philosophical," view of the nature of art. In Plato's work, literary criticism became a discipline, an intellectual enterprise requiring analytical rigor and sustained argumentation.

Much of Plato's literary criticism is marked by a strong hostility to art. First, as a metaphysician Plato argues that an artistic fiction is an "imitation," one degree removed from real experience, and thus two degrees removed from the ultimate reality which is ideal. Since for Plato the pursuit of this ultimate truth is the most significant of all human activities, he is extremely cautious about the "knowledge" that art conveys. Second, as a moralist Plato argues that poetry feeds and waters the passions, elements of personality that need to be

controlled and disciplined by reason. Viewing the epics as repositories of dangerous moral examples, Plato is finally led to declare a "feud" between poetry and
philosophy.

Once the distance between art and reality is recognized, however, Plato
can find a positive role for proper kinds of literary imitation. Abundant evidence
can be found in Plato's dialogues (themselves works of art) to demonstrate
that certain metaphors, myths, and fictions represent necessary stages in the
gradual progress men must make as they travel from spiritual darkness to
spiritual light. Moreover, Plato's apparent acceptance of the ancient notion of
divine inspiration would elevate the status of poetry. Although Plato's most
sustained discussion of inspiration, the dialogue *Ion,* may have ironic overtones,
the speaker Socrates decides that the real power possessed by the rhapsode Ion
must derive from a sacred "madness" imparted by the muse.

Aristotle (384–322 B.C.) began his philosophical career as one of Plato's
students, but in almost every area of intellectual inquiry he eventually diverged
radically from Plato, even while addressing himself to the very questions that
Plato raised. Aristotle's literary criticism follows this pattern. Although Plato
is never mentioned by name in Aristotle's *Poetics,* Plato's critical position seems
to be used as a point of departure. Like Plato, Aristotle defines poetic art as a
kind of "imitation," but he effectively rids this term of any pejorative connotations. Aristotle's orientation is aesthetic: he considers an artistic imitation
as the creation of an object with its own ontology and its own unique internal
logic. Moreover, he emphasizes the capacity of art to illuminate human existence.
In Chapter 4 of the *Poetics* he declares that the pleasure man obtains from all
forms of artistic imitation is predicated on a process of learning. In Chapter 9
Aristotle argues that poetry is more significant and more philosophical than
history: poetry aims at universals, whereas history is concerned with particulars.
For Aristotle poetry has an essentially intellectual goal, the unified presentation
of insights into human action.

Aristotle's controversial term *katharsis* (Chapter 6) seems directly related to his theory of imitation. Scholars have traditionally interpreted it as an
emotional process—for example, the "purging" of the audience's emotions of
pity and fear through their witnessing of an imitation in tragic form, the essential pleasure being a sense of relief from oppressive feelings. But Aristotle's
statement in Chapter 4 that a kind of "learning" is the essential pleasure produced by artistic imitations suggests an alternate, and more positive, interpretation. It is possible to render *katharsis* as "intellectual clarification," thus confirming a notion of art as illuminatory. Aristotle may have meant that a tragedy
gives clarity to incidents involving pity and fear, that the dramatist's particular
insight into the human condition becomes the "theme" around which the work
is organized.

The relationship of art and morality is not discussed explicitly in the

Poetics. In the treatment of the ideal tragic hero in Chapter 13 certain moral factors are relevant, but on the whole the *Poetics* deals strictly with questions of artistic effectiveness—emphasizing "probability" (internal coherence) rather than fidelity to some external norm. Aristotle does speak about the relation of art to morality in the *Politics,* where certain types of artistic imitation are accepted or excluded from the educational process in the state, on the basis of whether or not they contribute to social goals. This is an issue which Aristotle places outside the province of literary criticism itself, and he maintains a far stricter distinction between the aesthetic and ethical realms than any other critic of the classical era—or, for that matter, any Western theorist up to the time of Immanuel Kant.

Aristotle views poetry as a craft which the artist must master to achieve success. Thus the *Poetics* deals extensively with all aspects of the art of poetry, from larger philosophical and psychological questions to specific discussions of plot, characterization, and diction. This emphasis on the technical aspect of art was to reappear in the rhetorical orientation of later classical critics, but it is given its fullest and most aesthetic expression in the *Poetics.*

Unlike Plato, Aristotle has little to say about inspiration. His one reference to it in the *Poetics* appears in a disputed passage in Chapter 17, where he says either that the poet must be talented *or* mad, or that the poet must be talented *rather than* mad. The first interpretation might be related to the theme of divine "furor" described in Plato's *Ion,* but the idea of "talent" could also stand as a rationalized version of inspiration. Clearly Aristotle recognized, as did the early proto-critics, the existence of some innate power, beyond the diligent study of the rules of art, by which an individual artist performs effectively. Nevertheless, Aristotle's major emphasis remains on poetry as a *technê,* a body of knowledge governed by observable principles.

HELLENISTIC AND HORATIAN CRITICISM

Unfortunately, Aristotle's *Poetics* exerted no observable influence in the classical period. It appears likely that the treatise was unavailable to subsequent critics; but even if it had been known, the practical and didactic temper of later classical criticism would probably have insured the rejection of its aesthetic thesis. From the third to the first century B.C., as Greek culture itself became more diffuse, literary criticism—as distinguished (which it rarely was) from the study of rhetoric—belonged primarily to two groups: philosophical moralists and professional scholars.

The followers of the Epicurean school, like the members of the Platonic Academy, were hostile to poetry, considering it an emotional danger to the potentially wise man. One late Epicurean, however, offered a surprising alternative to this view: Philodemus of Gadara (ca. 110–40/35 B.C.) was himself a poet, and his fragmentary *Poetics* provides the closest Hellenistic analogue to Aristotelian criticism. Philodemus dismissed orthodox moral criticism, arguing that a true judgment of a poem cannot separate content from form. He insisted on the poet's freedom to treat any subject, even an imaginary one, and he rejected all rigid critical "rules" which would subvert the wholeness and integrity of the work of art.

More typical of Hellenistic philosophical criticism is the Stoic school, which usually drew a firm distinction between content and form. The Stoics tended to judge literature by ethical and utilitarian standards, although they were far less negative than most Platonists and Epicureans. Their main distinction was a penchant for allegorical interpretation.

The use of allegorizing as a critical method had begun early in classical criticism, perhaps with Theagenes of Rhegium (6th century B.C.), and it was occasionally used by the Sophists. It could serve as a defense for morally questionable poetry—for example, in taking the quarrels among Homer's gods as a cosmological allegory of the contention of the physical elements in nature. Plato, in Book II of the *Republic,* refers explicitly to this technique, but declares it useless: unsophisticated readers, especially impressionable youths, would still be vulnerable to bad moral examples as presented in poetry. The Stoics, however, carried out critical allegorizing on a large scale, using it not only to "rescue" allegedly dangerous poetry, but also to confirm specific Stoic beliefs. This trend is best illustrated by a work probably written in the first century A.D., the *Quaestiones Homericae* by Heraclitus (otherwise unknown). Treating the *Iliad* and the *Odyssey* in detail, Heraclitus extracts from the poems "hidden" meanings which adumbrate Stoic doctrines. Like other Stoic interpreters, Heraclitus not only focuses on major episodes, but also delves into stylistics: he examines figures of speech as means of conveying "secondary" meanings, and emphasizes etymologies as guides to allegorical intentions.

A more standard stylistic criticism was practiced by the Hellenistic scholars—many of them grammarians, editors of texts, and antiquarians associated with libraries and royal courts. Although little of their own criticism is extant, it is clear that they used stylistics as a means of discussing broader poetic issues. What set them apart from contemporaneous rhetorical critics was a thoroughgoing "classicism," with strong prescriptive and conservative attitudes. The scholars at Alexandria, for example, devised an elaborate schema of genres, with each poetic type governed by "rules" regarding subject matter, verse form, and diction. Their work seemed to suggest that all true examples of literary excellence lay in the Greek past; they venerated the ancients by drawing up official lists of the great models in each poetic form.

Horace (65–8 B.C.) transformed this kind of classicism into vital criticism. His eloquent and urbane *Ars Poetica* embodies a complex sensibility, balancing a classicist conservatism and penchant for rule-making with a lively wit, a tone of common sense, and an unremitting commitment to poetry as a demanding but noble craft. This sensibility is evident when Horace considers a critical commonplace of the Hellenistic period: whether natural aptitude or acquired technical skill is the more essential attribute for a poet. Horace takes a middle ground and asserts the need for both powers, but he concludes his verse-essay with a highly amusing caricature of the "mad" poet, vulgar and pompous, a disgrace both to his family name and to the discipline of literature.

Horace also takes a middle ground in regard to the ultimate value of poetry, asserting that the poet must both profit and please his audience. Both of these goals require an understanding of the truths of human nature. "Profit" for Horace means the moral advantages gained from precepts expressed in the poet's work, insights perhaps similar to those which dominate so many of Horace's own odes and humane satires. The "pleasure" Horace mentions is explicitly related to poetic realism ("verisimilitude") and decorum. Most of Horace's essay deals with techniques and procedures for achieving such literary propriety; despite his recognition of the moral aspects of art, it is this sense of poetry as a precise craft that controls the *Ars Poetica*.

RHETORICAL CRITICISM

The Alexandrian classicism on which Horace drew was deeply influenced by the study of rhetoric, but the *Ars Poetica* also owes a great debt to Roman rhetoric. The modern scholars George C. Fiske and Mary A. Grant have even approached Horace's treatise in terms of Cicero's *De Oratore* and *Orator* rather than earlier poetic treatises, pointing out such parallel topics as decorum of character, the dual goals of instruction and delight, and the emulation of great models as a means of training. This kind of overlap between poetry and rhetoric is typical of the classical tradition: both arts were usually subsumed under a larger concept—"effective expression"—and Aristotle's *Poetics* was the only major critical document of the period which did not rely heavily on rhetorical theory. The significance of classical rhetoric for the study of literature is most obvious in three areas: stylistics, moral issues, and motivation.

The discipline of rhetoric first attracted significant attention in Athens in 427 B.C., through the visit of Gorgias of Leontini. For Gorgias rhetoric was concerned only with style: as a Sophist he maintained that the effectiveness of a speech depended not on its truth value, but on the skill with which the orator used stylistic devices to appeal to his audience. Consequently, Gorgias' work emphasizes the importance of various sound effects and rhetorical figures.

The contribution to literary criticism of Gorgias' rhetorical approach was the development of a methodology and working vocabulary which could be used to study the verbal complexities of poetry. Such stylistic analysis was carried further by Aristotle's student Theophrastus (ca. 370–288/85 B.C.), Cicero (106–43 B.C.), and Demetrius (1st century B.C.?)—all of whom recommended to students of rhetoric well-chosen *poetic* illustrations of the subtle and telling ways that language can be manipulated. In fact, one justification for the study of poetry within the classical grammar curriculum was to illustrate rhetorical figures that the student might use in prose orations.

Cicero's early thinking on rhetoric is emphatically in the Gorgian tradition, and is typified by *De Inventione,* a treatise focusing on technical terms and formulae. Together with the anonymous *Rhetorica ad Herennium* (once thought erroneously to have been written by Cicero), *De Inventione* provided a terminology for the qualitative and quantitative parts of rhetoric—a terminology used extensively in the literary criticism of the Middle Ages and early Renaissance, when Aristotle's *Poetics* was unknown and the structural vocabulary of criticism was relatively impoverished.

Qualitatively, Cicero divides rhetoric into invention, arrangement, style, memory, and delivery. Quantitatively, he divides a speech into exordium, statement of the case (*narratio*), partition, proof, refutation, and peroration. He also treats rhetorical figures in detail, and discusses the three kinds of style—high, middle, and low (which the *Rhetorica ad Herennium* correlates with the various poetic genres). Demetrius, in the selection reprinted in this anthology, provides a good example of the late classical approach to high style. "Longinus," on the other hand, departs from purely stylistic rhetoric: his discussion of high style is really a discussion of a certain kind of moral excellence, and is related to a second major movement in rhetorical criticism.

The movement was begun by Gorgias' pupil Isocrates (436–338 B.C.) who, departing from the sophistic orientation of his teacher, viewed rhetoric as a subject as well as a method, a discipline involving genuine philosophical and moral principles. Isocrates insisted that the truly effective orator must possess moral goodness. Plato, in the dialogues *Gorgias* and *Phaedrus,* made clear his admiration for this idealized theory, and much of Plato's literary criticism is, for all intents and purposes, the application to literature of Isocrates' rhetorical approach—that is, literature as a means of moral education.

Cicero's mature writings on rhetoric follow this lead. In *De Oratore, Orator,* and *Brutus* he rejects the notion that rhetoric is merely a technical discipline, arguing that it has significant relationships to philosophy, law, and history, and that it requires a proper moral disposition. Other critics in the same tradition are Dionysius of Halicarnassus (1st century B.C.), Quintilian (ca. 30/35–100 A.D.), and Plutarch (before 50–after 120 A.D.). Although these writers are sensitive to stylistic issues, their real status as "rhetorical" critics derives from their view of literature as a form of ethical persuasion.

The third major force in classical rhetoric was Aristotle's systematic formulation of the principles of argumentation. Unlike the followers of Iso-crates, Aristotle denied that rhetoric has a specific subject matter and a moral basis; he viewed rhetoric as an amoral "faculty" which enables its possessor to express himself most effectively. But unlike the followers of Gorgias, Aristotle thought of style as much less important than other means of influencing an audience. In Book II of his *Rhetoric* he focuses on three major forms of rhetorical appeal: *ethos* (the character of the speaker), *pathos* (the audience's emotions), and *dianoia* (lines of logical argument). The last two of these modes of appeal are especially relevant to literature.

Although Aristotle always maintained the distinction between rhetoric (which aims at persuasion) and literature (which aims at imitation, and hence aesthetic experience), his rhetorical approach allows for a complex examination of two kinds of motivation in literature: the artist's control of audience-response, and his development of characterization within his work. In his analysis of *pathos* Aristotle treats specific emotions (such as pity, fear, and indignation), em-phasizing the stimuli most likely to arouse them. Many of Aristotle's examples constitute what Kenneth Burke has called "epitomized situations," and they seem closely related to the dynamics of drama. Aristotle's exploration of *pathos* continues with a discussion of various character-types in relation to age, fortune, and moral quality. These thumbnail sketches are offered ostensibly as abstracts of hypothetical audiences the orator may encounter, but they also provide handy formulae for literary figures, and they might be compared to Aristotle's re-quirements for dramatic characters in Chapter 15 of the *Poetics*.

Aristotle's subsequent discussion focuses on intellectual modes of appeal, and he explains twenty-eight "topics," lines of argument, that the expert orator should know how to use. Some of these topics, such as *a fortiori* argumentation, are analogous to the kinds of logic that may control a thematic work of literature, and Aristotle again seems to be offering many "epitomized situations." In ad-dition, it is noteworthy that the term *dianoia,* used to refer to the intellectual modes of appeal, is used in the *Poetics* as one of the six qualitative parts of drama: "thought," the substance and rhetorical form of the dramatic speeches. In Chapter 19 of the *Poetics* Aristotle develops this concept by referring ex-plicitly to his *Rhetoric*. His general meaning seems to be that the dramatist—in order to create "probable" speeches that reveal character, elucidate the action, and guide the audience's responses—must have a mastery of the faculty of rhetoric.

Because of its unusual approach, neither moral nor emphatically stylistic, Aristotle's *Rhetoric* exerted relatively little influence on the work of subsequent classical rhetoricians. And in the area of literary criticism its only direct effect stemmed from Aristotle's treatment (in Book I) of "epideictic" as one of the three main kinds of oratory. As contrasted with political and legal oratory, epideictic is primarily ceremonial: the listener is addressed not as a *kritēs,* a judge who must render a decision, but as a *theōros,* similar to a spectator at a play. Epideictic oratory is concerned with "praise and blame," and its character- istic form, according to Aristotle, is the encomium or panegyric. The *Rhetoric* analyzes this form in detail, recommending special techniques of amplification to the prospective orator.

Late classical rhetoricians—especially Aphthonius and Menander (4th century A.D.)—supplemented Aristotle by providing formulae for other epideictic types: the praise of seasons, cities, rulers, and so forth, with emphasis on special "occasions" (birthday, marriage, funeral). Many of the techniques of these epideictic types are similar to those of "occasional poetry," and it is significant that from the late classical period through the Middle Ages epideictic formulae were used in the teaching of poetry. They provided, in effect, standard "topics," offering rhetorical approaches to a rhetorically-oriented literature.

LONGINIAN AND NEOPLATONIC CRITICISM

"Longinus" is the name given to the unknown author of *On the Sublime,* a rhetorical treatise probably written in the first century A.D. This work typifies the classical overlap of literature and rhetoric, for "Longinus" treats sublime expression in general, instructing the prospective orator by pointing out passages of poetry worthy of emulation. His approach seems close to those of Isocrates and the mature Cicero: although most of the treatise examines such practical skills as rhetorical figures and the arrangement of words, the concept of "the sublime" goes far beyond the traditional notion of high style. "Longinus" frames his discussion by considering sublimity in philosophical terms. He insists that the true artist (poet or orator) must possess a sublime nature, a moral ele- vation, and greatness of soul. The pleasure which "Longinus" attributes to the experience of the sublime is that of "transport" (*ecstasis*), by which he seems to mean an exciting intensification of the audience's capacity for moral and intellectual judgment, a sense of elevation that unites reason and emotion.

"Longinus" was once believed to have been a third-century disciple of Plotinus, and much of *On the Sublime* is easily compatible with the Neoplatonic approach to art. The philosophical emphasis of the treatise is on a goal at once moral and aesthetic, a stage of consciousness in which truth and beauty are perceived as one. As a rhetorical theorist "Longinus" seems to be making a transition from morality to mysticism.

The first stirrings of Neoplatonic criticism appeared in Alexandria in the first century A.D., in the commentaries on Genesis written by the Jewish philoso- pher Philo Judaeus. These commentaries emphasize the compatibility of Moses' vision with Plato's philosophy, and they explore the possibilities of allegorical exegesis. A similar kind of exegesis was used by some early Christian writers—

Clement of Alexandria in the late second century, Origen in the early third century—who began to develop a method for interpreting the pagan classics (especially Homer) in Christian terms. Their theories were based largely on the Platonic notions of inspiration and the essential oneness behind all truth.

Neoplatonism first became a fully developed approach to art in the work of Plotinus (205–269/270 A.D.). According to Plotinus, the soul of the true artist is attuned to the "One," and his work is thus inspired, possessing an essentially moral quality of revelation. The work of art is beautiful because it participates in the transcendent "Idea" of beauty; it achieves and expresses a vision of ultimate reality. Plotinus thus uses Plato's remarks on inspiration (as found in the *Ion*) to surmount Plato's objections to art as a secondary imitation (as found in the *Republic*). This positive emphasis was carried from aesthetics into literary criticism by two of Plotinus' students, Proclus and Porphyry. And Plotinus' general method reappears in the work of most idealistic critics—Christians, humanists, or romantics—from the Middle Ages onward.

This introduction was prepared jointly
by Leon Golden and Kevin Kerrane.

ARISTOPHANES

(ca. 450–385 B.C.)

INTRODUCTION

In his play *The Frogs* Aristophanes expands the boundaries of classical poetics by providing an early and very perceptive example of practical criticism, a comparison of the world views and dramatic styles of Aeschylus and Euripides. The first part of the play centers on Dionysus' adventures as he attempts to bring Euripides back from the dead. In the second half of the play, Dionysus adjudicates a contest between Aeschylus and Euripides as to who is really the best poet and deserves to return to the world, and it is here that we find many important statements of Aristophanes' view of literature.

The struggle between Aeschylus and Euripides is based both on philosophical and stylistic issues. Euripides berates Aeschylus for his use of strange, new, and very long words which are difficult to understand. Aeschylus counters that the nobility of his themes requires such language. Euripides proudly claims that he has made tragedy more realistic by using everyday speech and characters out of ordinary life. Aeschylus, in turn, denounces Euripides for degrading the stage by introducing to it language and incidents from the more sordid aspects of life.

Aeschylus proudly points to the fact that he wrote plays such as the *Seven Against Thebes,* which inspired men to want to fight for their country, and the *Persians,* which filled them with patriotic fervor, while Euripides presented the morally and ethically degraded on the stage. Aeschylus sees himself as a part of the noble tradition of poet-teachers which includes Orpheus, who taught mystic religious rites and the horror of murder; Musaeus, who explained the healing of illnesses and the meaning of oracles; Homer, who described the art of war; and Hesiod, who taught the tilling of the soil. The Aeschylean position strongly affirms the role of the poet as priest and moral instructor to his people.

Euripides is placed by Aristophanes in the position of defending the view that art has a right to depict the sordid aspects of reality and to use appropriate diction and costuming in the process. When Aeschylus denounces him for in-

14

troducing psychologically abnormal and morally degraded figures into his dramas, Euripides demands to know if his description of Phaedra's love for her stepson was untrue. Aeschylus accepts the truth of Euripides' description but asserts that the task of the poet is to be the teacher of mankind and that he should not portray events which subvert the morality of the audience.

There is a deep philosophical difference in the attitudes toward art expressed by Aeschylus and Euripides. For Aeschylus the artist is, as we have indicated, both a priest and teacher of his fellow men and his essential task is to present in his artistic work themes and actions which will uplift his audience morally and instruct them in a proper social and personal ethic. Both subject matter and style must be chosen so as to conform to this essential goal. Euripides argues for a very different concept of art, one in which the poet's essential task is to express reality no matter how vile or immoral it may be. The Euripidean position sees art as an investigation into the nature of reality and not as a means for achieving moral and social goals. The serious problem raised by the clashing arguments of Aeschylus and Euripides will play a prominent role in the history of classical literary criticism.

Aeschylus' elevated diction and Euripides' more pedestrian style are attributed in this passage to the character of the themes the two poets present. Aristophanes uses this occasion for some very perceptive, but frequently quite technical, stylistic criticism of both poets. He parodies both the rugged, sometimes unclear, diction of Aeschylus and the plain, sometimes pedestrian and mechanical, style of Euripides. In having his characters cite and analyze specific passages, Aristophanes functions as the first practical critic in the classical poetic tradition.

The translation which follows (and most of the notes) are by Richmond Lattimore and taken from Aristophanes, *The Frogs* (Ann Arbor: University of Michigan Press, 1962) by permission of the publisher.

The numbers inserted in the translation give the approximate location of every tenth line in the Greek text.

from THE FROGS

AESCHYLUS
The whole business gives me a pain in the middle, my rage and resentment are
    heated
at the idea of having to argue with *him*. But so he can't say I'm defeated,
here, answer me, you. What's the poet's duty, and why is the poet respected?

EURIPIDES
Because he can write, and because he can think, but mostly because he's injected
some virtue into the body politic.

AESCHYLUS
                                        What if you've broken your trust, (1010)
and corrupted good sound right-thinking people and filled them with treacherous
    lust?
If poets do that, what reward should they get?

DIONYSOS
                                        The axe. That's what we should
    do with 'em.

AESCHYLUS
Then think of the people *I* gave him, and think of the people when he got
    through with 'em.
I left him a lot of heroic six-footers, a grand generation of heroes,
    unlike our new crop of street-corner loafers and gangsters and
    decadent queer-os.
Mine snorted the spirit of spears and splendor, of white-plumed helmets and
    stricken fields,
of warrior heroes in shining armor and greaves[1] and sevenfold-oxhide shields.

DIONYSOS
And that's a disease that never dies out. The munition-makers will kill me.

EURIPIDES
Just what did you do to make them so noble? Is that what you're trying to tell
    me?

DIONYSOS
Well, answer him, Aeschylus, don't withdraw into injured dignity. That won't
    go. (1020)

AESCHYLUS
I made them a martial drama.

DIONYSOS
                        Which?

AESCHYLUS
                                        Seven Against Thebes, if you
    want to know.
Any man in an audience sitting through that would aspire to heroic endeavor.

DIONYSOS

That was a mistake, man. Why did you make the Thebans more warlike than ever
and harder to fight with? By every right it should mean a good beating for you.

AESCHYLUS

To the audience

Well, *you* could have practiced austerity too. It's exactly what *you* wouldn't *do*.
Then I put on my *Persians*,[2] and anyone witnessing that would promptly be
    smitten
with longing for victory over the enemy. Best play I ever have written.

DIONYSOS

Oh, yes, I loved that, and I thrilled where I sat when I heard old Dareios was
    dead
and the chorus cried "wahoo" and clapped with their hands. I tell you, it went
    to my head.

AESCHYLUS

There, there is work for poets who also are MEN. From the earliest times (1030)
incitement to virtue and useful knowledge have come from the makers of rhymes.
There was Orpheus first. He preached against murder, and showed us the heavenly
    way.
Musaeus taught divination and medicine; Hesiod, the day-after-day cultivation
    of fields, the seasons, and plowings. Then Homer, divinely inspired,
is a source of indoctrination to virtue. Why else is he justly admired
    than for teaching how heroes armed them for battle?

DIONYSOS

He didn't teach Pantakles, though.

He can't get it right. I watched him last night. He was called to parade, don't
    you know,
and he put on his helmet and tried to tie on the plume when the helm was on top
    of his head.

AESCHYLUS

Ah, many have been my heroic disciples; the last of them, Lamachos (recently
    dead).
The man in the street simply has to catch something from all my heroics and
    braveries. (1040)
My Teucers and lion-hearted Patrokloses lift him right out of his knaveries
and make him thrill to the glory of war and spring to the sound of the trumpet.
But I never regaled you with Phaidra the floozie—or Sthenoboia[3] the strumpet.
I think I can say that a lovesick woman has never been pictured by me.

EURIPIDES
Aphrodite never did notice you much.

AESCHYLUS
                                        Aphrodite can go climb a tree.
But you'll never have to complain that she didn't bestow her attentions on you.
She got you in person, didn't she?

DIONYSOS
                              Yes, she did, and your stories came true.
The fictitious chickens came home to roost.

EURIPIDES
                              But tell me, o man without pity:
suppose I did write about Sthenoboia. What harm has she done to our city?

AESCHYLUS
Bellerophon-intrigues, as given by you, have caused the respectable wives (1050)
of respectable men, in shame and confusion, to do away with their lives.

EURIPIDES
But isn't my story of Phaidra a story that really has happened?

AESCHYLUS
                                              So be it.
It's true. But the poet should cover up scandal, and not let anyone see it.
He shouldn't exhibit it out on the stage. For the little boys have their teachers
to show them example, but when they grow up we poets must act as their
    preachers,
and what we preach should be useful and good.

EURIPIDES
                                    But you, with your massive con-
    struction,
huge words and mountainous phrases, is that what you call useful instruction?
You ought to make people talk like people.

AESCHYLUS
                              Your folksy style's for the birds.
For magnificent thoughts and magnificent fancies, we must have magnificent
    words.
It's appropriate too for the demigods of heroic times to talk bigger

than we. (1060) It goes with their representation as grander in costume and
     figure.
I set them a standard of purity. You've corrupted it.

EURIPIDES

How did I do it?

AESCHYLUS
By showing a royal man in a costume of rags, with his skin showing through it.
You played on emotions.

EURIPIDES

But why should it be so wrong to awaken their pity?

AESCHYLUS
The rich men won't contribute for warships.[4] You can't find one in the city
who's willing to give. He appears in his rags, and howls, and complains that
     he's broke.

DIONYSOS
But he always has soft and expensive underwear under the beggarman's cloak.
The liar's so rich and he eats so much that he has to feed some to the fishes.

AESCHYLUS
You've taught the young man to be disputatious. Each argues as long as he wishes.
You've emptied the wrestling yards of wrestlers. They all sit around on their
     fannies (1070)
and listen to adolescent debates. The sailormen gossip like grannies
     and question their officers' orders. In my time, all that they knew how to do
was to holler for rations, and sing "yeo-ho," and row, with the rest of the crew.

DIONYSOS
And blast in the face of the man behind, that's another thing too that they knew
     how to do.
And how to steal from the mess at sea, and how to be robbers ashore.
But now they argue their orders. We just can't send them to sea any more.

AESCHYLUS
That's what he's begun. What hasn't he done?
His nurses go propositioning others.
His heroines have their babies in church
or sleep with their brothers (1080)

or go around murmuring: *"Is* life life?"[5]
So our city is rife
with the clerk and the jerk,
the altar-baboon, the political ape,
and our physical fitness is now a disgrace
with nobody in shape
to carry a torch in a race.

PLATO

(ca. 429–347 B.C.)

INTRODUCTION

Alfred North Whitehead once observed that the history of Western philosophy is basically a series of "footnotes" to Plato. To a lesser extent, the same observation might be made about the history of Western poetics. Plato, the formulator of man's first general theory of art, has had an immense influence on nearly every generation of Western literary critics.

It is significant, however, that this influence has been so diverse. On the one hand, Plato's position is reflected in the antagonism of religious, radically humanistic, and politically totalitarian forces to aesthetic freedom and to art as an end in itself. On the other hand, Plato has served as the patron saint of scores of critics who wish to glorify the artist and the role of art in human life. These strikingly different emphases are possible because of the rich complexity of Plato's theory of art.

Plato's most famous statements about art occur in Book X of the *Republic*, where the decision is made to banish nearly all poetry from the ideal state. The surprisingly intense opposition to art exhibited in Book X derives from two kinds of Platonic premises: metaphysical and ethical. First, as a philosophical idealist principally concerned with the apprehension of ultimate reality, Plato is antagonistic to artistic *fictions*, which necessarily distort what limited vision of truth man possesses. In Book X of the *Republic* Plato argues that works of art are at best trivial, being merely imperfect reflections of the literal world, which is in turn a pale reflection of the ideal. Using the example of a bed, Plato cites the necessary existence of the idea of the bed, an eternally existing model for all actual beds—which can themselves be called "imitations" of this idea. Thus, a painting or a literary description of a bed would be an "imitation of an imitation," standing three degrees removed from reality itself.

Plato's second basis of opposition to art also appears in Book X of the *Republic*: he suggests that art is not only inherently trivial but also potentially dangerous, that it poses ethical as well as metaphysical problems. Imitative art has a powerful emotional effect on its audience. Plato, unlike Aristotle, identifies this effect as unhealthy, a reversal of the control that reason should always have over the passions. According to Plato, the imitative poet establishes a "badly governed state" within the soul of each member of the audience. Moreover, the power of art to mold men's attitudes and values means that the philosopher has the right to object to (and to censor) any artistic imitation which deviates from approved themes and representations.

Many discussions of Plato's theory of art begin and end with Book X of the *Republic*, but distinguished work by Richard McKeon and W. J. Verdenius, among others, has shown that Plato's view of art is deeper and much more complex than the preceding summary might suggest.[1] Plato's remarks in Book X cannot be isolated from the logic that controls the *Republic* as a whole, or from the general attitudes expressed in other dialogues.

In contrast to the *Laws*, where an attempt is made to depict a fairly realistic state, the *Republic* is an inquiry into the principles of an ideal state, one existing in accordance with *absolute* truth and justice. Thus, whereas the *Laws* significantly modifies most of the "Platonic" restrictions against art, the *Republic* denies toleration to any activities which might subvert the absolute social, moral, and philosophical goals of the state. In Book III of the *Republic* Plato not only justifies stringent censorship (e. g., of poems which portray wickedness triumphant), but also demands that poets tell "profitable" stories which can help to inculcate such virtues as courage and temperance.

Plato also sees the form or style of a literary work as having a moral potency. He argues that the completely imitative mode (i. e., drama) is the worst; in tragedies and comedies evil is represented directly, and thus becomes more potentially attractive to the audience. On the other hand, a totally narrative style, while avoiding the direct representation of evil, also prevents the direct representation of the morally good. Plato finally affirms a mixed style, in which there is a small amount of direct representation of the morally good and a large amount of narration. (Plato's remarks in Book III provide an interesting counterpoint to those of Aristotle in the *Poetics*. Aristotle, who sees as "imitative" *all* the styles that Plato mentions, argues on aesthetic grounds for the superiority of the dramatic mode. Moreover, Plato's insistence in Book III on "poetic justice"—goodness rewarded and vice punished—would seem to make Aristotle's ideal literary form, tragedy, almost impossible.)

Many of Plato's negative comments about art are repeated in other dialogues. Poetry is attacked for one of two reasons—its moral dangers or its distance from absolute truth. In the *Gorgias*, for example, poetry and music are described as forms of flattery, in that their goal is "pleasure" rather than the moral improvement of the audience. In the *Phaedrus* Plato uses the myth of Theuth to contrast the stasis of art with the dynamism of philosophical dialectic; artistic imitations, and the "written word" in general, are compared unfavorably to the "living word" of the never-ending dialectical process.

Nevertheless, it is precisely this concern with a dialectic of spiritual growth that leads Plato to allow for a more positive view of art. In Book V of the *Republic* (516 A-B) Plato compares the intellectual process of moving from opinion to knowledge with the sense experience of moving from the depths of a cave to open sunlight. He notes that a person could not endure the blinding light of the sun after long exposure to darkness: such a person would have to accommodate himself *gradually* to increasing levels of light before he could view the bright sun. Similarly, the person who is proceeding from spiritual darkness to spiritual light must adjust himself to the new experience gradually. He will need, therefore, to traverse a series of imitations of reality that come ever closer to absolute truth. Artistic imitations which perform this role thus have a significant place in the Platonic system.

As long as a man maintains a clear and absolute distinction between the imitation and reality, a work of art may provide him with a means of spiritual growth. In the *Laws* (668 A-B) such worthwhile imitations are identified as having truth (similarity to the model) rather than pleasure as their goal. Obviously, the poet should have sound knowledge of his subject matter. In the *Sophist* (267 B) we are told that some imitators have knowledge of what they imitate, while others do not; imitations accomplished by those who have knowledge will, by virtue of similarity to models, be able to illuminate reality itself. In the *Symposium* Diotima eloquently praises the "children of the spirit"—by which she means all of the intellectual achievements of man, including the works of Hesiod and Homer. Diotima's remarks make it clear that literary works can be a useful (though lower) stage in the quest for an understanding of absolute beauty.

The *Laws*, which—as has been noted—delineates the concept of a political state more realistic than that of the *Republic*, presents a liberalization of many strictures against art—again because of Plato's concern with a dialectic of spiritual growth. Plato deals with literature and music as elements of the educational process, stressing the moral possibilities of various kinds of art. In the state envisioned by the *Laws* both comedy and tragedy have a place, and the reasoning that Plato uses to "defend" them indicates that he is concerned with the moral dimension of literature in a newer, more subtle way. Comedy is to be admitted because man, in learning the nature of the ignoble and the ridiculous, may be better able to understand and pursue the noble and the virtuous. Tragedy is to be allowed because, when it conforms to the morality approved by the state, it illuminates the noble aspects of human existence. The standard for judging tragedy is to be found in the wisdom of the philosopher-statesman, for the *Laws* tells us that the whole state "is an imitation of the best and noblest life, which we affirm to be indeed the very truth of tragedy."

Plato's positive view of artistic imitation is supported by the formal qualities of his own dialogues. His frequent use of key images, such as the cave, is an example of imitation used to express a truth that could not be expressed in any other way. Moreover, the larger and more extended metaphors that we call "myths" occur at many crucial places in the dialogues, providing imaginative clarification of Plato's themes. Finally, it is significant that Aristotle (in Chapter I of the *Poetics*) classified the Platonic dialogues themselves as forms of "imitation." Plato is, in fact, one of the most poetic of all philosophers.

Admitting all of this, however, Plato's theory remains troublesome: its didactic emphasis seems too crude to be aesthetically satsifying. Generations of Neoplatonic critics, from Plotinus to Shelley, have attempted to remedy this problem by locating another, more powerful positive emphasis in Plato's poetic: a doctrine of inspiration, in which the poet is seen as the direct imitator of ultimate reality, not a mere copier of the images of physical nature. This doctrine, which makes of the poet a mystic visionary, accords art a supreme role in human life, far beyond that of a "beginning stage" for spiritual growth.

The putative basis for this doctrine is Plato's *Ion*, an investigation into the nature of the skill and knowledge of the poet and rhapsode. Ion, an elocutionist extremely talented in interpreting Homer, is nevertheless puzzled by his inability to interpret other poets equally well. Socrates proceeds to show that Ion lacks a truly scientific command of his subject matter—i.e., medicine, military strategy, and other areas of knowledge within the Homeric poems. (When Ion momentarily anticipates Aristotle by asking whether the province of poetic knowledge is really "the entire poems" rather than any separable discipline discussed in the poems, Socrates disregards the question.) According to Socrates, the kind of knowledge possessed by a poet or rhapsode must be based on divine inspiration, since it obviously cannot be based on scientific expertise. Socrates uses the image of a magnetic field to explain the nature of inspiration. The muse of poetry is the source of a power which pulls the poet's soul toward the ideal; the poet in turn influences the rhapsode (Ion) who finally communicates this influence to the audience.

Despite the strong possibility that Plato is being ironic, that he is using the disjunction which concludes *Ion* to satirize the pretentiousness of poets and rhapsodes,[2] the concept of *furor poeticus*, inspiration in which the poet is "possessed" and unconscious of what he is doing, has become a commonplace of literary theory. In the two great periods of Plato's critical influence—the Italian Renaissance and the romantic movements of the nineteenth century—*furor poeticus* has been used as a supplement for Plato's didacticism—rendering more aesthetically palatable a theory of poetry as metaphysical or ethical "truth." Renaissance Neoplatonists (e.g., Ficino and Politian) sometimes spoke of art almost as a humanistic religion, an inspired presentation of ultimate reality. For romantic critics (especially Shelley and Emerson) Plato's didactic and inspirational emphases were almost perfectly consonant with the concept of the transcendental imagination.

Generally speaking, the poetic world-view of twentieth-century criticism is far more Aristotelian than Platonic. Nevertheless, whenever a critic tries to deal fully with the truth-value, the ethical implications, or the social significance of literature, he is almost certain to provide one more "footnote" to Plato.

The translations of the selections used here (and most of the notes) are Benjamin Jowett's. They are reprinted from *The Dialogues of Plato*, 4th ed. (Oxford: Clarendon Press, 1953) by permission of the publisher. The numbers inserted in the translations are those of Stephanus (the sixteenth century scholar-printer Henri Estienne) and are generally given in editions of Plato. In the following English selections, these numbers appear in the approximate location in which they occur in the original. Stephanus' subdivisions (A, B, etc.) have been omitted.

from THE SYMPOSIUM

[*Socrates*] "Assuming Love to be such as you say, what is the use of him to men?" [*Diotima*] "That, Socrates," she replied, "I will attempt to unfold: of his nature and birth I have already spoken; and you acknowledge that love is of the beautiful. But someone will say: What does it consist in, Socrates and Diotima? Or rather let me put the question more clearly, and ask: When a man loves the beautiful, what does his love desire?" I answered her "That the beautiful may be his." "Still," she said, "the answer suggests a further question: What is given by the possession of beauty?" "To what you have asked," I replied, "I have no answer ready." "Then," she said, "let me put the word 'good' in the place of the beautiful, and repeat the question once more: If he who loves loves the good, what is it then that he loves?" "The possession of the good." "And what does he gain who possesses the good?" "Happiness," I replied; "there is less difficulty in answering that question." (205) "Yes," she said, "the happy are made happy by the acquisition of good things. Nor is there any need to ask why a man desires happiness; the answer is already final." "You are right," I said. "And is this wish and this desire common to all? And do all men always desire their own good, or only some men?—What say you?" "All men," I replied; "the desire is common to all." "Why, then," she rejoined, "are not all men, Socrates, said to love, but only some of them? whereas you say that all men are always loving the same things." "I myself wonder," I said, "why this is." "There is nothing to wonder at," she replied; "the reason is that one part of love is separated off and receives the name of the whole, but the other parts have other names." "Give an illustration," I said. She answered me as follows: "There is creative activity which, as you know, is complex and manifold. All that causes the passage of non-being into being is a 'poesy' or creation, and the processes of all art are creative; and the masters of arts are all poets or creators." "Very true." "Still," she said, "you know that they are not called poets, but have other names; only that one portion of creative activity which is separated off from the rest, and is concerned with music and meter is called by the name of the whole and is termed poetry, and they who possess poetry in this sense of the word are called poets." "Very true," I said. "And the same holds of love. For you may say generally that all desire of good and happiness is only the great and subtle power of love; but they who are drawn towards him by any other path, whether the path of money-making or gymnastics or philosophy, are not called lovers—the name of the whole is appropriated to those whose desire takes one form only—they alone are said to love, or to be lovers." "I dare say," I replied, "that you are right." "Yes," she added, "and you hear people say that lovers are seeking for their other half; but I say that they are seeking neither for the half of themselves, nor for the whole, unless the half or the whole be also a good; men will cut off their own hands and feet and cast them away, if they think them evil. They do not, I imagine, each cling to what is his own, unless perchance there be someone who calls what belongs to him the good, and what belongs to another the evil; (206) for there is nothing which men love but the good. Is there anything?" "Certainly, I should say, that there is nothing." "Then," she said, "the simple truth is, that men love the good." "Yes," I said. "To which must be added that they love the possession of the good?" "Yes, that must be added." "And not only the possession, but the everlasting possession of the good?" "That must be added too." "Then love," she said, "may be described generally as the love of the everlasting possession of the good?" "That is most true."

"Then if this be always the nature of love, can you tell me further," she went on, "what is the manner of the pursuit? what are they doing who show all this eagerness and heat which is called love? And what is the object which they have in view? Answer me." "Nay, Diotima," I replied, "if I knew, I should not be wondering at your wisdom, neither should I come to learn from you about this very matter." "Well," she said, "I will teach you: The object which they have in view is birth in beauty, whether of body or soul." "I do not understand you," I said; "the oracle requires an explanation." "I will make my meaning clearer," she replied. "I mean to say, that all men are bringing to the birth in their bodies and in their souls. There is a certain age at which human nature is desirous of procreation—procreation which must be in beauty and not in deformity. The union of man and woman is a procreation; it is a divine thing, for conception and generation are an immortal principle in the mortal creature, and in the inharmonious they can never be. But the deformed is inharmonious with all divinity, and the beautiful harmonious. Beauty, then, is the destiny or goddess of parturition who presides at birth, and therefore, when approaching beauty, the procreating power is propitious, and expansive, and benign, and bears and produces fruit: at the sight of ugliness she frowns and contracts and has a sense of pain, and turns away, and shrivels up, and not without a pang refrains from procreation. And this is the reason why, when the hour of procreation comes, and the teeming nature is full, there is such a flutter and ecstasy about beauty whose approach is the alleviation of the bitter pain of travail. For love, Socrates, is not, as you imagine, the love of the beautiful only." "What then?" "The love of generation and of birth in beauty." "Yes," I said. "Yes, indeed," she replied. "But why of generation? Because to the mortal creature, generation is a sort of eternity and immortality, and if, as has been already admitted, love is of the everlasting possession of the good, all men will necessarily desire immortality together with good: (207) whence it must follow that love is of immortality."

All this she taught me at various times when she spoke of love. And I remember her once saying to me, "What is the cause, Socrates, of love, and the attendant desire? See you not how all animals, birds as well as beasts, in their desire of procreation, are in agony when they take the infection of love, which begins with the desire of union and then passes to the care of offspring, on whose behalf the weakest are ready to battle against the strongest even to the uttermost, and to die for them, and will let themselves be tormented with hunger, or make any other sacrifice, in order to maintain their young. Man may be supposed to act thus from reason; but why should animals have these passionate feelings? Can you tell my why?" Again I replied that I did not know. She said to me: "And do you expect ever to become a master in the art of love, if you do not know this?" "But I have told you already, Diotima, that my ignorance is the reason why I come to you, for I am conscious that I want a teacher; tell me then the cause of this and of the other mysteries of love." "Marvel not," she said, "if you believe that love is of the immortal, as we have several times acknowledged; for here again, and on the same principle too, the mortal nature is seeking as far as is possible to be everlasting and immortal: and this is only to be attained by generation, because generation always leaves behind a new and different existence in the place of the old. Nay, even in the life of the same individual there is succession and not absolute uniformity: a man is called the same, and yet in the interval between youth and age, during which every animal is said to have life and identity, he is undergoing a perpetual process of loss and reparation—hair, flesh, bones, blood, and the whole body are always changing. Which is true not only of the body, but also of the soul, whose habits, tempers, opinions, desires, pleasures, pains, fears, never remain the same way in any one of us, but are always coming and going. What is still more surprising, it is equally true of science; (208) not only do some of the sciences come to life in our minds, and others die away, so that we are never the same in regard to them either, but the same fate happens to each of them individually. For what is implied in the word 'recollection,' but the departure of knowledge, which is ever being forgotten, and is renewed and preserved by recollection, and appears to be the same although in reality new, according to that law by which all mortal things are preserved, not absolutely the same, but by substitution, the old worn-out mortality leaving another new and similar existence behind—unlike the divine, which is wholly and eternally the same? And in this way, Socrates, the mortal body, or mortal anything, partakes of immortality; but the immortal in another way. Marvel not then at the love which all men have of their offspring; for that universal love and interest is for the sake of immortality."

I was astonished at her words, and said: "Is this really true, O most wise Diotima?" And she answered with all the authority of an accomplished sophist: "Of that, Socrates, you may be assured; think only of the ambition of men, and you will wonder at the senselessness of their ways, unless you consider how they are stirred by the passionate love of fame. They are ready to run all risks, even greater than they would have run for their children, and to pour out money and undergo any sort of toil, and even to die, 'if so they leave an everlasting name.' Do you imagine that Alcestis would have died to save Admetus, or Achilles to avenge Patroclus, or your own Codrus in order to preserve the kingdom for his sons, if they had not imagined that the memory of their virtues, which still survives among us, would be immortal? Nay," she said, "I am persuaded that all men do all things, and the better they are the more they do them, in hope of the glorious fame of immortal virtue; for they desire the immortal.

"Those who are pregnant in the body only, betake themselves to women and beget children—this is the the character of their love; their offspring, as they hope, will preserve their memory and give them the blessedness and immortality which they desire for all future time. (209) But souls which are pregnant— for there certainly are men who are more creative in their souls than in their bodies, creative of that which is proper for the soul to conceive and bring forth: and if you ask me what are these conceptions, I answer, wisdom, and virtue in general—among such souls are all creative poets and all artists who are deserving of the name inventor. But the greatest and fairest sort of wisdom by far is that which is concerned with the ordering of states and families, and which is called temperance and justice. And he who in youth has the seed of these implanted in his soul, when he grows up and comes to maturity desires to beget and generate. He wanders about seeking beauty that he may get offspring —for from deformity he will beget nothing—and naturally embraces the beautiful rather than the deformed body; above all, when he finds a fair and noble and well-nurtured soul, he embraces the two in one person, and to such a one he is full of speech about virtue and the nature and pursuits of a good man, and he tries to educate him. At the touch and in the society of the beautiful which is ever present to his memory, even when absent, he brings forth that which he had conceived long before, and in company with him tends that which he brings forth; and they are married by a far nearer tie and have a closer friendship than those who beget mortal children, for the children who are their common offspring are fairer and more immortal. Who, when he thinks of Homer and Hesiod and other great poets, would not rather have their children than ordinary human ones? Who would not emulate them in the creation of children such as theirs, which have preserved their memory and given them everlasting glory? Or who would not have such children as Lycurgus left behind him to be the saviors, not only of Lacedaemon, but of Hellas, as one may say? There is Solon, too, who is the revered father of Athenian laws; and many others there are in many other places, both among Hellenes and barbarians, who have given to the world many noble works, and have been the parents of virtue of every kind; and many temples have been raised in their honor for the sake of children such as theirs; which were never raised in honor of anyone, for the sake of his mortal children.

"These are the lesser mysteries of love, into which even you, Socrates, may enter; (210) to the greater and more hidden ones which are the crown of these, and to which, if you pursue them in a right spirit, they will lead, I know not whether you will be able to attain. But I will do my utmost to inform you, and do you follow if you can. For he who would proceed aright in this matter should begin in youth to seek the company of corporeal beauty; and first, if he be guided by his instructor aright, to love one beautiful body only—out of that he should create fair thoughts; and soon he will of himself perceive that the beauty of one body is akin to the beauty of another; and then if beauty of form in general is his pursuit, how foolish would he be not to recognize that the beauty in every body is one and the same! And when he perceives this he will abate his violent love of the one, which he will despise and deem a small thing, and will become a steadfast lover of all beautiful bodies. In the next stage he will consider that the beauty of the soul is more precious than the beauty of the outward form; so that if a virtuous soul have but a little comeliness, he will be content to love and tend him, and will search out and bring to the birth thoughts which may improve the young, until he is compelled next to contemplate and see the beauty in institutions and laws, and to understand that the beauty of them all is of one family, and that personal beauty is a trifle; and after institutions his guide will lead him on to the sciences, in order that, beholding the wide region already occupied by beauty, he may cease to be like a servant in love with one beauty only, that of a particular youth or man or institution, himself a slave mean and narrow-minded; but drawing towards and contemplating the vast sea of beauty, he will create many fair and noble thoughts and discourses in boundless love of wisdom, until on that shore he grows and waxes strong, and at last the vision is revealed to him of a single science, which is the science of beauty everywhere. To this I will proceed; please give me your very best attention:

"He who has been instructed thus far in the things of love, and who has learned to see the beautiful in due order and succession, when he comes toward the end will suddenly perceive a nature of wondrous beauty (and this, Socrates, is the final cause of all our former toils)—a nature which in the first place is everlasting, (211) knowing not birth or death, growth or decay; secondly, not fair in one point of view and foul in another, or at one time or in one relation or at one place fair, at another time or in another relation or at another place foul, as if fair to some and foul to others, or in the likeness of a face or hands or any other part of the bodily frame, or in any form of speech or knowledge, or existing in any individual being, as for example, in a living creature, whether in heaven, or in earth, or anywhere else; but beauty absolute, separate, simple, and everlasting, which is imparted to the ever growing and perishing beauties of all other beautiful things, without itself suffering diminution, or increase, or any change. He who, ascending from these earthly things under the influence of true love, begins to perceive that beauty, is not far from the end. And the true order of going, or being led by another, to the things of love, is to begin from the beauties of earth and mount upwards for the sake of that other beauty, using these as steps only, and from one going on to two, and from two to all fair bodily forms, and from fair bodily forms to fair practices, and from fair practices to fair sciences, until from fair sciences he arrives at the science of which I have spoken, the science which has no other object than absolute beauty, and at last knows that which is beautiful by itself alone. This, my dear Socrates," said the stranger of Mantinea [Diotima], "is that life above all others which man should live, in the contemplation of beauty absolute; a beauty which if you once beheld, you would see not to be after the measure of gold, and garments, and fair boys and youths, whose presence now entrances you; and you and many a one would be content to live seeing them only and conversing with them without meat or drink, if that were possible—you only want to look at them and to be with them. But what if a man had eyes to see the true beauty—the divine beauty, I mean, pure and clear and unalloyed, not infected with the pollutions of the flesh and all the colors and vanities of mortal life—thither looking, and holding converse with the true beauty simple and divine? (212) Remember how in that communion only, beholding beauty with that by which it can be beheld, he will be enabled to bring forth, not images of beauty, but realities (for he has hold not of an image but of a reality), and bringing forth and nourishing true virtue will properly become the friend of God and be immortal, if mortal man may. Would that be an ignoble life?"

from PHAEDRUS

SOCRATES. I dare say that you are thoroughly at home in the views of Tisias. Now we have one more thing to ask him. Does he not define probability to be that which the many think?

PHAEDRUS. Certainly, he does.

SOC. I believe that he has a clever and ingenious case of this sort: He supposes a feeble and valiant man to have assaulted a strong and cowardly one, and to have robbed him of his coat or of something or other; he is brought into court, and then Tisias says that both parties should tell lies: the coward should say that he was assaulted by more men than one; the other should prove that they were alone, and should argue thus: "How could a weak man like me have assaulted a strong man like him?" The complainant will not like to confess his own cowardice, and will therefore invent some other lie which his adversary will thus gain an opportunity of refuting. And there are other devices of the same kind which have a place in the system. Am I not right, Phaedrus?

PHAEDR. Certainly.

SOC. Bless me, what a wonderfully mysterious art is this which Tisias or some other gentleman, in whatever name or country he rejoices, has discovered. Shall we say a word to him or not?

PHAEDR. What shall we say to him?

SOC. Let us tell him that, before he appeared, you and I were saying that the probability of which he speaks was engendered in the minds of the many by the likeness of the truth, and we had just been affirming that he who knew the truth would always know best how to discover the resemblances of the truth. If he has anything else to say about the art of speaking we should like to hear him; but if not, we are satisfied with the view recently expressed, that unless a man estimates the various characters of his hearers and is able to divide all things into classes and to comprehend every one under single ideas, he will never be a skillful rhetorician even within the limits of human power. And this skill he will not attain without a great deal of trouble, which a good man ought to undergo, not for the sake of speaking and acting before men, but in order that he may be able to say what is acceptable to God and always to act acceptably to Him as far as in him lies; for there is a saying of wiser men than ourselves, that a man of sense should not try to please his fellow servants (at least this should not be his first object) but his good and noble masters; (274) and therefore, Tisias, if the way is long and circuitous, marvel not at this, for, where the end is great, there we may take the longer road, but not for lesser ends such as yours. However, our argument says that even these are best secured as the consequence of higher aims.

PHAEDR. I think, Socrates, that this is admirable, if only practicable.

SOC. But provided one's aim is honorable, so is any ill success which may ensue.

PHAEDR. True.

SOC. Enough appears to have been said by us of a true and false art of speaking.

PHAEDR. Certainly.

SOC. But there is something yet to be said of propriety and impropriety of writing.

PHAEDR. Yes.

SOC. Do you know how you can speak or act about rhetoric in a manner which will be acceptable to God?

PHAEDR. No, indeed. Do you?

SOC. I have heard a tradition of the ancients, whether true or not they only know; although if we had found the truth ourselves, do you think that we should care much about the opinions of men?

PHAEDR. Your question needs no answer; but simply tell me what you say that you have heard.

SOC. At the Egyptian city of Naucratis there was a famous old god whose name was Theuth; the bird which is called the Ibis is sacred to him, and he was the inventor of many arts, such as arithmetic and calculation and geometry and astronomy as well as draughts and dice, but his great discovery was the use of letters. Now in those days [the god] Thamus was the king of the whole country of Egypt; and he dwelt in that great city of Upper Egypt which the Hellenes call Egyptian Thebes, and the god himself is called by them Ammon. To him came Theuth and showed his inventions, desiring that the other Egyptians might be allowed to have the benefit of them; he enumerated them, and Thamus inquired about their several uses, and praised some of them and censured others, as he approved or disapproved of them. It would take a long time to repeat all that Thamus said to Theuth in praise or blame of the various arts. But when they came to letters, Theuth said: O king, here is a study which will make the Egyptians wiser and give them better memories; it is a specific both for the memory and for the wit. Thamus replied: O most ingenious Theuth, the parent or inventor of an art is not always the best judge of the utility or inutility of his own inventions to the users of them. (275) And in this instance, you who are the father of letters, from a paternal love of your own children have been led to attribute to them a quality which they cannot have; for this discovery of yours will create forgetfulness in the learners' souls, because they will not use their memories; they will trust to the external written characters and not remember of themselves. And so the specific which you have discovered is an aid not to memory, but to reminiscence. As for wisdom, it is the reputation, not the reality, that you have to offer to those who learn from you; they will have heard many things and yet received no teaching; they will appear to be omniscient and will generally know nothing; they will be tiresome company, having acquired not wisdom, but the show of wisdom.

PHAEDR. Yes, Socrates, you can easily invent tales of Egypt, or of any other country.

SOC. There was a tradition in the temple of Dodona[1] that oaks first gave prophetic utterances. The men of old, far simpler than you sophisticated young men, deemed that if they heard the truth even from "oak or rock," it was enough; whereas you seem to consider not whether a thing is or is not true, but who the speaker is and from what country the tale comes.

PHAEDR. I acknowledge the justice of your rebuke; and I think that the Theban is right in his view about letters.

SOC. He would be a very simple person, and quite a stranger to the oracles of Thamus or Ammon, who should suppose that he had left his "Art" in writings or who should accept such an inheritance in the hope that the written word would give anything intelligible or certain; or who deemed that writing could be any more than a reminder to one who already knows the subject.

PHAEDR. That is most true.

SOC. I cannot help feeling, Phaedrus, that writing has one grave fault in common with painting; for the creations of the painter have the attitude of life, and yet if you ask them a question they preserve a solemn silence. And the same may be said of books. You would imagine that they had intelligence, but if you require any explanation of something that has been said, they preserve one unvarying meaning. And when they have been once written down they are tumbled about anywhere, all alike, among those who understand them and among strangers, and do not know to whom they should or should not reply: and, if they are maltreated or abused, they have no parent to protect them; for the book cannot protect or defend itself.

PHAEDR. That again is most true.

(276) SOC. Is there not another kind of word or speech far better than this, and having far greater power—a son of the same family, but lawfully begotten?

PHAEDR. Whom do you mean, and what is his origin?

SOC. I mean an intelligent word graven in the soul of the learner, which can defend itself, and knows with whom to speak and with whom to be silent.

PHAEDR. You mean the living word of knowledge which has a soul, and of which the written word is properly no more than an image?

SOC. Yes, of course that is what I mean. And now may I be allowed to ask you a question?: Would a husbandman, who is a man of sense, take seeds which he values and which he wishes to bear fruit, and in sober seriousness plant them during the heat of summer, in some garden of Adonis, that he may rejoice when he sees them in eight days appearing in beauty? At least he would do so, if at all, only for the sake of amusement and for show. But when he is in earnest he employs his art of husbandry and sows in fitting soil, and is satisfied if in eight months the seeds which he has sown arrive at perfection?

PHAEDR. Yes, Socrates, that will be his way when he is in earnest; he might act otherwise for the reasons which you give.

SOC. And can we suppose that he who knows the just and good and honorable has less understanding than the husbandman about his own seeds?

PHAEDR. Certainly not.

SOC. Then he will not seriously incline to "write" his thoughts "in water" with pen and ink, sowing words which can neither speak for themselves nor teach the truth adequately to others?

PHAEDR. No, that is not likely.

SOC. No, that is not likely—in the garden of letters he will sow and plant, but only for the sake of recreation and amusement; he will write them down as memorials to be treasured against the forgetfulness of old age, by himself, or by any other man who is treading the same path. He will rejoice in beholding their tender growth; and while others are refreshing their souls with banqueting and the like, this will be the pastime in which his days are spent.

PHAEDR. A pastime, Socrates, as noble as the other is ignoble, the pastime of a man who can be amused by serious talk, and can discourse merrily about justice and the like.

SOC. True, Phaedrus. But nobler far is the serious pursuit of the dialectician, who, finding a congenial soul, by the help of science sows and plants therein words which are able to defend themselves and him who planted them, (277) and are not unfruitful, but have in them a seed which others brought up in different soils render immortal, making the possessors of it happy to the utmost extent of human happiness.

PHAEDR. Far nobler, certainly.

SOC. And now at last, Phaedrus, having agreed upon this, we may decide the original question.

PHAEDR. What question was that?

SOC. I mean those problems, in trying to solve which we have made our way hither; we wished to examine the censure passed on Lysias for his professional speech-writing, and to distinguish the speech composed with art from that which is composed without art. And I think that we have now pretty well distinguished the artistic from its opposite.

PHAEDR. Yes, I thought so, but I wish that you would repeat what was said.

SOC. Until a man knows the truth of the several particulars of which he is writing or speaking, and is able to define them as they are, and having defined them again to divide them until they can be no longer divided; and until in like manner he is able to discern the nature of the soul, and discover the different modes of discourse which are adapted to different natures, and to arrange and dispose them in such a way that the simple form of speech may be addressed to the simpler nature, and the complex form, with many variations of key, to the more complex nature—until he has accomplished all this, he will be unable to handle arguments according to rules of art, as far as their nature allows them to be subjected to art, either for the purpose of teaching or persuading;—such is the view which is implied in the whole preceding argument.

PHAEDR. Yes, that was our view, certainly.

SOC. Secondly, as to the censure which was passed on the speaking or writing of discourses, and when they might be rightly or wrongly censured—did not our previous argument show—?

PHAEDR. Show what?

SOC. That whether Lysias or any other writer that ever was or will be, whether private man or statesman, proposes laws and so becomes the author of a political treatise, fancying that there is any great certainty and clearness in his performance, the fact of his so writing is only a disgrace to him, whatever men may say. For not to know the nature of justice and injustice, and good and evil, and not to be able to distinguish the dream from the reality, cannot in truth be otherwise than disgraceful to him, even though he have the applause of the whole world.

PHAEDR. Certainly.

SOC. But he who thinks that in the written word, whatever its subject, there is neccessarily much which is not serious, and that no discourse worthy of study has ever yet been written in poetry or prose, and that spoken ones are no better if, like the recitations of rhapsodes, they are delivered for the sake of persuasion, and not with any view to criticism or instruction; (278) and who thinks that even the best of writings are but a memorandum for those who know, and that only in principles of justice and goodness and nobility taught and communicated orally for the sake of instruction and graven in the soul, which is the true way of writing, is there clearness and perfection and seriousness, and that such principles should be deemed a man's own and his legitimate offspring;—being, in the first place, the word which he finds in his own bosom; secondly, the brethren and descendants and relations of his idea which have been duly implanted by him in the souls of others;—and who cares for them and no others—this is the right sort of man; and you and I, Phaedrus, would pray that we may become like him.

PHAEDR. That is most assuredly my desire and prayer.

SOC. And now the play is played out; and of rhetoric enough. Go and tell Lysias that to the fountain and school of the Nymphs we went down, and were bidden by them to convey a message to him and to other composers of speeches—to Homer and other writers of poems, whether set to music or not; and to Solon and others who have composed writings in the form of political discourses which they would term laws—to all of them we are to say that if their compositions are based on knowledge of the truth, and they can defend or prove them, when they are put to the test, by spoken arguments, which leave their writings poor in comparison of them, then they are to be called, not only poets, orators, legislators, but are worthy of a higher name, befitting the serious pursuit of their life.

PHAEDR. What name would you assign to them?

SOC. Wise, I may not call them; for that is a great name which belongs to God alone,—lovers of wisdom or philosophers is their modest and befitting title.

PHAEDR. Very suitable.

SOC. And he who cannot rise above his own compilations and compositions, which he has been long patching and piecing, adding some and taking away some, may be justly called poet or speech-maker or law-maker.

from GORGIAS

SOCRATES. Can you tell me the pursuits which delight mankind—or rather, if you would prefer, let me ask, and do you answer, which of them belong to the pleasurable class, and which of them not? In the first place, what do you say of flute-playing? Does not that appear to be an art which seeks only pleasure, Callicles, and thinks of nothing else?

CALLICLES. I assent.

SOC. And is not the same true of all similar arts, as, for example, the art of playing the lyre at festivals?

CAL. Yes.

SOC. And what do you say of the choral art and of dithyrambic poetry? Are not they of the same nature? Do you imagine that Cinesias the son of Meles cares about what will tend to the moral improvement of his hearers, or about what will give pleasure to the multitude? (502)

CAL. There can be no mistake about Cinesias, Socrates.

SOC. And what do you say of his father, Meles the harp-player? When he sang to the harp, did you suppose that he had his eye on the highest good? Perhaps he indeed could scarcely be said to regard even the greatest pleasure, since his singing was an infliction to his audience? In fact, would you not say that all music of the harp and dithyrambic poetry in general have been invented for the sake of pleasure?

CAL. I should.

SOC. And as for the Muse of Tragedy, that solemn and august personage —what are her aspirations? Is all her aim and desire only to give pleasure to the spectators, or does she strive to refrain her tongue from all that pleases and charms them but is vicious? To proclaim, in speech and song, truth that is salutary but unpleasant, whether they welcome it or not? Which in your judgment is of the nature of tragic poetry?

CAL. There can be no doubt, Socrates, that Tragedy has her face turned towards pleasure and the gratification of the audience.

SOC. And is not that the sort of thing, Callicles, which we were just now describing as flattery?

CAL. Quite true.

SOC. Well now, suppose that we strip all poetry of melody and rhythm and meter, there will remain speech?

CAL. To be sure.

SOC. And this speech is addressed to a crowd of people?

CAL. Yes.

SOC. Then poetry is a sort of public speaking?

CAL. True.

SOC. And it is a rhetorical sort of public speaking; do not the poets in the theatres seem to you to be rhetoricians?

CAL. Yes.

SOC. Then now we have discovered a sort of rhetoric which is addressed to a crowd of men, women, and children, freemen and slaves. And it is not much to our taste, for we have described it as having the nature of flattery.

CAL. Quite true.

SOC. Very good. And what do you say of that other rhetoric which addresses the Athenian Assembly and the assemblies of freemen in other states? Do the rhetoricians appear to you always to aim at what is best, and do they seek to improve the citizens by their speeches, or are they too, like the rest of mankind, bent upon giving them pleasure, forgetting the public good in the thought of their own interest, playing with the people as with children, and trying only to gratify them, but never considering whether they will be better or worse for this? (503)

CAL. The question does not admit of a simple answer. There are some who have a real care of the public in what they say, while others are such as you describe.

SOC. That is enough for me. If rhetoric also is twofold, one part of it will be mere flattery and disgraceful declamation; the other noble, aiming at the improvement of the souls of the citizens, and striving to say what is best, whether welcome or unwelcome to the audience. But you have never known such a rhetoric; or if you have, and can point out any rhetorician who is of this stamp, who is he?

CAL. But, indeed, I am afraid that I cannot tell you of any such among the orators who are at present living.

ION

(530) SOCRATES. Welcome, Ion. Are you from your native city of Ephesus?

ION. No, Socrates; but from Epidaurus, where I attended the festival of Aesculapius.

SOC. Indeed! Do the Epidaurians have a contest of rhapsodes[1] in his honor?

ION. O yes; and of other kinds of music.

SOC. And were you one of the competitors—and did you succeed?

ION. I—we—obtained the first prize of all, Socrates.

SOC. Well done; now we must win another victory, at the Panathenaea.[2]

ION. It shall be so, please heaven.

SOC. I have often envied the profession of a rhapsode, Ion; for it is a part of your art to wear fine clothes and to look as beautiful as you can, while at the same time you are obliged to be continually in the company of many good poets, and especially of Homer, who is the best and most divine of them, and to understand his mind, and not merely learn his words by rote; all this is a thing greatly to be envied. I am sure that no man can become a good rhapsode who does not understand the meaning of the poet. For the rhapsode ought to interpret the mind of the poet to his hearers, but how can he interpret him well unless he knows what he means? All this is much to be envied, I repeat.

ION. Very true, Socrates; interpretation has certainly been the most laborious part of my art; and I believe myself able to speak about Homer better than any man; and that neither Metrodorus of Lampsacus, nor Stesimbrotus of Thasos, nor Glaucon, nor anyone else who ever was, had as good ideas about Homer as I have, or as many.

SOC. I am glad to hear you say so, Ion; I see that you will not refuse to acquaint me with them.

ION. Certainly, Socrates; and you really ought to hear how exquisitely I display the beauties of Homer. I think that the Homeridae should give me a golden crown.[3]

SOC. I shall take an opportunity of hearing your embellishments of him at some other time. (531) But just now I should like to ask you a question: Does your art extend to Hesiod and Archilochus, or to Homer only?

ION. To Homer only; he is in himself quite enough.

SOC. Are there any things about which Homer and Hesiod agree?

ION. Yes; in my opinion there are a good many.

SOC. And can you interpret what Homer says about these matters better than what Hesiod says?

ION. I can interpret them equally well, Socrates, where they agree.

SOC. But what about matters in which they do not agree? For example, about divination of which both Homer and Hesiod have something to say—

ION. Very true.

SOC. Would you or a good prophet be a better interpreter of what these two poets say about divination, not only when they agree, but when they disagree?

ION. A prophet.

SOC. And if you were a prophet, and could interpret them where they agree, would you not know how to interpret them also where they disagree?

ION. Clearly.

SOC. But how did you come to have this skill about Homer only, and not about Hesiod or the other poets? Does not Homer speak of the same themes which all other poets handle? Is not war his great argument? And does he not speak of human society and of intercourse of men, good and bad, skilled and unskilled, and of the gods conversing with one another and with mankind, and about what happens in heaven and in the world below, and the generations of gods and heroes? Are not these the themes of which Homer sings?

ION. Very true, Socrates.

SOC. And do not the other poets sing of the same?

ION. Yes, Socrates; but not in the same way as Homer.

SOC. What, in a worse way?

ION. Yes, in a far worse.

SOC. And Homer in a better way?

ION. He is incomparably better.

SOC. And yet surely, my dear friend Ion, where many people are discussing numbers, and one speaks better than the rest, there is somebody who can judge which of them is the good speaker?

ION. Yes.

SOC. And he who judges of the good will be the same as he who judges of the bad speakers?

ION. The same.

SOC. One who knows the science of arithmetic?

ION. Yes.

SOC. Or again, if many persons are discussing the wholesomeness of food, and one speaks better than the rest, will he who recognizes the better speaker be a different person from him who recognizes the worse, or the same?

Ion. Clearly the same.

Soc. And who is he, and what is his name?

Ion. The physician.

Soc. And speaking generally, in all discussions in which the subject is the same and many men are speaking, will not he who knows the good know the bad speaker also? (532) For obviously if he does not know the bad, neither will he know the good, when the same topic is being discussed.

Ion. True.

Soc. We find, in fact, that the same person is skillful in both?

Ion. Yes.

Soc. And you say that Homer and the other poets, such as Hesiod and Archilochus, speak of the same things, although not in the same way; but the one speaks well and the other not so well?

Ion. Yes; and I am right in saying so.

Soc. And if you know the good speaker, you ought also to know the inferior speakers to be inferior?

Ion. It would seem so.

Soc. Then, my dear friend, can I be mistaken in saying that Ion is equally skilled in Homer and in other poets, since he himself acknowledges that the same person will be a good judge of all those who speak of the same things; and that almost all poets do speak of the same things?

Ion. Why then, Socrates, do I lose attention and have absolutely no ideas of the least value and practically fall asleep when anyone speaks of any other poet; but when Homer is mentioned, I wake up at once and am all attention and have plenty to say?

Soc. The reason, my friend, is not hard to guess. No one can fail to see that you speak of Homer without any art or knowledge. If you were able to speak of him by rules of art, you would have been able to speak of all other poets; for poetry is a whole.

Ion. Yes.

Soc. And when anyone acquires any other art as a whole, the same may be said of them. Would you like me to explain my meaning, Ion?

Ion. Yes, indeed, Socrates; I very much wish that you would: for I love to hear you wise men talk.

Soc. O that we were wise, Ion, and that you could truly call us so; but you rhapsodes and actors, and the poets whose verses you sing, are wise; whereas I am a common man, who only speak the truth. For consider what a very commonplace and trivial thing is this which I have said—a thing which any man might say: that when a man has acquired a knowledge of a whole art, the inquiry into good and bad is one and the same. Let us consider this matter; is not the art of painting a whole?

Ion. Yes.

Soc. And there are and have been many painters good and bad?

ION. Yes.

SOC. And did you ever know anyone who was skillful in pointing out the excellences and defects of Polygnotus the son of Aglaophon, but incapable of criticizing other painters; (533) and when the work of any other painter was produced, went to sleep and was at a loss, and had no ideas; but when he had to give his opinion about Polygnotus, or whoever the painter might be, and about him only, woke up and was attentive and had plenty to say?

ION. No indeed, I have never known such a person.

SOC. Or take sculpture—did you ever know of anyone who was skillful in expounding the merits of Daedalus the son of Metion, or of Epeius the son of Panopeus, or of Theodorus the Samian, or of any individual sculptor; but when the works of sculptors in general were produced, was at a loss and went to sleep and had nothing to say?

ION. No indeed; no more than the other.

SOC. And if I am not mistaken, you never met with anyone among flute-players or harp-players or singers to the harp or rhapsodes who was able to discourse of Olympus or Thamyras or Orpheus, or Phemius the rhapsode of Ithaca, but was at a loss when he came to speak of Ion of Ephesus, and had no notion of his merits or defects?

ION. I cannot deny what you say, Socrates. Nevertheless I am conscious in my own self, and the world agrees with me, that I do speak better and have more to say about Homer than any other man; but I do not speak equally well about others. After all, there must be some reason for this; what is it?

SOC. I see the reason, Ion; and I will proceed to explain to you what I imagine it to be. The gift which you possess of speaking excellently about Homer is not an art, but, as I was just saying, an inspiration; there is a divinity moving you, like that contained in the stone which Euripides calls a magnet, but which is commonly known as the stone of Heraclea. This stone not only attracts iron rings, but also imparts to them a similar power of attracting other rings; and sometimes you may see a number of pieces of iron and rings suspended from one another so as to form quite a long chain: and all of them derive their power of suspension from the original stone. In like manner the Muse first of all inspires men herself; and from these inspired persons a chain of other persons is suspended, who take the inspiration. For all good poets, epic as well as lyric, compose their beautiful poems not by art, but because they are inspired and possessed. (534) And as the Corybantian revelers[4] when they dance are not in their right mind, so the lyric poets are not in their right mind when they are composing their beautiful strains: but when falling under the power of music and meter they are inspired and possessed; like Bacchic maidens who draw milk and honey from the rivers when they are under the influence of Dionysus but not when they are in their right mind. And the soul of the lyric poet does the same, as they themselves say; for they tell us that they bring songs from honeyed fountains, culling them out of the gardens and dells of the Muses; they, like the bees, wing-ing their way from flower to flower. And this is true. For the poet is a light and winged and holy thing, and there is no invention in him until he has been inspired and is out of his senses, and reason is no longer in him: no man, while he retains that faculty, has the oracular gift of poetry.

Many are the noble words in which poets speak concerning the actions of men; but like yourself when speaking about Homer, they do not speak of them by any rules of art: they are simply inspired to utter that to which the Muse impels them, and that only; and when inspired, one of them will make dithyrambs,[5] another hymns of praise, another choral strains, another epic or iambic verses, but not one of them is of any account in the other kinds. For not by art does the poet sing, but by power divine; had he learned by rules of art, he would have known how to speak not of one theme only, but of all; and therefore God takes away reason from poets, and uses them as his ministers, as he also uses the pronouncers of oracles and holy prophets, in order that we who hear them may know them to be speaking not of themselves, who utter these priceless words while bereft of reason, but that God himself is the speaker, and that through them he is addressing us. And Tynnichus the Chalcidian affords a striking instance of what I am saying: he wrote no poem that anyone would care to remember but the famous paean[6] which is in everyone's mouth, one of the finest lyric poems ever written, simply an invention of the Muses, as he himself says. For in this way God would seem to demonstrate to us and not to allow us to doubt that these beautiful poems are not human, nor the work of man, but divine and the work of God; and that the poets are only the interpreters of the gods by whom they are severally possessed. (535) Was not this the lesson which God intended to teach when by the mouth of the worst of poets he sang the best of songs? Am I not right, Ion?

ION. Yes, indeed, Socrates, I feel that you are; for your words touch my soul, and I am persuaded that in these works the good poets, under divine inspiration, interpret to us the voice of the gods.

Soc. And you rhapsodists are the interpreters of the poets?

ION. There again you are right.

Soc. Then you are the interpreters of interpreters?

ION. Precisely.

Soc. I wish you would frankly tell me, Ion, what I am going to ask of you: When you produce the greatest effect upon the audience in the recitation of some striking passage, such as the apparition of Odysseus leaping forth on the floor, recognized by the suitors and shaking out his arrows at his feet, or the description of Achilles springing upon Hector, or the sorrows of Andromache, Hecuba, or Priam—are you in your right mind? Are you not carried out of yourself, and does not your soul in an ecstasy seem to be among the persons or places of which you are speaking, whether they are in Ithaca or in Troy or whatever may be the scene of the poem?

ION. That proof strikes home to me, Socrates. For I must frankly confess that at the tale of pity my eyes are filled with tears, and when I speak of horrors, my hair stands on end and my heart throbs.

SOC. Well, Ion, and what are we to say of a man who at a sacrifice or festival, when he is dressed in an embroidered robe, and has golden crowns upon his head, of which nobody has robbed him, appears weeping or panic-stricken in the presence of more than twenty thousand friendly faces, when there is no one despoiling or wronging him—is he in his right mind or is he not?

ION. No indeed, Socrates, I must say that, strictly speaking, he is not in his right mind.

SOC. And are you aware that you produce similar effects on most of the spectators?

ION. Only too well; for I look down upon them from the stage, and behold the various emotions of pity, wonder, sternness, stamped upon their countenances when I am speaking: and I am obliged to give my very best attention to them; for if I make them cry I myself shall laugh, and if I make them laugh I myself shall cry, when the time of payment arrives.

SOC. Do you know that the spectator is the last of the rings which, as I am saying, receive the power of the original magnet from one another? The rhapsode like yourself and the actor are intermediate links, and the poet himself is the first of them. (536) Through all these God sways the souls of men in any direction which He pleases, causing each link to communicate the power to the next. Thus there is a vast chain of dancers and masters and undermasters of choruses, who are suspended, as if from the stone, at the side of the rings which hang down from the Muse. And every poet has some Muse from whom he is suspended, and by whom he is said to be possessed, which is nearly the same thing; for he is taken hold of. And from these first rings, which are the poets, depend others, some deriving their inspiration from Orpheus, others from Musaeus; but the greater number are possessed and held by Homer. Of whom, Ion, you are one, and are possessed by Homer; and when anyone repeats the words of another poet you go to sleep, and know not what to say; but when anyone recites a strain of Homer you wake up in a moment, and your soul leaps within you, and you have plenty to say; for not by art or knowledge about Homer do you say what you say, but by divine inspiration and by possession; just as the Corybantian revelers too have a quick perception of that strain only which is appropriated to the god by whom they are possessed, and have plenty of dances and words for that, but take no heed of any other. And you, Ion, when the name of Homer is mentioned have plenty to say, and have nothing to say of others. You ask, "Why is this?" The answer is that your skill in the praise of Homer comes not from art but from divine inspiration.

ION. That is good, Socrates; and yet I doubt whether you will ever have eloquence enough to persuade me that I praise Homer only when I am mad and possessed; and if you could hear me speak of him I am sure you would never think this to be the case.

SOC. I should like very much to hear you, but not until you have answered a question which I have to ask. On what part of Homer do you speak well?—not surely about every part?

ION. There is no part, Socrates, about which I do not speak well: of that I can assure you.

SOC. Surely not about things in Homer of which you have no knowledge?

ION. And what is there in Homer of which I have no knowledge?

(537) SOC. Why, does not Homer speak in many passages about arts? For example, about driving; if I can only remember the lines I will repeat them.

ION. I remember, and will repeat them.

SOC. Tell me then, what Nestor says to Antilochus, his son, where he bids him be careful of the turn at the horse-race in honor of Patroclus.

ION. "Bend gently," he says, "in the polished chariot to the left of them, and urge the horse on the right hand with whip and voice; and slacken the rein. And when you are at the goal, let the left horse draw near, so that the nave of the well-wrought wheel may appear to graze the extremity; but have a care not to touch the stone."[7]

SOC. Enough. Now, Ion, will the charioteer or the physician be the better judge of the propriety of these lines?

ION. The charioteer, clearly.

SOC. And will the reason be that this is his art, or will there be any other reason?

ION. No, that will be the reason.

SOC. And every art is appointed by God to have knowledge of a certain work; for that which we know by the art of the pilot we shall not succeed in knowing also by the art of medicine?

ION. Certainly not.

SOC. Nor shall we know by the art of the carpenter that which we know by the art of medicine?

ION. Certainly not.

SOC. And this is true of all the arts—that which we know with one art we shall not know with the other? But let me ask a prior question: You admit that there are differences of arts?

ION. Yes.

SOC. You would argue, as I should, that if there are two kinds of knowledge, dealing with different things, these can be called different arts?

ION. Yes.

SOC. Yes, surely; for if the object of knowledge were the same, there would be no meaning in saying that the arts were different—since they both gave the same knowledge. For example, I know that here are five fingers, and you know the same. And if I were to ask whether I and you became acquainted with this fact by the help of the same art of arithmetic, you would acknowledge that we did?

ION. Yes.

(538) SOC. Tell me, then, what I was intending to ask you—whether in your opinion this holds universally? If two arts are the same, must not they necessarily have the same objects? And if one differs from another, must it not be because the object is different?

ION. That is my opinion, Socrates.

SOC. Then he who has no knowledge of a particular art will have no right judgment of the precepts and practice of that art?

ION. Very true.

SOC. Then which will be the better judge of the lines which you were reciting from Homer, you or the charioteer?

ION. The charioteer.

SOC. Why, yes, because you are a rhapsode and not a charioteer.

ION. Yes.

SOC. And the art of the rhapsode is different from that of the charioteer?

ION. Yes.

SOC. And if a different knowledge, then a knowledge of different matters?

ION. True.

SOC. You know the passage in which Hecamede, the concubine of Nestor, is described as giving to the wounded Machaon a posset, as he says, "made with Pramnian wine; and she grated cheese of goat's milk with a grater of bronze, and at his side placed an onion which gives a relish to drink."[8] Now would you say that the art of the rhapsode or the art of medicine was better able to judge of the propriety of these lines?

ION. The art of medicine.

SOC. And when Homer says, "And she descended into the deep like a leaden plummet, which, set in the horn of ox that ranges the fields, rushes along carrying death among the ravenous fishes,"[9] will the art of the fisherman or of the rhapsode be better able to judge what these lines mean, and whether they are accurate or not?

ION. Clearly, Socrates, the art of the fisherman.

SOC. Come now, suppose that you were to say to me: "Since you, Socrates, are able to assign different passages in Homer to their corresponding arts, I wish that you would tell me what are the passages of which the excellence ought to be judged by the prophet and prophetic art"; and you will see how readily and truly I shall answer you. For there are many such passages, particularly in the Odyssey; as, for example, the passage in which Theoclymenus the prophet of the house of Melampus says to the suitors:

(539) Wretched men! what is happening to you? Your heads
and your faces and your limbs underneath are shrouded in night;

and the voice of lamentation bursts forth, and your cheeks are wet with tears. And the vestibule is full, and the court is full, of ghosts descending into the darkness of Erebus, and the sun has perished out of heaven, and an evil mist is spread abroad.[10]

And there are many such passages in the Iliad also; as for example in the description of the battle near the rampart, where he says:

> As they were eager to pass the ditch, there came to them an omen: a soaring eagle, skirting the people on his left, bore a huge blood-red dragon in his talons, still living and panting; nor had he yet resigned the strife, for he bent back and smote the bird which carried him on the breast by the neck, and he in pain let him fall from him to the ground into the midst of the multitude. And the eagle, with a cry, was borne afar on the wings of the wind.[11]

These are the sort of things which I should say that the prophet ought to consider and determine.

ION. And you are quite right, Socrates, in saying so.

SOC. Yes, Ion, and you are right also. And as I have selected from the Iliad and Odyssey for you passages which describe the office of the prophet and the physician and the fisherman, do you, who know Homer so much better than I do, Ion, select for me passages which relate to the rhapsode and the rhapsode's art, and which the rhapsode ought to examine and judge of better than other men.

ION. All passages, I should say, Socrates.

SOC. Not all, Ion, surely. Have you already forgotten what you were saying? A rhapsode ought to have a better memory.

(540) ION. Why, what am I forgetting?

SOC. Do you not remember that you declared the art of the rhapsode to be different from the art of the charioteer?

ION. Yes, I remember.

SOC. And you admitted that being different they would know different objects?

ION. Yes.

SOC. Then upon your own showing the rhapsode, and the art of the rhapsode, will not know everything?

ION. I should exclude such things as you mention, Socrates.

SOC. You mean to say that you would exclude pretty much the subjects of the other arts. As he does not know all of them, which of them will he know?

ION. He will know what a man and what a woman ought to say, and what a freeman and what a slave ought to say, and what a ruler and what a subject.

Soc. Do you mean that a rhapsode will know better than the pilot what the ruler of a sea-tossed vessel ought to say?

Ion. No; the pilot will know best.

Soc. Or will the rhapsode know better than the physician what the ruler of a sick man ought to say?

Ion. Again, no.

Soc. But he will know what a slave ought to say?

Ion. Yes.

Soc. Suppose the slave to be a cowherd; the rhapsode will know better than the cowherd what he ought to say in order to soothe infuriated cows?

Ion. No, he will not.

Soc. But he will know what a spinning-woman ought to say about the working of wool?

Ion. No.

Soc. At any rate he will know what a general ought to say when exhorting his soldiers?

Ion. Yes, that is the sort of thing which the rhapsode will be sure to know.

Soc. What! Is the art of the rhapsode the art of the general?

Ion. I am sure that I should know what a general ought to say.

Soc. Why, yes, Ion, because you may possibly have the knowledge of a general as well as that of a rhapsode; and you might also have a knowledge of horsemanship as well as of the lyre, and then you would know when horses were well or ill managed. But suppose I were to ask you: By the help of which art, Ion, do you know whether horses are well managed, by your skill as a horseman or as a performer on the lyre—what would you answer?

Ion. I should reply, by my skill as a horseman.

Soc. And if you judged of performers on the lyre, you would admit that you judged of them as a performer on the lyre, and not as a horseman?

Ion. Yes.

Soc. And in judging of the general's art, do you judge as a general, or as a good rhapsode?

Ion. To me there appears to be no difference between them.

(541) Soc. What do you mean? Do you mean to say that the art of the rhapsode and of the general is the same?

Ion. Yes, one and the same.

Soc. Then he who is a good rhapsode is also a good general?

Ion. Certainly Socrates.

Soc. And he who is a good general is also a good rhapsode?

Ion. No; I do not agree to that.

Soc. But you do agree that he who is a good rhapsode is also a good general.

ION. Certainly.

SOC. And you are the best of Hellenic rhapsodes?

ION. Far the best, Socrates.

SOC. And are you also the best general, Ion?

ION. To be sure, Socrates; and Homer was my master.

SOC. But then, Ion, why in the name of goodness do you, who are the best of generals as well as the best of rhapsodes in all Hellas, go about reciting rhapsodies when you might be a general? Do you think that the Hellenes are in grave need of a rhapsode with his golden crown, and have no need at all of a general?

ION. Why, Socrates, the reason is that my countrymen, the Ephesians, are the servants and soldiers of Athens, and do not need a general; and that you and Sparta are not likely to appoint me, for you think that you have enough generals of your own.

SOC. My good Ion, did you never hear of Apollodorus of Cyzicus?

ION. Who may he be?

SOC. One who, though a foreigner, has often been chosen their general by the Athenians: and there is Phanosthenes of Andros, and Heraclides of Clazomenae, whom they have also appointed to the command of their armies and to other offices, although aliens, after they had shown their merit. And will they not choose Ion the Ephesian to be their general, and honor him, if they deem him qualified? Were not the Ephesians originally Athenians, and Ephesus is no mean city? But, indeed, Ion, if you are correct in saying that by art and knowledge you are able to praise Homer, you do not deal fairly with me, and after all your professions of knowing many glorious things about Homer, and promises that you would exhibit them, you only deceive me, and so far from exhibiting the art of which you are a master, will not, even after my repeated entreaties, explain to me the nature of it. You literally assume as many forms as Proteus, twisting and turning up and down, until at last you slip away from me in the disguise of a general, in order that you may escape exhibiting your Homeric lore. (542) And if you have art, then, as I was saying, in falsifying your promise that you would exhibit Homer, you are not dealing fairly with me. But if, as I believe, you have no art, but speak all these beautiful words about Homer unconsciously under his inspiring influence, then I acquit you of dishonesty, and shall only say that you are inspired. Which do you prefer to be thought, dishonest or inspired?

ION. There is a great difference, Socrates, between the two alternatives; and inspiration is by far the nobler.

SOC. Then, Ion, I shall assume the nobler alternative; and attribute to you in your praises of Homer inspiration, and not art.

THE REPUBLIC

from BOOK III
Persons of the Dialogue
Socrates   Adeimantus   Glaucon

(386) Then as far as the gods are concerned, I said, such tales are to be told, and such others are not to be told to our disciples from their youth upwards, if we mean them to honor the gods and their parents, and to value friendship with one another.

Yes; and I think that our principles are right, he said.

But if they are to be courageous, must they not learn other lessons besides these, and lessons of such a kind as will take away the fear of death? Can any man be courageous who has the fear of death in him?

Certainly not, he said.

And can he be fearless of death, or will he choose death in battle rather than defeat and slavery, who believes the world below to be real and terrible?

Impossible.

Then we must assume a control over the narrators of this class of tales as well as over the others, and beg them not simply to revile, but rather to commend the world below, intimating to them that their descriptions are untrue, and will do harm to our future warriors.

That will be our duty, he said.

Then, I said, we shall have to obliterate many obnoxious passages, beginning with the verses, "I would rather be a serf on the land of a poor and portionless man than rule over all the dead who have come to nought."[1] We must also expunge the verse, which tells us how Pluto feared: "Lest the mansions grim and squalid which the gods abhor should be seen both of mortals and immortals."[2] And again: "O heavens! verily in the house of Hades there is soul and ghostly form, but no mind at all in them!"[3] Again of Tiresias: "[To him even after death did Persephone grant mind] that he alone should be wise; but the other souls are flitting shades."[4] Again: "The soul flying from the limbs had gone to Hades, lamenting her fate, leaving manhood and youth."[5] Again: "And the soul, with shrilling cry, passed like smoke beneath the earth."[6] (387) And, "As bats in hollow of mystic cavern, whenever any of them has dropped out of the string and falls from the rock, fly shrilling and cling to one another, so did they with shrilling cry hold together as they moved."[7] And we must beg Homer and the other poets not to be angry if we strike out these and similar passages, not because they are unpoetical, or unattractive to the popular ear, but because the greater the poetical charm of them, the less are they meet[8] for the ears of boys and men who are meant to be free, and who should fear slavery more than death.

Undoubtedly.

Also we shall have to reject all the terrible and appalling names which describe the world below—Cocytus and Styx, ghosts under the earth, and sapless shades, and any similar words of which the very mention causes a shudder to pass through the inmost soul[4] of him who hears them. I do not say that these horrible stories may not have a use of some kind; but there is a danger that our guardians may be rendered too excitable and effeminate by them.

There is a real danger, he said.

Then we must have no more of them.

True.

Our poets must sing in another and a nobler strain.

Clearly.

And shall we proceed to get rid of the weepings and wailings of famous men?

They will go with the rest.

But shall we be right in getting rid of them? Reflect: our principle is that the good man will not consider death terrible to any other good man who is his comrade.

Yes; that is our principle.

And therefore he will not sorrow for his departed friend as though he had suffered anything terrible?

He will not.

Another thing which we should say of him is that he is the most sufficient for himself and his own happiness, and therefore is least in need of other men.

True, he said.

And for this reason the loss of a son or brother, or any deprivation of fortune, is to him of all men least terrible.

Assuredly.

And therefore he will be least likely to lament, and will bear with the greatest equanimity any misfortune of this sort which may befall him.

Yes, he will feel such a misfortune far less than another.

Then we shall be right in getting rid of the lamentations of famous men, and making them over to women (and not even to women who are good for anything), (388) or to men of a baser sort, that those who are being educated by us to be the defenders of their country may scorn to do the like.

That will be very right.

Then we will once more entreat Homer and the other poets not to depict Achilles,[9] who is the son of a goddess, first lying on his side, then on his back, and then on his face; then starting up and sailing[10] in a frenzy along the shores of the barren sea; now taking the sooty ashes in both his hands and pouring them over his head, or weeping and wailing[11] in the various modes which Homer has delineated. Nor should he describe Priam the kinsman of the gods as praying and beseeching, "rolling in the dirt, calling each man loudly by his name."[12] Still more earnestly will we beg of him at all events not to introduce the gods lamenting and saying, "Alas! my misery! Alas! that I bore the bravest to my sorrow."[13] But if he must introduce the gods, at any rate let him not dare so completely to misrepresent the greatest of the gods, as to make him say: "O heavens! with my eyes verily I behold a dear friend of mine chased round and round the city, and my heart is sorrowful."[14] Or again: "Woe is me that I am fated to have Sarpedon, dearest of men to me, subdued at the hands of Patroclus the son of Menoetius."[15] For if, my dear Adeimantus, our young men seriously listen to such unworthy representations of the gods, instead of laughing at them as they ought, hardly will any of them deem that he himself, being but a man, can be dishonored by similar actions; neither will he rebuke any inclination which may arise in his mind to say and do the like. And instead of having any shame or endurance, he will be always whining and lamenting on slight occasions.

Yes, he said, that is most true.

Yes, I replied; but that surely is what ought not to be, as the argument has just proved to us; and by that proof we must abide until it is disproved by a better.

It ought not to be.

Neither ought our guardians to be given to laughter. For a fit of laughter which has been indulged to excess almost always demands a violent reaction.

So I believe.

Then persons of worth, even if only mortal men, must not be represented as overcome by laughter, and still less must such a representation of the gods be allowed.

(389) Still less of the gods, as you say, he replied.

Then we shall not suffer such an expression to be used about the gods as that of Homer when he describes how "inextinguishable laughter arose among the blessed gods, when they saw Hephaestus bustling about the mansion."[16] On your views, we must not admit them.

On my views, if you like to father them on me; that we must not admit them is certain.

Again, truth should be highly valued; if we were right in saying that falsehood is useless to the gods, and useful only as a medicine to men, then the use of such medicines should be restricted to physicians; private individuals have no business with them.

Clearly not, he said.

Then if anyone at all is to have the privilege of lying, the rulers of the state should be the persons; and they, in their dealings either with enemies or with their own citizens, may be allowed to lie for the public good. But nobody else should meddle with anything of the kind; and although the rulers have this privilege, for a private man to lie to them in return is to be deemed a more heinous fault than for the patient or the pupil of a gymnasium not to speak the truth about his own bodily illnesses to the physician or to the trainer, or for a sailor not to tell the captain what is happening about the ship and the rest of the crew, and how things are going with himself or his fellow sailors.

Most true, he said.

If, then, the ruler catches in a lie anybody beside himself in the state, "any of the craftsmen, whether he be priest or physician or carpenter,"[17] he will punish him for introducing a practice which is equally subversive and destructive of ship or state.

Most certainly, he said, if our talk about the state is ever translated into action.[18]

In the next place our youth must be temperate?

Certainly.

Are not the chief elements of temperance, speaking generally, obedience to commanders and command of oneself in the pleasures of eating and drinking, and of sexual relations?

True.

Then we shall approve such language as that of Diomede in Homer, "Friend, sit still and obey my word,"[19] and the verses which follow, "The Greeks marched breathing prowess,[20] . . . in silent awe of their leaders,"[21] and other sentiments of the same kind.

We shall.

What of this line, "O heavy with wine, who hast the eyes of a dog and the heart of a stag,"[22] and of the words which follow? (390) Would you say that these, or any similar impertinences which private individuals are supposed to address to their rulers, whether in verse or prose, are well or ill spoken?

They are ill spoken.

They may very possibly afford some amusement, but they do not conduce to temperance. And therefore they are likely to do harm to our young men—you would agree with me there?

Yes.

And then, again, to make the wisest of men say that nothing in his opinion is more glorious than "When the tables are full of bread and meat, and the cup-bearer carries round wine which he draws from the bowl and pours into the cups";[23] is it fit or conducive to self-control for a young man to hear such words? Or the verse "The saddest of fates is to die and meet destiny from hunger"?[24] What would you say again to the tale of Zeus, who, while other gods and men were asleep and he the only person awake, lay devising plans, but forgot them all in a moment through his lust, and was so completely overcome at the sight of Hera that he would not even go into the hut, but wanted to lie with her on the ground, declaring that he had never been in such a state of rapture before, even when they first used to meet one another "without the knowledge of their parents";[25] or that other tale of how Hephaestus, because of similar goings-on, cast a chain around Ares and Aphrodite?[26]

Indeed, he said, I am strongly of opinion that they ought not to hear that sort of thing.

But any instances of endurance of various ills by famous men which are recounted or represented in drama, these they ought to see and hear; as, for example, what is said in the verses, "He smote his breast and thus reproached his heart,/ Endure, my heart; far worse hast thou endured!"[27]

Certainly, he said.

In the next place, we must not let them be receivers of bribes or lovers of money.

Certainly not.

Neither must we sing to them of "gifts persuading gods, and persuading reverend kings."[28] Neither is Phoenix, the tutor of Achilles, to be approved or deemed to have given his pupil good counsel when he told him that if the Greeks offered him gifts he should assist them;[29] but that without a gift he should not lay aside his anger. Neither will we believe or acknowledge Achilles himself to have been such a lover of money that he took Agamemnon's gifts, or that when he had received payment he restored the dead body of Hector, but that without payment he was unwilling to do so.[30]

(391) Undoubtedly, he said, these are not sentiments which can be approved.

Loving Homer as I do,[31] I hardly like to say that to attribute these feelings to Achilles, or to accept such a narrative from others, is downright impiety. As little can I believe the narrative of his insolence to Apollo, where he says, "Thou hast wronged me, O far-darter, most abominable of deities. Verily I would be even with thee, if I had only the power";[32] or his insubordination to the river-god,[33] on whose divinity he is ready to lay hands; or his offering to the dead Patroclus of his own hair,[34] which had been previously dedicated to the other river-god Spercheius, and that he actually performed this vow; or that he dragged Hector round the tomb of Patroclus,[35] and slaughtered the captives at the pyre;[36] all this we shall declare to be untrue, and shall not allow our citizens to be persuaded that he, the wise Cheiron's pupil, the son of a goddess and of Peleus who was the most modest of men and third in descent from Zeus, was so confused within as to be affected with two seemingly inconsistent diseases, meanness, not untainted by avarice, and overweening contempt of gods and men.

You are quite right, he replied.

And let us equally refuse to believe, or allow to be repeated, the tale of Theseus son of Poseidon, and Peirithous son of Zeus, going forth as they did to perpetrate a horrid rape; or of any other hero or son of a god daring to do such impious and dreadful things as they falsely ascribe to them in our day: and let us further compel the poets to declare either that these acts were not done by them, or that they were not the sons of gods—both in the same breath they shall not be permitted to affirm. We will not have them trying to persuade our youth that the gods are the authors of evil, and that heroes are no better than men—sentiments which, as we were saying, are neither pious nor true, for we have already proved that evil cannot come from the gods.

Assuredly not.

And further they are likely to have a bad effect on those who hear them; for everybody will begin to excuse his own vices when he is convinced that similar wickednesses are always being perpetrated by "the kindred of the gods, near descendants of Zeus, who worship him their ancestor at his altar, aloft in air on the peak of Ida," and who have "the blood of deities yet flowing in their veins."[37] And therefore let us put an end to such tales, lest they engender laxity of morals among the young. (392)

By all means, he replied.

But now that we are determining what classes of tales are or are not to be told, let us see whether any have been omitted by us. The manner in which gods and demigods and heroes and the world below should be treated has been already laid down.

Very true.

And it remains for us to decide what to say about men?

Clearly so.

But we are not in a condition to answer this question at present, my friend.

Why not?

Because, if I am not mistaken, we shall have to say that, about men, poets and story-tellers are guilty of making the gravest misstatements when they tell us that wicked men are often happy and the good miserable; and that injustice is profitable when undetected, but that justice is a man's own loss and another's gain—these things we shall forbid them to utter, and command them to sing and describe the opposite.

To be sure we shall, he replied.

But if you admit that I am right in this, then I shall maintain that you have implied the principle for which we have been all along contending.

I grant the truth of your inference.

That such things are or are not to be said about men is a question which we cannot determine until we have discovered what justice is, and how naturally advantageous to the possessor, whether he seem to be just or not.

Most true, he said.

Enough of the subjects of poetry: let us now speak of the style; and when this has been considered, both matter and manner will have been completely treated.

I do not understand what you mean, said Adeimantus.

Then I must make you understand; and perhaps I may be more intelligible if I put the matter in this way. You are aware, I suppose, that all mythology and poetry is a narration of events, either past, present, or to come?

Certainly, he replied.

And narration may be either simple narration, or imitation, or a union of the two?

That again, he said, I do not quite understand.

I fear that I must be an absurdly vague teacher. Like a bad speaker, therefore, I will not take the whole of the subject, but will break a piece off in illustration of my meaning. You know the first lines of the Iliad, in which the poet says that Chryses prayed Agamemnon to release his daughter, and that Agamemnon flew into a passion with him; whereupon Chryses, failing of his object, invoked the anger of the god against the Achaeans. (393) Now as far as these lines, "And he prayed all the Greeks, but especially the two sons of Atreus, the chiefs of the people,"[38] the poet is speaking in his own person; he never even tries to distract us by assuming another character. But in what follows he takes the person of Chryses, and then he does all that he can to make us believe that the speaker is not Homer, but the aged priest himself. And in this double form he has cast the entire narrative of the events which occurred at Troy and in Ithaca and throughout the Odyssey.

Yes.

And a narrative it remains both in the speeches which the poet recites from time to time and in the intermediate passages?

Quite true.

But when the poet speaks in the person of another, may we not say that he assimilates his style to that of the person who, as he informs you, is going to speak?

Certainly we may.

And this assimilation of himself to another, either by the use of voice or gesture, is the imitation of the person whose character he assumes?

Of course.

Then in this case the narrative of the poet, whether Homer or another, may be said to proceed by way of imitation?

Very true.

Or, if the poet were at no time to disguise himself, then again the imitation would be dropped, and his poetry become simple narration. However, in order that you may not have to repeat that you do not understand, I will show how the change might be effected. If Homer had said, "The priest came, having his daughter's ransom in his hands, supplicating the Achaeans, and above all the kings"; and then if, instead of speaking in the person of Chryses, he had continued in his own person, the words would have been, not imitation, but simple narration. The passage would have run as follows (I am no poet, and therefore I drop the meter), "The priest came and prayed the gods on behalf of the Greeks that they might capture Troy and return safely home, but begged that they would give him back his daughter, and take the ransom which he brought, and respect the god. Thus he spoke, and the other Greeks revered the priest and assented. But Agamemnon was wroth, and bade him depart and not come again, lest the staff and chaplets[39] of the god should be of no avail to him, and told him that before his daughter should be released, she should grow old with him in Argos. And then he told him to go away and not to provoke him, if he intended to get home un-scathed. (394) And the old man went away in fear and silence, and, when he had left the camp, he called upon Apollo by his many names, reminding him of everything which he had done pleasing to him, whether in building his temples or in offering sacrifice, and praying that his good deeds might be returned to him and that the Achaeans might expiate his tears by the arrows of the god,"—and so on. In this way the whole becomes simple narrative.

I understand, he said.

And you must realize that an opposite case occurs, when the poet's com-ments are omitted and the passages of dialogue only are left.

That also, he said, I understand; you mean, for example, as in tragedy.

You have conceived my meaning perfectly; and I think I can now make clear what you failed to apprehend before, that some poetry and mythology are wholly imitative (and, as you say, I mean tragedy and comedy); there is likewise the opposite style, in which the poet is the only speaker—of this the dithyramb affords the best example; and the combination of both is found in epic, and in several other styles of poetry. Do I take you with me?

Yes, he said; I see now what you meant.

I will ask you to remember also what I began by saying, that we had done with the subject and might proceed to the style.

Yes, I remember.

In saying this, I intended to imply that we must come to an understanding about the mimetic art—whether the poets, in narrating their stories, are to be al-lowed by us to imitate, and if so, whether in whole or in part, and if the latter, in what parts; or should all imitation be prohibited?

You mean, I suspect, to ask whether tragedy and comedy shall be admitted into our state?

Perhaps, I said; but there may be more than this in question: I really do not know as yet, but whither the argument may blow, thither we go.

And go we will, he said.

Then, Adeimantus, let me ask you to consider whether our guardians should or should not be fond of imitation; or rather, has not this question been decided by the rule already laid down that one man can only do one thing well, and not many; and that one who grasps at many will altogether fail of gaining much reputation in any?

Certainly.

And this is equally true of imitation; no one man can imitate many things as well as he would imitate a single one?

He cannot.

(395) Then the same person will hardly be able to play a serious part in life, and at the same time to be an imitator and imitate many other parts as well; for even when two species of imitation are nearly allied, the same persons cannot succeed in both, as for example, the writers of tragedy and comedy—did you not just now call them imitations?

Yes, I did; and you are right in thinking that the same persons cannot succeed in both.

Any more than they can be rhapsodists and actors at once?

True.

Neither do comic and tragic writers employ the same actors; yet all these things are imitations.

They are so.

And human nature, Adeimantus, appears to have been coined into yet smaller pieces, and to be as incapable of imitating many things well, as of performing well the actions of which the imitations are copies.

Quite true, he replied.

If then we adhere to our original notion and bear in mind that our guardians, released from every other business, are to dedicate themselves wholly to the maintenance of the freedom of the state, making this their craft and engaging in no work which does not bear on this end, then they ought not to practice or even imitate anything else; if they imitate at all, they should imitate from youth upward only those characters which are suitable to their profession—the courageous, temperate, holy, free, and the like; but they should not depict or be skillful at imitating any kind of illiberality or baseness, lest the fruit of imitation should be reality. Did you never observe how imitations, beginning in early youth and continuing far into life, at length grow into habits and become a second nature, affecting body, voice, and mind?

Yes, certainly, he said.

Then, I said, we will not allow those for whom we profess a care and of whom we say that they ought to be good men, to imitate a woman, whether young or old, quarrelling with her husband, or striving and vaunting against the gods in conceit of her happiness, or when she is in affliction, or sorrow, or weeping; and certainly not one who is in sickness, love, or labor.

Very right, he said.

Neither must they represent slaves, male or female, performing the offices of slaves?

They must not.

And surely not bad men, whether cowards or any others, who do the reverse of what we have just been prescribing, who scold or mock or revile one another in drink or out of drink, (396) or who in any other manner sin against themselves and their neighbors in word or deed, as the manner of such is. Neither should they be trained to imitate the action or speech of madmen; they must be able to recognize madness and vice in man or woman, but none of these things is to be practiced or imitated.

Very true, he replied.

Neither may they imitate smiths or other artificers, or oarsmen, or boat-swains, or the like?

How can they, he said, when they are not allowed to apply their minds to the callings of any of these?

Nor may they imitate the neighing of horses, the bellowing of bulls, the murmur of rivers and roll of the ocean, thunder, and all that sort of thing?

Nay, he said, if madness be forbidden, neither may they copy the behavior of madmen.

You mean, I said, if I understand you aright, that there is one sort of narrative style which is likely to be employed by an upright and good man when he has anything to say, and another sort, very unlike it, which will be preferred by a man of an opposite character and education.

And which are these two sorts? he asked.

As for the man of orderly life, I answered, when the time comes to describe some saying or action of another good man,—I think he will be willing to personate him, and will not be ashamed of this sort of imitation: he will be most ready to play the part of the good man when he is acting firmly and wisely; less often and in a less degree when he is overtaken by illness or love or drink, or has met with any other disaster. But when he comes to a character which is unworthy of him, he will not seriously assume the likeness of his inferior, and will do so, if at all, for a moment only when he is performing some good action; at other times he will be ashamed, both because he is not trained in imitation of such characters, and because he disdains to fashion and frame himself after the baser models; he feels the employment of such an art, unless in jest, to be beneath him.

So I should expect, he replied.

Then he will adopt a mode of narration such as we have illustrated out of Homer, that is to say, his style will be both imitative and narrative; but there will be, in a long story, only a small proportion of the former. Do you agree?

Certainly, he said; that is the model which such a speaker must necessarily take. (397)

But there is another sort of character who will narrate anything, and, the worse he is, the more unscrupulous he will be; nothing will be too bad for him: and he will be ready to imitate anything, in right good earnest, and before a large company. As I was just now saying, he will attempt to represent the roll of thunder, the noise of wind and hail, or the creaking of wheels, and pulleys, and the various sounds of flutes, pipes, trumpets, and all sorts of instruments: he will bark like a dog, bleat like a sheep, or crow like a cock; his entire art will consist in imitation of voice and gesture, or will be but slightly blended with narration.

That, he said, will be his mode of speaking.

These, then, are the two kinds of style I had in mind.

Yes.

And you would agree with me in saying that one of them is simple and has but slight changes; and that if an author expresses this style in fitting harmony and rhythm, he will find himself, if he does his work well, keeping pretty much within the limits of a single harmony (for the changes are not great), and in like manner he will make a similar choice of rhythm?

That is quite true, he said.

Whereas the other requires all sorts of harmonies and all sorts of rhythms if the music and the style are to correspond, because the style has all sorts of changes.

That is also perfectly true, he replied.

And do not the two styles, or the mixture of the two, comprehend all poetry and every form of expression in words? No one can say anything except in one or other of them or in both together.

They include all, he said.

And shall we receive into our state all the three styles, or one only of the two unmixed styles? Or would you include the mixed?

I should prefer only to admit the pure imitator of virtue.

Yes, I said, Adeimantus; and yet the mixed style is also charming: and indeed the opposite style to that chosen by you is by far the most popular with children and their attendants, and with the masses.

I do not deny it.

But I suppose you would argue that such a style is unsuitable to our state, in which human nature is not twofold or manifold, for one man plays one part only?

Yes; quite unsuitable.

And this is the reason why in our state, and in our state only, we shall find a shoemaker to be a shoemaker and not a pilot also, and a husbandman to be a husbandman and not a dicast[40] also, and a soldier a soldier and not a trader also, and the same throughout?

True, he said.

(398) And therefore when any one of these pantomimic gentlemen, who are so clever that they can imitate anything, comes to us and makes a proposal to exhibit himself and his poetry, we will fall down and worship him as a sacred, marvellous and delightful being; but we must also inform him that in our state such as he are not permitted to exist; the law will not allow them. And so when we have anointed him with myrrh, and set a garland of wool upon his head, we

shall send him away to another city. For we mean to employ for our souls' health the rougher and severer poet or storyteller, who will imitate the style of the virtuous only, and will follow those models which we prescribed at first when we began the education of our soldiers.

We certainly will, he said, if we have the power.

Then now, my friend, I said, that part of music or literary education which relates to the story or myth may be considered to be finished; for the matter and manner have both been discussed.

I think so too, he said.

Next in order will follow melody and song.

That is obvious.

Everyone now would be able to discover what we ought to say about them, if we are to be consistent with ourselves.

I fear, said Glaucon, laughing, that the word "everyone" hardly includes me, for I cannot at the moment say what they should be, though I have a suspicion.

At any rate you are aware that a song or ode has three parts—the words, the melody, and the rhythm.

Yes, he said; so much as that I know.

And as for the words, there will surely be no difference between words which are and which are not set to music; both will conform to the same laws, and these have been already determined by us?

Yes.

And the melody and rhythm will be in conformity with the words?

Certainly.

We were saying, when we spoke of the subject-matter, that we had no need of lamentation and strains of sorrow?

True.

And which are the harmonies expressive of sorrow? You are musical, and can tell me.

The harmonies which you mean are the mixed or tenor Lydian, and the full-toned or bass Lydian, and such-like.

These then, I said, must be banished; even to women who have a character to maintain they are of no use, and much less to men.

Certainly.

In the next place, drunkenness and softness and indolence are utterly unbecoming the character of our guardians.

Utterly unbecoming.

And which are the soft and convivial harmonies?

The Ionian, he replied, and some of the Lydian which are termed "relaxed."

(399) Well, and are these of any use for warlike men?

Quite the reverse, he replied; and if so the Dorian and the Phrygian are the only ones which you have left.

I answered: Of the harmonies I know nothing, but would have you leave me one which can render the note or accent which a brave man utters in warlike action and in stern resolve; and when his cause is failing, and he is going to wounds or death or is overtaken by disaster in some other form, at every such crisis he meets the blows of fortune with firm step and a determination to endure; and an opposite kind for times of peace and freedom of action, when there is no pressure of necessity, and he is seeking to persuade God by prayer, or man by instruction and admonition, or when on the other hand he is expressing his willingness to yield to the persuasion of entreaty or admonition of others. And when in this manner he has attained his end, I would have the music show him not carried away by his success, but acting moderately and wisely in all circumstances, and acquiescing in the event. These two harmonies I ask you to leave; the strain of necessity and the strain of freedom, the strain of the unfortunate and the strain of the fortunate, the strain of courage, and the strain of temperance; these, I say, leave.

And these, he replied, are the Dorian and Phrygian harmonies of which I was just now speaking.

Then, I said, if these and these only are to be used in our songs and melodies, we shall not want multiplicity of strings or a panharmonic scale?

I suppose not.

Then we shall not maintain the artificers of lyres with three corners and complex scales, or the makers of any other many-stringed, curiously harmonized instruments?

Certainly not.

But what do you say to flute-makers and flute-players? Would you admit them into our state when you reflect that in this composite use of harmony the flute is worse than any stringed instrument; even the panharmonic music is only an imitation of the flute?

Clearly not.

There remain then only the lyre and the harp for use in the city, and the shepherds in the country may have some kind of pipe.

That is surely the conclusion to be drawn from the argument.

The preferring of Apollo and his instruments to Marsyas and his instruments is not at all strange, I said.

Not at all, he replied.

And so, by the dog of Egypt, we have been unconsciously purging the state, which not long ago we termed luxurious.

And we have done wisely, he replied.

Then let us now finish the purgation, I said. Next in order to harmonies, rhythms will naturally follow, and they should be subject to the same rules, for we ought not to seek out complex systems of meter, and a variety of feet, but rather to discover what rhythms are the expressions of a courageous and harmonious life; (400) and when we have found them, we shall adapt the foot and the melody to words having a like spirit, not the words to the foot and melody. To say what these rhythms are will be your duty—you must teach me them, as you have already taught me the harmonies.

But, indeed, he replied, I cannot tell you. I know from observation that there are some three principles of rhythm out of which metrical systems are framed, just as in sounds there are four notes[41] out of which all the harmonies are composed. But of what sort of lives they are severally the imitations I am unable to say.

Then, I said, we must take Damon into our counsels; and he will tell us what rhythms are expressive of meanness, or insolence, or fury, or other unworthiness, and what are to be reserved for the expression of opposite feelings. And I think that I have an indistinct recollection of his mentioning a complex Cretic rhythm; also a dactylic or heroic, and he arranged them in some manner which I do not quite understand, making the rhythms equal in the rise and fall of the foot, long and short alternating; and, unless I am mistaken, he spoke of an iambic as well as of a trochaic rhythm, and assigned to them short and long quantities.[42] Also in some cases he appeared to praise or censure the movement of the foot quite as much as the rhythm; or perhaps a combination of the two; for I am not certain what he meant. These matters, however, as I was saying, had better be referred to Damon himself, for the analysis of the subject would be difficult, you know?

Rather so, I should say.

But it does not require much analysis to see that grace or the absence of grace accompanies good or bad rhythm.

None at all.

And also that good and bad rhythm naturally assimilate to a good and bad style; and that harmony and discord in like manner follow style; for our principle is that rhythm and harmony are regulated by the words, and not the words by them.

Just so, he said, they should follow the words.

And will not the words and the character of the style depend on the temper of the soul?

Yes.

And everything else on the style?

Yes.

Then beauty of style and harmony and grace and good rhythm depend on simplicity—I mean the true simplicity of a rightly and nobly ordered mind and character, not that other simplicity which is only a euphemism for folly?

Very true, he replied.

And if our youth are to do their work in life, must they not make these graces and harmonies their perpetual aim?

They must.

(401) And surely the art of the painter and every other creative and constructive art are full of them—weaving, embroidery, architecture, and every kind of manufacture; also nature, animal and vegetable—in all of them there is grace or the absence of grace. And ugliness and discord and inharmonious motion are nearly allied to ill words and ill nature, as grace and harmony are the twin sisters of goodness and self-restraint and bear their likeness.

That is quite true, he said.

But shall our superintendence go no further, and are the poets only to be required by us to express the image of the good in their works, on pain, if they do anything else, of expulsion from our state? Or is the same control to be extended to other artists, and are they also to be prohibited from exhibiting the opposite forms of vice and intemperance and meanness and deformity in sculpture and building and the other creative arts; and is he who cannot conform to this rule of ours to be prevented from practicing his art in our state, lest the taste of our citizens be corrupted by him? We would not have our guardians grow up amid images of moral deformity, as in some noxious pasture, and there browse and feed upon many a baneful herb and flower day by day, little by little, until they silently gather a festering mass of corruption in their own soul. Let us rather search for artists who are gifted to discern the true nature of the beautiful and graceful; then will our youth dwell in a land of health, amid fair sights and sounds, and receive the good in everything; and beauty, the effluence of fair works, shall flow into the eye and ear, like a health-giving breeze from a purer region, and insensibly draw the soul from earliest years into likeness and sympathy with the beauty of reason.

There can be no nobler training than that, he replied.

And therefore, I said, Glaucon, musical training is a more potent instrument than any other, because rhythm and harmony find their way into the inward places of the soul, on which they mightily fasten, imparting grace, and making the soul of him who is rightly educated graceful, or of him who is ill-educated ungraceful; and also because he who has received this true education of the inner being will most shrewdly perceive omissions or faults in art and nature, (402) and with a true taste, while he praises and rejoices over and receives into his soul the good, and becomes noble and good, he will justly blame and hate the bad, now in the days of his youth, even before he is able to know the reason why; and when reason comes he will recognize and salute the friend with whom his education has made him long familiar.

Yes, he said, I quite agree with you in thinking that it is for such reasons that they should be trained in music.

Just as in learning to read, I said, we were satisfied when we knew the letters of the alphabet, few as they are, in all their recurring combinations; not slighting them as unimportant whether they occupy a space large or small, but everywhere eager to make them out, because we knew we should not be perfect in the art of reading until we could do so:

True—

And as we recognize the reflection of letters in water, or in a mirror, only when we know the letters themselves, the same art and study giving us the knowledge of both:

Exactly—

Even so, as I maintain, neither we nor the guardians, whom we say that we have to educate, can ever become musical until we and they know the essential forms of temperance, courage, liberality, magnanimity, and their kindred, as well as the contrary forms, in all their combinations, and can recognize them and their images wherever they are found, not slighting them either in small things or great, but believing them all to be within the sphere of one art and study.

Most assuredly.

And when nobility of soul is observed in harmonious union with beauty of form, and both are cast from the same mold, that will be the fairest of sights to him who has an eye to see it?

The fairest indeed.

And the fairest is also the loveliest?

That may be assumed.

And it is with human beings who most display such harmony that a musical man will be most in love; but he will not love any who do not possess it.

That is true, he replied, if the deficiency be in the soul; but if there be any bodily defect he will be patient of it, and may even approve it.

BOOK X
Persons of the Dialogue
Socrates   Glaucon

(595) Of the many excellences which I perceive in the order of our state, there is none which upon reflection pleases me better than the rule about poetry.

To what do you refer?

To our refusal to admit the imitative kind of poetry, for it certainly ought not to be received; as I see far more clearly now that the parts of the soul have been distinguished.

What do you mean?

Speaking in confidence, for you will not denounce me to the tragedians and the rest of the imitative tribe, all poetical imitations are ruinous to the understanding of the hearers, unless as an antidote they possess the knowledge of the true nature of the originals.

Explain the purport of your remark.

Well, I will tell you, although I have always from my earliest youth had an awe and love of Homer which even now makes the words falter on my lips, for he seems to be the great captain and teacher of the whole of that noble tragic company[1]; but a man is not to be reverenced more than the truth, and therefore I will speak out

Very good, he said.

Listen to me then, or rather, answer me.

Put your question.

Can you give me a general definition of imitation? for I really do not myself understand what it professes to be.

A likely thing, then, that I should know.

(596) There would be nothing strange in that, for the duller eye may often see a thing sooner than the keener.

Very true, he said; but in your presence, even if I had any faint notion, I could not muster courage to utter it. Will you inquire yourself?

Well then, shall we begin the inquiry at this point, following our usual method: Whenever a number of individuals have a common name, we assume that there is one corresponding idea or form[2]—do you understand me?

I do.

Let us take, for our present purpose, any instance of such a group; there are beds and tables in the world—many of each, are there not?

Yes.

But there are only two ideas or forms of such furniture—one the idea of a bed, the other of a table.

True.

And the maker of either of them makes a bed or he makes a table for our use, in accordance with the idea—that is our way of speaking in this and similar instances—but no artificer makes the idea itself: how could he?

Impossible.

And there is another artificer—I should like to know what you would say of him.

Who is he?

One who is the maker of all the works of all other workmen.

What an extraordinary man!

Wait a little, and there will be more reason for your saying so. For this is the craftsman who is able to make not only furniture of every kind, but all that grows out of the earth, and all living creatures, himself included; and besides these he can make earth and sky and the gods, and all the things which are in heaven or in the realm of Hades under the earth.

He must be a wizard and no mistake.

Oh! you are incredulous, are you? Do you mean that there is no such maker or creator, or that in one sense there might be a maker of all these things but in another not? Do you see that there is a way in which you could make them all yourself?

And what way is this? he asked.

An easy way enough; or rather, there are many ways in which the feat might be quickly and easily accomplished, none quicker than that of turning a mirror round and round—you would soon enough make the sun and the heavens, and the earth and yourself, and other animals and plants, and furniture and all the other things of which we were just now speaking, in the mirror.

Yes, he said, but they would be appearances only.

Very good, I said, you are coming to the point now. And the painter too is, as I conceive, just such another—a creator of appearances, is he not?

Of course.

But then I suppose you will say that what he creates is untrue. And yet there is a sense in which the painter also creates a bed? Is there not?

Yes, he said, but here again, an appearance only.

(597) And what of the maker of the bed? Were you not saying that he too makes, not the idea which according to our view is the real object denoted by the word bed, but only a particular bed?

Yes, I did.

Then if he does not make a real object he cannot make what *is*, but only some semblance of existence; and if any one were to say that the work of the maker of the bed, or of any other workman, has real existence, he could hardly be supposed to be speaking the truth.

Not, at least, he replied, in the view of those who make a business of these discussions.

No wonder, then, that his work too is an indistinct expression of truth.

No wonder.

Suppose now that by the light of the examples just offered we inquire who this imitator is?

If you please.

Well then, here we find three beds: one existing in nature, which is made by God, as I think that we may say—for no one else can be the maker?

No one, I think.

There is another which is the work of the carpenter?

Yes.

And the work of the painter is a third?

Yes.

Beds, then, are of three kinds, and there are three artists who super-intend them: God, the maker of the bed, and the painter?

Yes, there are three of them.

God, whether from choice or from necessity, made one bed in nature and one only; two or more such beds neither ever have been nor ever will be made by God.

Why is that?

Because even if He had made but two, a third would still appear behind them of which they again both possessed the form, and that would be the real bed and not the two others.

Very true, he said.

God knew this, I suppose, and He desired to be the real maker of a real bed, not a kind of maker of a kind of bed, and therefore He created a bed which is essentially and by nature one only.

So it seems.

Shall we, then, speak of Him as the natural author or maker of the bed?

Yes, he replied; inasmuch as by the natural process of creation He is the author of this and of all other things.

And what shall we say of the carpenter—is not he also the maker of a bed?

Yes.

But would you call the painter an artificer and maker?

Certainly not.

Yet if he is not the maker, what is he in relation to the bed?

I think, he said, that we may fairly designate him as the imitator of that which the others make.

Good, I said; then you call him whose product is third in the descent from nature, an imitator?

Certainly, he said.

And so if the tragic poet is an imitator, he too is thrice removed from the king and from the truth; and so are all other imitators.

That appears to be so.

Then about the imitator we are agreed. And what about the painter? (598) Do you think he tries to imitate in each case that which originally exists in nature, or only the creations of artificers?

The latter.

As they are or as they appear? You have still to determine this.

What do you mean?

I mean to ask whether a bed really becomes different when it is seen from different points of view, obliquely or directly or from any other point of view? Or does it simply appear different, without being really so? And the same of all things.

Yes, he said, the difference is only apparent.

Now let me ask you another question: Which is the art of painting designed to be—an imitation of things as they are, or as they appear—of appearance or of reality?

Of appearance, he said.

Then the imitator is a long way off the truth, and can reproduce all things because he lightly touches on a small part of them, and that part an image. For example: A painter will paint a cobbler, carpenter, or any other artisan, though he knows nothing of their arts; and, if he is a good painter, he may deceive children or simple persons when he shows them his picture of a carpenter from a distance, and they will fancy that they are looking at a real carpenter.

Certainly.

And surely, my friend, this is how we should regard all such claims: whenever anyone informs us that he has found a man who knows all the arts, and all things else that anybody knows, and every single thing with a higher degree of accuracy than any other man—whoever tells us this, I think that we can only retort that he is a simple creature who seems to have been deceived by some wizard or imitator whom he met, and whom he thought all-knowing, because he himself was unable to analyse the nature of knowledge and ignorance and imitation.

Most true.

And next, I said, we have to consider tragedy and its leader, Homer; for we hear some persons saying that these poets know all the arts; and all things human; where virtue and vice are concerned, and indeed all divine things too; because the good poet cannot compose well unless he knows his subject, and he who has not this knowledge can never be a poet. We ought to consider whether here also there may not be a similar illusion. Perhaps they may have come across imitators and been deceived by them; they may not have remembered when they saw their works that these were thrice removed from the truth, (599) and could easily be made without any knowledge of the truth, because they are appearances only and not realities? Or, after all, they may be in the right, and good poets do really know the things about which they seem to the many to speak so well?

The question, he said, should by all means be considered.

Now do you suppose that if a person were able to make the original as well as the image, he would seriously devote himself to the image-making branch? Would he allow imitation to be the ruling principle of his life, as if he had nothing higher in him?

I should say not.

But the real artist, who had real knowledge of those things which he chose also to imitate, would be interested in realities and not in imitations; and would desire to leave as memorials of himself works many and fair; and, instead of being the author of encomiums, he would prefer to be the theme of them.

Yes, he said, that would be to him a source of much greater honor and profit.

Now let us refrain, I said, from calling Homer or any other poet to account regarding those arts to which his poems incidentally refer: we will not ask them, in case any poet has been a doctor and not a mere imitator of medical parlance, to show what patients have been restored to health by a poet, ancient or modern, as they were by Asclepius; or what disciples in medicine a poet has left behind him, like the Asclepiads. Nor shall we press the same question upon them about the other arts. But we have a right to know respecting warfare, strategy, the administration of states and the education of man, which are the chiefest and noblest subjects of his poems, and we may fairly ask him about them. "Friend Homer," then we say to him, "if you are only in the second remove from truth in what you say of virtue, and not in the third—not an image maker, that is, by our definition, an imitator—and if you are able to discern what pursuits make men better or worse in private or public life, tell us what state was ever better governed by your help? The good order of Lacedaemon is due to Lycurgus, and many other cities great and small have been similarly benefited by others; but who says that you have been a good legislator to them and have done them any good? Italy and Sicily boast of Charondas, and there is Solon who is renowned among us; but what city has anything to say about you?" Is there any city which he might name?

I think not, said Glaucon; not even the Homerids themselves pretend that he was a legislator.

(600) Well, but is there any war on record which was carried on successfully owing to his leadership or counsel?

There is not.

Or is there anything comparable to those clever improvements in the arts, or in other operations, which are said to have been due to men of practical genius such as Thales the Milesian or Anacharsis the Scythian?

There is absolutely nothing of the kind.

But, if Homer never did any public service, was he privately a guide or teacher of any? Had he in his lifetime friends who loved to associate with him, and who handed down to posterity an Homeric way of life, such as was established by Pythagoras who was especially beloved for this reason and whose followers are to this day conspicuous among others by what they term the Pythagorean way of life?

Nothing of the kind is recorded of him. For surely, Socrates, Creophylus, the companion of Homer, that child of flesh, whose name always makes us laugh, might be more justly ridiculed for his want of breeding, if what is said is true, that Homer was greatly neglected by him in his own day when he was alive?

Yes, I replied, that is the tradition. But can you imagine, Glaucon, that if Homer had really been able to educate and improve mankind—if he had been capable of knowledge and not been a mere imitator—can you imagine, I say, that he would not have attracted many followers, and been honored and loved by them? Protagoras of Abdera, and Prodicus of Ceos, and a host of others, have only to whisper to their contemporaries: "You will never be able to manage either your own house or your own state until you appoint us to be your ministers of education"—and this ingenious device of theirs has such an effect in making men love them that their companions all but carry them about on their shoulders. And is it conceivable that the contemporaries of Homer, or again of Hesiod, would have allowed either of them to go about as rhapsodists, if they had really been able to help mankind forward in virtue? Would they not have been as unwilling to part with them as with gold, and have compelled them to stay at home with them? Or, if the master would not stay, then the disciples would have followed him about everywhere, until they had got education enough?

Yes, Socrates, that, I think, is quite true.

Then must we not infer that all these poetical individuals, beginning with Homer, are only imitators, who copy images of virtue and the other themes of their poetry, but have no contact with the truth? (601) The poet is like a painter who, as we have already observed, will make a likeness of a cobbler though he understands nothing of cobbling; and his picture is good enough for those who know no more than he does, and judge only by colors and figures.

Quite so.

In like manner the poet with his words and phrases[3] may be said to lay on the colors of the several arts, himself understanding their nature only enough to imitate them; and other people, who are as ignorant as he is, and judge only from his words, imagine that if he speaks of cobbling, or of military tactics, or of anything else, in meter and harmony and rhythm, he speaks very well—such is the sweet influence which melody and rhythm by nature have. For I am sure that you know what a poor appearance the works of poets make when stripped of the colors which art puts upon them, and recited in simple prose. You have seen some examples?

Yes, he said.

They are like faces which were never really beautiful, but only blooming, seen when the bloom of youth has passed away from them?

Exactly.

Come now, and observe this point: The imitator or maker of the image knows nothing, we have said, of true existence; he knows appearances only. Am I not right?

Yes.

Then let us have a clear understanding, and not be satisfied with half an explanation.

Proceed.

Of the painter we say that he will paint reins, and he will paint a bit?

Yes.

And the worker in leather and brass will make them?

Certainly.

But does the painter know the right form of the bit and reins? Nay, hardly even the workers in brass and leather who make them; only the horseman who knows how to use them—he knows their right form.

Most true.

And may we not say the same of all things?

What?

That there are three arts which are concerned with all things: one which uses, another which makes, a third which imitates them?

Yes.

And the excellence and beauty and rightness of every structure, animate or inanimate, and of every action of man, is relative solely to the use for which nature or the artist has intended them.

True.

Then beyond doubt it is the user who has the greatest experience of them, and he must report to the maker the good or bad qualities which develop themselves in use; for example, the flute-player will tell the flute-maker which of his flutes is satisfactory to the performer; he will tell him how he ought to make them, and the other will attend to his instructions?

Of course.

So the one pronounces with knowledge about the goodness and badness of flutes, while the other, confiding in him, will make them accordingly?

True.

The instrument is the same, but about the excellence or badness of it the maker will possess a correct belief, since he associates with one who knows, and is compelled to hear what he has to say; (602) whereas the user will have knowledge?

True.

But will the imitator have either? Will he know from use whether or no that which he paints is correct or beautiful? Or will he have right opinion from being compelled to associate with another who knows and gives him instructions about what he should paint?

Neither.

Then an imitator will no more have true opinion than he will have knowledge about the goodness or badness of his models?

I suppose not.

The imitative poet will be in a brilliant state of intelligence about the theme of his poetry?

Nay, very much the reverse.

And still he will go on imitating without knowing what makes a thing good or bad, and may be expected therefore to imitate only that which appears to be good to the ignorant multitude?

Just so.

Thus far then we are pretty well agreed that the imitator has no knowledge worth mentioning of what he imitates. Imitation is only a kind of play or sport, and the tragic poets, whether they write in iambic or in heroic verse,[4] are imitators in the highest degree?

Very true.

And now tell me, I conjure you—this imitation is concerned with an object which is thrice removed from the truth?

Certainly.

And what kind of faculty in man is that to which imitation makes its special appeal?

What do you mean?

I will explain: The same body does not appear equal to our sight when seen near and when seen at a distance?

True.

And the same objects appear straight when looked at out of the water, and crooked when in the water; and the concave becomes convex, owing to the illusion about colors to which the sight is liable. Thus every sort of confusion is revealed within us; and this is that weakness of the human mind on which the art of painting in light and shadow, the art of conjuring, and many other ingenious devices impose, having an effect upon us like magic.

True.

And the arts of measuring and numbering and weighing come to the rescue of the human understanding—there is the beauty of them—with the result that the apparent greater or less, or more or heavier, no longer have the mastery over us, but give way before the power of calculation and measuring and weighing?

Most true.

And this, surely, must be the work of the calculating and rational principle in the soul?

To be sure.

And often when this principle measures and certifies that some things are equal, or that some are greater or less than others, it is, at the same time, contradicted by the appearance which the objects present?

True.

But did we not say that such a contradiction is impossible—the same faculty cannot have contrary opinions at the same time about the same thing?

We did; and rightly.

(603) Then that part of the soul which has an opinion contrary to measure

can hardly be the same with that which has an opinion in accordance with measure?

True.

And the part of the soul which trusts to measure and calculation is likely to be the better one?

Certainly.

And therefore that which is opposed to this is probably an inferior principle in our nature?

No doubt.

This was the conclusion at which I was seeking to arrive when I said that painting or drawing, and imitation in general, are engaged upon productions which are far removed from truth, and are also the companions and friends and associates of a principle within us which is equally removed from reason, and that they have no true or healthy aim.

Exactly.

The imitative art is an inferior who from intercourse with an inferior has inferior offspring.

Very true.

And is this confined to the sight only, or does it extend to the hearing also, relating in fact to what we term poetry?

Probably the same would be true of poetry.

Do not rely, I said, on a probability derived from the analogy of painting; but let us once more go directly to that faculty of the mind with which imitative poetry has converse, and see whether it is good or bad.

By all means.

We may state the question thus: Imitation imitates the actions of men, whether voluntary or involuntary, on which, as they imagine, a good or bad result has ensued, and they rejoice or sorrow accordingly. Is there anything more?

No, there is nothing else.

But in all this variety of circumstances is the man at unity with himself —or rather, as in the instance of sight there was confusion and opposition in his opinions about the same things, so here also is there not strife and inconsistency in his life? Though I need hardly raise the question again, for I remember that all this has been already admitted; and the soul has been acknowledged by us to be full of these and ten thousand similar oppositions occurring at the same moment?

And we were right, he said.

Yes, I said, thus far we were right; but there was an omission which must now be supplied.

What was the omission?

Were we not saying that a good man, who has the misfortune to lose his son or anything else which is most dear to him, will bear the loss with more equanimity than another?

Yes, indeed.

But will he have no sorrow, or shall we say that although he cannot help sorrowing, he will moderate his sorrow?

The latter, he said, is the truer statement.

(604) Tell me: will he be more likely to struggle and hold out against his sorrow when he is seen by his equals, or when he is alone in a deserted place?

The fact of being seen will make a great difference, he said.

When he is by himself he will not mind saying many things which he would be ashamed of any one hearing, and also doing many things which he would not care to be seen doing?

True.

And doubtless it is the law and reason in him which bids him resist; while it is the affliction itself which is urging him to indulge his sorrow?

True.

But when a man is drawn in two opposite directions, to and from the same object, this, as we affirm, necessarily implies two distinct principles in him?

Certainly.

One of them is ready to follow the guidance of the law?

How do you mean?

The law would say that to be patient under calamity is best, and that we should not give way to impatience, as the good and evil in such things are not clear, and nothing is gained by impatience; also, because no human thing is of serious importance, and grief stands in the way of that which at the moment is most required.

What is most required? he asked.

That we should take counsel about what has happened, and when the dice have been thrown, according to their fall, order our affairs in the way which reason deems best; not, like children who have had a fall, keeping hold of the part struck and wasting time in setting up a howl, but always accustoming the soul forthwith to apply a remedy, raising up that which is sickly and fallen, banishing the cry of sorrow by the healing art.

Yes, he said, that is the true way of meeting the attacks of fortune.

Well then, I said, the higher principle is ready to follow this suggestion of reason?

Clearly.

But the other principle, which inclines us to recollection of our troubles and to lamentation, and can never have enough of them, we may call irrational, useless, and cowardly?

Indeed, we may.

Now does not the principle which is thus inclined to complaint, furnish a great variety of materials for imitation? Whereas the wise and calm temperament, being always nearly equable, is not easy to imitate or to appreciate when imitated, especially at a public festival when a promiscuous crowd is assembled in a theatre. For the feeling represented is one to which they are strangers.

Certainly.

(605) Then the imitative poet who aims at being popular is not by nature made, nor is his art intended, to please or to affect the rational principle in the soul; but he will appeal rather to the lachrymose and fitful temper, which is easily imitated?

Clearly.

And now we may fairly take him and place him by the side of the painter, for he is like him in two ways: first, inasmuch as his creations have an inferior degree of truth—in this, I say, he is like him; and he is also like him in being the associate of an inferior part of the soul; and this is enough to show that we shall be right in refusing to admit him into a state which is to be well ordered, because he awakens and nourishes this part of the soul, and by strengthening it impairs the reason. As in a city when the evil are permitted to wield power and the finer men are put out of the way, so in the soul of each man, as we shall maintain, the imitative poet implants an evil constitution, for he indulges the irrational nature which has no discernment of greater and less, but thinks the same thing at one time great and at another small—he is an imitator of images and is very far removed from the truth.

Exactly.

But we have not yet brought forward the heaviest count in our accusation—the power which poetry has of harming even the good (and there are very few who are not harmed), is surely an awful thing?

Yes, certainly, if the effect is what you say.

Hear and judge: The best of us, as I conceive, when we listen to a passage of Homer or one of the tragedians, in which he represents some hero who is drawling out his sorrows in a long oration, or singing, and smiting his breast—the best of us, you know, delight in giving way to sympathy, and are in raptures at the excellence of the poet who stirs our feelings most.

Yes, of course I know.

But when any sorrow of our own happens to us, then you may observe that we pride ourselves on the opposite quality—we would fain be quiet and patient; this is considered the manly part, and the other which delighted us in the recitation is now deemed to be the part of a woman.

Very true, he said.

Now can we be right in praising and admiring another who is doing that which any one of us would abominate and be ashamed of in his own person?

No, he said, that is certainly not reasonable.

(606) Nay, I said, quite reasonable from one point of view.

What point of view?

If you consider, I said, that when in misfortune we feel a natural hunger and desire to relieve our sorrow by weeping and lamentation, and that this very feeling which is starved and suppressed in our own calamities is satisfied and delighted by the poets—the better nature in each of us, not having been sufficiently trained by reason or habit, allows the sympathetic element to break loose because the sorrow is another's; and the spectator fancies that there can be no disgrace to himself in praising and pitying any one who while professing to be a brave man, gives way to untimely lamentation; he thinks that the pleasure is a gain, and is far from wishing to lose it by rejection of the whole poem. Few persons ever reflect, as I should imagine, that the contagion must pass from others to themselves. For the pity which has been nourished and strengthened in the misfortunes of others is with difficulty repressed in our own.

How very true!

And does not the same hold also of the ridiculous? There are jests which you would be ashamed to make yourself, and yet on the comic stage, or indeed in private, when you hear them, you are greatly amused by them, and are not at all disgusted at their unseemliness—the case of pity is repeated—there is a principle in human nature which is disposed to raise a laugh, and this, which you once restrained by reason because you were afraid of being thought a buffoon, is now let out again; and having stimulated the risible faculty at the theater, you are betrayed unconsciously to yourself into playing the comic poet at home.

Quite true, he said.

And the same may be said of lust and anger and all the other affections, of desire and pain and pleasure, which are held to be inseparable from every action—in all of them poetry has a like effect; it feeds and waters the passions instead of drying them up; she lets them rule, although they ought to be controlled if mankind are ever to increase in happiness and virtue.

I cannot deny it.

Therefore, Glaucon, I said, whenever you meet with any of the eulogists of Homer declaring that he has been the educator of Hellas, and that he is profitable for education and for the ordering of human things, and that you should take him up again and again and get to know him and regulate your whole life according to him, we may love and honor those who say these things —they are excellent people, as far as their lights extend; (607) and we are ready to acknowledge that Homer is the greatest of poets and first of tragedy writers; but we must remain firm in our conviction that hymns to the gods and praises of famous men are the only poetry which ought to be admitted into our state. For if you go beyond this and allow the honeyed Muse to enter, either in epic or lyric verse, not law and the reason of mankind, which by common consent have ever been deemed best,[5] but pleasure and pain will be the rulers in our state.

That is most true, he said.

And now since we have reverted to the subject of poetry, let this our defense serve to show the reasonableness of our former judgment in sending away out of our state an art having the tendencies which we have described; for reason constrained us. But that she may not impute to us any harshness or want of politeness, let us tell her that there is an ancient quarrel between philosophy and poetry; of which there are many proofs, such as the saying of "the yelping hound howling at her lord," or of one "mighty in the vain talk of fools," and "the mob of sages circumventing Zeus," and the "subtle thinkers who are beggars after all";[6] and there are innumerable other signs of ancient enmity between them. Notwithstanding this, let us assure the poetry which aims at pleasure, and the art of imitation, that if she will only prove her title to exist in a well-ordered state we shall be delighted to receive her—we are very conscious of her charms; but it would not be right on that account to betray the truth. I dare say, Glaucon, that you are as much charmed by her as I am, especially when she appears in Homer?

Yes, indeed, I am greatly charmed.

Shall I propose, then, that she be allowed to return from exile, but upon this condition only—that she make a defense of herself in some lyrical or other meter?

Certainly.

And we may further grant to those of her defenders who are lovers of poetry and yet not poets the permission to speak in prose on her behalf: let them show not only that she is pleasant but also useful to states and to human life, and we will listen in a kindly spirit; for we shall surely be the gainers if this can be proved, that there is a use in poetry as well as a delight?

Certainly, he said, we shall be the gainers.

If her defense fails, then, my dear friend, like other persons who are enamored of something, but put a restraint upon themselves when they think their desires are opposed to their interests, so too must we after the manner of lovers give her up, though not without a struggle. We too are inspired by that love of such poetry which the education of noble states has implanted in us, (608) and therefore we shall be glad if she appears at her best and truest; but so long as she is unable to make good her defense, this argument of ours shall be a charm to us, which we will repeat to ourselves while we listen to her strains; that we may not fall away into the childish love of her which captivates the many. At all events we are well aware that poetry,[7] such as we have described, is not to be regarded seriously as attaining to the truth; and he who listens to her, fearing for the safety of the city which is within him, should be on his guard against her seductions and make our words his law.

Yes, he said, I quite agree with you.

Yes, I said, my dear Glaucon, for great is the issue at stake, greater than appears, whether a man is to be good or bad. And what will any one be profited if under the influence of honor or money or power, aye, or under the excitement of poetry, he neglect justice and virtue?

Yes, he said; I have been convinced by the argument, as I believe that anyone else would have been.

And yet we have not described the greatest prizes and rewards which await virtue.

What, are there any greater still? If there are, they must be of an inconceivable greatness.

Why, I said, what was ever great in a short time? The whole period from childhood to age is surely but a little thing in comparison with eternity?

Say rather "nothing," he replied.

And should an immortal being be anxious for this little time rather than for the whole?

For the whole, certainly. But why do you ask?

Are you not aware, I said, that the soul of man is immortal and imperishable?

He looked at me in astonishment, and said: No, by heaven: And are you really prepared to maintain this?

Yes, I said, I ought to be, and you too—there is no difficulty in proving it.

I see a great difficulty; but I should like to hear you state this argument of which you make so light.

Listen then.

I am attending.

There is a thing which you call good and another which you call evil?

Yes, he replied.

Would you agree with me in thinking that the corrupting and destroying element is the evil, and the saving and improving element the good?

True.

And you admit that everything has a good and also an evil; (609) as ophthalmia is the evil of the eyes and disease of the whole body; as blight is of corn, and rot of timber, or rust of copper and iron: in everything, or in almost everything, there is an inherent evil and disease?

Yes, he said.

And any of these evils, when it attacks a thing, first makes it rotten and at last wholly dissolves and destroys it?

True.

The vice and evil which is inherent in each is the destruction of each; or if this does not destroy them there is nothing else that will; for good certainly will never destroy anything, nor, again, will that which is neither good nor evil.

Certainly not.

If, then, we find any nature which has indeed some inherent corruption, but of a kind whereby it cannot be dissolved or destroyed, we many be certain that of such a nature there is no destruction?

That may be assumed.

Well, I said, and is there no evil which corrupts the soul?

Yes, he said, there are all the evils which we were just now passing in review: unrighteousness, intemperance, cowardice, ignorance.

But does any of these dissolve and destroy her? And here do not let us fall into the error of supposing that the unjust and foolish man, when he is detected, perishes through his own injustice, which is an evil of the soul. You should represent it rather in this way: The evil of the body is a disease which dissolves and wastes it, till it is no longer a body at all; and all the things of which we were just now speaking come to annihilation through their own corruption attaching to them and inhering in them and so destroying them. Is not this true?

Yes.

Consider the soul in like manner. Does injustice, or vice in some other form, waste and consume her? Do they by attaching to the soul and inhering in her at last bring her to death, and so separate her from the body?

Certainly not.

And yet, I said, it is unreasonable to suppose that anything can perish under a disease proper to another thing, which could not be destroyed by a corruption of its own?

It is, he replied.

Consider, I said, Glaucon, that even the badness of food, whether staleness, decomposition, or any other bad quality, when confined to the actual food, is not supposed to destroy the body; although, if the badness of food causes the body to become corrupt in its own fashion, then we should say that the body has been destroyed by a corruption of itself, which is disease, brought on by this; (610) but that the body, being one thing, can be destroyed by the badness of food, which is another, unless it has implanted the corruption peculiar to the body—this we shall absolutely deny?

Very true.

On the same principle, then, unless some bodily evil can produce in the soul an evil of the soul, we must not suppose that the soul, which is one thing, can be dissolved, in the absence of its own disease, by an evil which belongs to another?

Yes, he said, there is reason in that.

Either, then, let us refute this conclusion, or, while it remains unrefuted, let us never say that fever, or any other disease, or the knife put to the throat, or even the cutting up of the whole body into the minutest pieces, can destroy the soul, until she herself is proved to become more unholy or unrighteous in consequence of these things being done to the body; but that the soul or anything else can be free from its special evil and yet be destroyed because a foreign evil is found in something else, is not to be affirmed by any man.

And surely, he replied, no one will ever prove that the souls of dying men become more unjust in consequence of death.

But if someone, lest he be obliged to admit the immortality of the soul, boldly goes out to meet our argument, and says that the dying do really become more evil and unrighteous, then, if the speaker is right, I suppose that injustice, like disease, must be assumed to be fatal to the unjust, and that those who take this disorder die by the natural inherent power of destruction which evil has, and which kills them sooner or later, but in quite another way from that in which, at present, the wicked receive death at the hands of others as the penalty of their deeds?

Nay, he said, in that case injustice, if fatal to the unjust, will not be so very terrible to him, for he will thus be delivered from evil. But I rather suspect the opposite will prove to be the truth, and that injustice which, if it have the power, will murder others, gives the murderer greater vitality—aye, and keeps him well awake too; so far removed is her dwelling-place from being a house of death.

True, I said; if the inherent natural vice or evil of the soul has not the force to kill or destroy her, hardly will that which is appointed to be the destruction of some other body destroy a soul, or anything else except that of which it was appointed to be the destruction.

Yes, that can hardly be.

(611) But the soul which cannot be destroyed by any evil, whether its own or that of something else, must exist for ever, and if existing for ever, must be immortal?

Certainly.

Let that be our conclusion, I said; and, if it is a true conclusion, you will observe that the souls must always be the same, for if none be destroyed they will not diminish in number. Neither will they increase, for the increase of the immortal natures must, as you know, come from something mortal, and all things would thus end in immortality.

Very true.

But this we cannot believe—reason will not allow us—any more than we can believe the soul, in her truest nature, to be a thing full of variety and internal difference and dissimilarity.

What do you mean? he said.

It is not easy, I said, for that thing to be immortal which is a compound of many elements not perfectly adapted to each other, as the soul has appeared to us to be.

Certainly not.

Her immortality is demonstrated by the previous argument, and there are many other proofs; but to see her as she really is, not, as we now behold her, marred by association with the body and other miseries, you must contemplate her with the eye of reason, in her original purity; and then her greater beauty will be revealed, and the forms of justice and injustice and all the things which we have described will be more vividly discerned. Thus far, we have spoken the truth concerning her as she appears at present, but we have seen her only in a condition which may be compared to that of the sea-god Glaucus, whose original nature could hardly be discerned by those who saw him because his natural members were either broken off or crushed and damaged by the waves in all sorts of ways, and incrustations had grown over them of seaweed and shells and stones, so that he was more like some monster than to his own natural form. And the soul which we behold is in a similar condition, disfigured by ten thousand ills. But not there, Glaucon, not there must we look.

Where then?

At her love of wisdom. Let us see whom she affects, and what society and converse she seeks in virtue of her near kindred with the immortal and eternal and divine; also how different she would become if wholly following this superior principle, and borne by a divine impulse out of the ocean in which she now is, and disengaged from the stones and shells and things of earth and rock which in wild variety spring up around her because she feeds upon earth, (612) and is overgrown by the good things of this life as they are termed: then you would see her as she is, and know whether she have one shape only or many, or what her nature and state may be. Of her affections and of the forms which she takes in this present life I think that we have now given a very fair description.

True, he replied.

And thus, I said, we have disproved the charges brought against justice without introducing the rewards and glories, which, as you were saying, are to be found ascribed to her in Homer and Hesiod; but justice in her own nature has been shown to be best for the soul in her own nature. Let a man do what is just, whether he have the ring of Gyges or not, and even if in addition to the ring of Gyges he put on the helmet of Hades.

Very true.

And now, Glaucon, there will be no harm in further enumerating how many and how great are the rewards which justice and the other virtues procure to the soul from gods and men, both in life and after death.

Certainly not, he said.

Will you repay me, then, what you borrowed in the argument?

What did I borrow?

The assumption that the just man should appear unjust and the unjust just: for you were of opinion[8] that even if the true state of the case could not possibly escape the eyes of gods and men, still this admission ought to be made for the sake of the argument, in order that pure justice might be weighed against pure injustice. Do you remember?

The injustice would be mine if I had forgotten.

Then, as the cause is decided, I demand on behalf of justice that we should admit the estimation in which she is held by gods and men to be what it really is; since she has been shown to confer the blessings which come from reality, and not to deceive those who truly possess her, let what has been taken from her be given back, that so she may win that palm of appearance which is hers also, and which she gives to her own.

The demand, he said, is just.

In the first place, I said—and this is the first thing which you will have to give back—the nature both of the just and unjust is truly known to the gods.

Granted.

And if they are both known to them, one must be the friend and the other the enemy of the gods, as we admitted from the beginning?

True.

(613) And the friend of the gods may be supposed to receive in its best form whatever the gods bestow, excepting only such evil as may have been the necessary consequence of former sins?

Certainly.

Then this must be our notion of the just man, that even when he is in poverty or sickness, or any other seeming misfortune, these things will bring him finally to some good end, either in life, or perhaps in death; for the gods surely will not neglect anyone whose earnest desire is to become just and by the pursuit of virtue to be like God, as far as man can attain the divine likeness?

Yes, he said; if he is like God he will surely not be neglected by Him.

And of the unjust must not the opposite be supposed?

Certainly.

Such, then, are the palms of victory which the gods give the just?

That, at least, is my conviction.

And what do they receive of men? Look at things as they really are, and you will see that the clever unjust are in the case of runners, who run well from the starting-place to the goal but not back again from the goal: they go off at a great pace, but in the end only look foolish, slinking away with their ears draggling on their shoulders, and without a crown; but the true runner comes to the finish and receives the prize and is crowned. And this is the way with the just; they endure to the end of every action and association, and of life itself, and so win a good report and carry off the prizes which men have to bestow.

True.

Will you then allow me to repeat of the just the blessings which you were attributing to the fortunate unjust? I shall say of them that as they grow older they become rulers in their own city if they care to be; they marry whom they like and give in marriage to whom they will; all that you said of the others I now say of these. And, on the other hand, of the unjust I say that the greater number, even though they escape in their youth, are found out at last and look foolish at the end of their course, and when they come to be old and miserable are flouted alike by stranger and citizen; they are beaten, and then come those things unfit for ears polite, as you truly term them; they will be racked and have their eyes burned out, as you were saying. And you may suppose that I have repeated the remainder of your tale of horrors. I ask once more, will you allow all this?

Certainly, he said, for what you say is true.

(614) These, then, are the prizes and rewards and gifts which are bestowed upon the just by gods and men in this present life, in addition to the other good things which justice of herself provides.

Yes, he said; and they are fair and lasting.

And yet, I said, all these are as nothing either in number or greatness in comparison with those other recompenses which await both just and unjust after death. And you ought to hear them, and then both just and unjust will have received from us a full payment of the debt which the argument owes to them.

Speak, he said; there are few things which I would more gladly hear.

Well, I said, I will tell you a tale; not one of the tales which Odysseus tells[9] to the hero Alcinous, yet this too is a tale of a hero, Er the son of Armenius, a Pamphylian by birth. He was slain in battle, and ten days afterwards, when the bodies of the dead were taken up already in a state of corruption, his body was found unaffected by decay, and carried away home to be buried. And on the twelfth day, as he was lying on the funeral pile, he returned to life and told them what he had seen in the other world. He said that when his soul left the body it went on a journey with a great company, and that they came to a mysterious place at which there were two openings in the earth; they were near together, and over against them were two other openings in the heaven above. In the intermediate space there were judges seated, who commanded the just, after they had given judgment on them and had bound their sentences in front of them, to ascend by the way up through the heaven on the right hand; and in like manner the unjust were bidden by them to descend by the lower way on the left hand; these also bore tokens of all their deeds, but fastened on their backs. He drew near, and they told him that he was to be the messenger who would carry the report of the other world to men, and they bade him hear and see all that was to be heard and seen in that place. Then he beheld and saw on one side the souls departing at either opening of heaven and earth when sentence had been given on them; and at the two other openings other souls, some ascending out of the earth dusty and worn with travel, some descending out of heaven clean and bright. And arriving ever and anon they seemed to have come from a long journey, and they went forth with gladness into the meadow, where they encamped as at a festival; and those who knew one another embraced and conversed, the souls which came from earth curiously inquiring about the things above, and the souls which came from heaven about the things beneath. And they told one another of what had happened by the way, (615) those from below weeping and sorrowing at the remembrance of the things which they had endured and seen in their journey beneath the earth (now the journey lasted a thousand years), while those from above were describing heavenly delights and visions of inconceivable beauty. The full story, Glaucon, would take too long to tell; but the sum was this: He said that for every wrong which they had done and every person whom they had injured they had suffered tenfold; or once in a hundred years—such being reckoned to be the length of man's life, and the penalty being thus paid ten times in a thousand years. If, for example, there were any who had been the cause of many deaths by the betrayal of cities or armies, or had cast many into slavery, or been accessory to any other ill treatment, for all their offences, and on behalf of each man wronged, they were afflicted with tenfold pain, and the rewards of beneficence and justice and holiness were in the same proportion. I need hardly repeat what he said concerning young children dying almost as soon as they were born. Of piety and impiety to gods and parents, and of murder, there were retributions other and greater far which he described. He mentioned that he was present when one of the spirits asked another, "Where is Ardiaeus the Great?" (Now this Ardiaeus lived a thousand years before the time of Er: he had been the tyrant of some city of Pamphylia and had murdered his aged father and his elder brother, and was said to have committed many other abominable crimes.) The answer of the other spirit was: "He comes not hither and will never come. And this," said he, "was one of the dreadful sights which we ourselves witnessed. We were at the mouth of the cavern, and, having completed all our experiences, were about to reascend, when of a sudden, we saw Ardiaeus and several others, most of whom were tyrants; but there were also some private individuals who had been great criminals: they were just, as they fancied, about to return into the upper world, but the mouth, instead of admitting them, gave a roar, whenever any of these whose wickedness was incurable or who had not been sufficiently punished tried to ascend; and then wild men of fiery aspect, who were standing by and heard the sound, seized and carried them[10] off; (616) but Ardiaeus and others they bound head and foot and hand, and threw them down, and flayed them with scourges, and dragged them along the road outside the entrance, carding them on thorns like wool, and declaring to the passers-by what were their crimes, and that they were being taken away to be cast into Tartarus." And of all the many terrors of every kind which they had endured, he said that there was none like the terror which each of them felt at that moment, lest they should hear the voice; and when there was silence, one by one they ascended with exceeding joy. These, said Er, were the penalties and retributions, and there were blessings as great.

Now when each band which was in the meadow had tarried seven days, on the eighth they were obliged to proceed on their journey, and, on the fourth day after, he said that they came to a place where they could see from above a line of light, straight as a column, extending right through the whole heaven and through the earth, in color resembling the rainbow, only brighter and purer; another day's journey brought them to the place, and there, in the midst of the light, they saw the ends of the chains of heaven let down from above: for this light is the belt of heaven, and holds together the circumference of the universe, like the under-girders of a trireme.[11] From these ends is extended the spindle of Necessity, on which all the revolutions turn. The shaft and hook of this spindle are made of adamant, and the whorl is made partly of steel and also partly of other materials. The nature of the whorl is as follows; it is, in outward shape, like the whorl used on earth; and his description of it implied that there is one large hollow whorl which is quite scooped out, and into this is fitted another lesser one, and another, and another, and four others, making eight in all, like vessels which fit into one another; the whorls show their circular edges on the upper side, and on their lower side all together form one continuous whorl. This is pierced by the shaft which is driven home through the centre of the eighth. The first and outermost whorl has the rim broadest, and the seven inner whorls are narrower, in the following proportions—the sixth is next to the first in size, the fourth next to the sixth; then comes the eighth; the seventh is fifth, the fifth is sixth, the third is seventh, last and eighth comes the second. The largest [or fixed stars] is spangled, and the seventh [or sun] is brightest; (617) the eighth [or moon] colored by the reflected light of the seventh; the second and fifth [Saturn and Mercury] are in color like one another, and yellower than the preceding; the third [Venus] has the whitest light; the fourth [Mars] is reddish; the sixth [Jupiter] is in whiteness second. Now the whole spindle has the same motion; but, as the whole revolves in one direction, the seven inner circles move slowly in the other, and of these the swiftest is the eighth; next in swiftness are the seventh, sixth, and fifth, which move together; third in swiftness appeared to move, because of this contrary motion, the fourth; the third appeared fourth and the second fifth. The spindle turns on the knees of Necessity; and on the upper surface of each circle stands a siren, who goes round with them, chanting a single tone or note. The eight together form one harmony; and round about, at equal intervals, there is another band, three in number, each sitting upon her throne: these are the Fates, daughters of Necessity, who are clothed in white robes and have chaplets upon their heads, Lachesis and Clotho and Atropos, who accompany with their voices the harmony of the sirens—Lachesis singing of the past, Clotho of the present,

Atropos of the future; Clotho from time to time assisting with a touch of her right hand the revolution of the outer circle of the whorl or spindle, and Atropos with her left hand touching and guiding the inner ones, and Lachesis laying hold of either in turn, first with one hand and then with the other.

When Er and the spirits arrived, their duty was to go at once to Lachesis; but first of all there came a prophet who arranged them in order; then he took from the knees of Lachesis lots and samples of lives, and having mounted a high pulpit, spoke as follows: "Hear the word of Lachesis, the daughter of Necessity. Mortal souls, behold a new cycle of life and mortality. Your genius will not be allotted to you, but you will choose your genius; and let him who draws the first lot have the first choice, and the life which he chooses shall be his destiny. Virtue is free, and as a man honors or dishonors her he will have more or less of her; the responsibility is with the chooser—God is not responsible." When the Interpreter had thus spoken he scattered lots indifferently among them all, and each of them took up the lot which fell near him, (618) all but Er himself (he was not allowed), and each as he took his lot perceived the number which he had obtained. Then the Interpreter placed on the ground before them the patterns of lives; and there were many more lives than the souls present, and they were of all sorts. There were lives of every animal and of man in every condition. And there were tyrannies among them, some lasting out the tyrant's life, others which broke off in the middle and came to an end in poverty and exile and beggary; and there were lives of famous men, some who were famous for their form and beauty as well as for their strength and success in games, or, again, for their birth and the qualities of their ancestors; and some who were the reverse of famous for the opposite qualities. And of women likewise. The disposition of the soul was not, however, included in them, because the soul, when choosing a new life, must of necessity become different. But there was every other quality, and they all mingled with one another, and also with elements of wealth and poverty, and disease and health; and there were also states intermediate in these respects.

And here, my dear Glaucon, is the supreme peril of our human state; and therefore each one of us must take the utmost care to forsake every other kind of knowledge and seek and study one thing only, if peradventure he may be able to discover someone who will make him able to discern between a good and an evil life, and so to choose always and everywhere the better life as he has opportunity. He should consider the bearing of all these things which have been mentioned severally and collectively upon the excellence of a life; he should know what the effect of beauty is, for good or evil, when combined with poverty or wealth in this or that kind of soul, and what are the good and evil consequences of noble and humble birth, of private and public station, of strength and weakness, of cleverness and dullness, and of all the natural and acquired gifts of the soul, and the operation of them when blended with one another;

he will then look at the nature of the soul, and from the consideration of all these qualities he will be able to determine which is the better and which is the worse; and so he will choose, giving the name of evil to the life which will tend to make his soul more unjust, and good to the life which will make his soul more just; all else he will disregard. For we have seen and know that this is the best choice both in life and after death. (619) A man must take with him into the world below an adamantine faith in truth and right, that there too he may be undazzled by the desire of wealth or the other allurements of evil, lest he be drawn into tyrannies and similar activities, and do irremediable wrongs to others and suffer yet worse himself; but may know how to choose a life moderate in these respects and avoid the extremes on either side, as far as possible, not only in this life but in all that which is to come. For this way brings men to their greatest happiness.

And according to the report of the messenger from the other world this was what the prophet said at the time: "Even for the last comer, if he chooses wisely and will live diligently, there is appointed a happy and not undesirable existence. Let not him who chooses first be careless, and let not the last despair." And when he had spoken, he who had the first choice came forward and in a moment chose the greatest tyranny; his mind having been darkened by folly and sensuality, he had not made any thorough inspection before he chose, and did not perceive that he was fated, among other evils, to devour his own children. But when he had time to examine the lot and saw what was in it, he began to beat his breast and lament over his choice, forgetting the proclamation of the prophet; for, instead of throwing the blame of his misfortune on himself, he accused chance and the gods, and everything rather than himself. Now he was one of those who came from heaven, and in a former life had dwelt in a well-ordered state, virtuous from habit only, and without philosophy. And for the most part it was true of others who were caught in this way, that the greater number of them came from heaven and therefore they had never been schooled by trial, whereas the pilgrims who came from earth having themselves suffered and seen others suffer were not in a hurry to choose. And owing to this inexperience of theirs, and also to the accident of the lot, the majority of the souls exchanged a good destiny for an evil or an evil for a good. For if a man had always on his arrival in this world dedicated himself from the first to sound philosophy, and had been moderately fortunate in the number of the lot, he might, as the messenger reported, be happy here, and also his journey to another life and return to this, instead of being rough and underground, would be smooth and heavenly. Most curious, he said, was the spectacle—sad and laughable and strange; for the choice of the souls was in most cases based on their experience of a previous life. (620) There he saw the soul which had once been Orpheus choosing the life of a swan out of enmity to the race of women, hating to be born of a woman because they had been his murderers; he beheld also the soul of Thamyras choosing the life of a nightingale; birds, on the other hand, like the swan and other musicians, wanting to be men. The soul which obtained the twentieth lot chose the life of a lion, and this was the soul of Ajax the son of Telamon, who would not be a man, remembering the injustice which was done him in the judgment about the arms. The next was Agamemnon, who took the life of an eagle, because, like Ajax, he hated human nature by reason of his sufferings. About the middle came the lot of Atalanta; she, seeing the great fame of an athlete, was unable to resist the temptation: and after her there followed the soul of Epeus the son of Panopeus passing into the nature of a woman skilled in some craft; and far away among the last who chose, the soul of the jester Thersites was putting on the form of a monkey. There came also the soul of Odysseus having yet to make a choice, and his lot happened to be the last of them all. Now the recollection of former toils had disenchanted him of ambition, and he went about for a considerable time in search of the life of a private man who had no cares; he had some difficulty in finding this, which was lying about and had been neglected by everybody else; and when he saw it, he said that he would have done the same had his lot been first instead of last, and gladly chose it. And not only did men pass into animals, but I must also mention that there were animals tame and wild who changed into one another and into corresponding human natures—the righteous into the gentle and the unrighteous into the savage, in all sorts of combinations.

All the souls had now chosen their lives, and they went in the order of their choice to Lachesis, who sent with them the genius whom they had severally chosen, to be the guardian of their lives and the fulfiller of the choice: this genius led the souls first to Clotho, and drew them within the revolution of the spindle impelled by her hand, thus ratifying the destiny of each; and then, when they were fastened to this, carried them to Atropos, who spun the threads and made them irreversible, (621) whence without turning round they passed beneath the throne of Necessity; and when they had all passed, they marched on to the plain of Forgetfulness, in intolerable scorching heat, for the plain was a barren waste destitute of trees and verdure; and then towards evening they encamped by the river of Unmindfulness, whose water no vessel can hold; of this they were all obliged to drink a certain quantity, and those who were not saved by wisdom drank more than was necessary; and each one as he drank forgot all things. Now after they had gone to rest, about the middle of the night there was a thunderstorm and earthquake, and then in an instant they were driven upwards in all manner of ways to their birth, like stars shooting. He himself was hindered from drinking the water. But in what manner or by what means he returned to the body he could not say; only in the morning, awaking suddenly, he found himself lying on the pyre.

And thus, Glaucon, the tale has been saved and has not perished, and will save us if we are obedient to the word spoken; and we shall pass safely over the river of Forgetfulness and our soul will not be defiled. Wherefore my counsel is that we hold fast ever to the heavenly way and follow after justice and virtue always, considering that the soul is immortal and able to endure every sort of good and every sort of evil. Thus shall we live dear to one another and to the gods, both while remaining here and when, like conquerors in the games who go round to gather gifts, we receive our reward. And it shall be well with us both in this life and in the pilgrimage of a thousand years which we have been describing.

LAWS

from BOOK VII

ATHENIAN STRANGER. Let us then affirm the paradox that strains of music are our laws (*nomoi*), and this latter being the name which the ancients gave to lyric songs, they probably would not have very much objected to our proposed application of the word. (800) Some one, either asleep or awake, must have had a dreamy suspicion of their nature. And let our decree be as follows: No one in singing or dancing shall offend against public and consecrated models, and the general fashion among the youth, any more then he would offend against any other law. And he who observes this law shall be blameless; but he who is disobedient, as I was saying, shall be punished by the guardians of the laws, and by the priests and priestesses. Suppose that we imagine this to be our law.

CLEINIAS. Very good.

ATH. Can anyone who makes such laws escape ridicule? Let us see. I think that our only safety will be in first framing certain models for composers. One of these models shall be as follows: If a sacrifice has been offered, and the victims burnt according to law—if, I say, anyone who may be a son or brother, standing by another at the altar and over the victims, horribly blasphemes, will not his words inspire despondency and evil omens and forebodings in the mind of his father and of his other kinsmen?

CLE. Of course.

ATH. And this is just what takes place in almost all our cities. A magistrate offers a public sacrifice, and there come in not one but many choruses, who take up a position a little way from the altar, and from time to time pour forth all sorts of horrible blasphemies on the sacred rites, exciting the souls of the audience with words and rhythms and melodies most sorrowful to hear; and he who at the moment when the city has offered sacrifice makes the citizens weep most, carries away the palm of victory. Now, ought we not to forbid such strains as these? And if ever our citizens must hear such lamentations, then on some unblest and inauspicious day let there be choruses of foreign and hired minstrels, like those hirelings who accompany the departed at funerals with barbarous Carian chants. That is the sort of thing which will be appropriate if we have such strains at all; and let the apparel of the singers of the funeral dirge be, not circlets and ornaments of gold, but the reverse. Enough of all this. I will simply ask once more whether we shall lay down as one of our principles of song——

CLE. What?

(801) ATH. That we should avoid every word of evil omen; let that kind of song which is of good omen be heard everywhere and always in our state. I need hardly ask again, but shall assume that you agree with me.

CLE. By all means; that law is approved by the suffrages of us all.

ATH. But what shall be our next musical law or type? Ought not prayers to be offered up to the gods when we sacrifice?

CLE. Certainly.

ATH. And our third law, if I am not mistaken, will be to the effect that our poets, understanding prayers to be requests which we make to the gods, will take especial heed that they do not by mistake ask for evil instead of good. To make such a prayer would surely be too ridiculous.

CLE. Very true.

ATH. Were we not a little while ago quite convinced that no silver or golden Plutus should dwell in our state?[1]

CLE. To be sure.

ATH. And what has it been the object of our argument to show? Did we not imply that the poets are not always quite capable of knowing what is good or evil? And if one of them utters a mistaken prayer in song or words, he will make our citizens pray for the opposite of what we ordain in matters of the highest import; than which, as I was saying, there can be few greater mistakes. Shall we then propose as one of our laws and models relating to the Muses——

CLE. What? Will you explain the law more precisely?

ATH. Shall we make a law that the poet shall compose nothing contrary to the ideas of the lawful, or just, or beautiful, or good, which are allowed in the state? Nor shall he be permitted to communicate his compositions to any private individuals, until he shall have shown them to the appointed judges and the guardians of the law, and they are satisfied with them. As to the persons whom we appoint to be our legislators about music[2] and as to the director of education,[3] these have been already indicated. Once more then, as I have asked more than once, shall this be our third law, and type, and model—what do you say?

CLE. Let it be so, by all means.

ATH. Then it will be proper to have hymns and praises of the gods,[4] intermingled with prayers; and after the gods prayers and praises should be offered in like manner to demigods and heroes, suitable to their several characters.

CLE. Certainly.

ATH. In the next place there will be no objection to a law, that citizens who are departed and have done good and energetic deeds, either with their souls or with their bodies, and have been obedient to the laws, should receive eulogies; this will be very fitting.

CLE. Quite true. (802)

ATH. But to honor with hymns and panegyrics those who are still alive is not safe; a man should run his course, and make a fair ending, and then we will praise him; and let praise be given equally to women as well as men who have been distinguished in virtue. The order of songs and dances shall be as follows: There are many ancient musical compositions and dances which are excellent, and from these it is fair to select what is proper and suitable to the newly-founded city; and they shall choose judges of not less than fifty years of age, who shall make the selection, and any of the old poems which they deem sufficient they shall include; any that are deficient or altogether unsuitable, they shall either utterly throw aside, or examine and amend, taking into their counsel poets and musicians, and making use of their potential genius; but explaining to them the wishes of the legislator in order that they may regulate dancing, music, and all choral strains, according to the mind of the judges; and not allowing them to indulge, except in some few matters, their individual pleasures and fancies. Now the irregular strain of music is always made ten thousand times better by attaining to law and order, and rejecting the honeyed Muse[5]—not however that we mean wholly to exclude pleasure, which is the characteristic of all music. And if a man be brought up from childhood to the age of discretion and maturity in the use of the orderly and severe music, when he hears the opposite he detests it, and calls it illiberal; but if trained in the sweet and vulgar music, he deems the severer kind cold and displeasing. So that, as I was saying before, while he who hears them gains no more pleasure from the one than from the other, the one has the advantage of making those who are trained in it better men, whereas the other makes them worse.

CLE. Very true.

ATH. Again, we must distinguish and determine on some general principle what songs are suitable to women, and what to men, and must assign to them their proper melodies and rhythms. It is shocking for a whole harmony to be inharmonical, or for a rhythm to be unrhythmical, and this will happen when the melody is inappropriate to them. And therefore the legislator must assign to these also their forms. Now both sexes have melodies and rhythms which of necessity belong to them; and those of women are clearly enough indicated by their natural difference. The grand, and that which tends to courage, may be fairly called manly; (803) but that which inclines to moderation and temperance, may be declared both in law and in ordinary speech to be the more womanly quality. This, then, will be the general order of them.

Let us now speak of the manner of teaching and imparting them, and the persons to whom, and the time when, they are severally to be imparted. As the shipwright first lays down the lines of the keel, and thus, as it were, draws the ship in outline, so do I seek to distinguish the patterns of life, and lay down their keels according to the nature of different men's souls; seeking truly to consider by what means, and in what ways, we may go through the voyage of life best. Now human affairs are hardly worth considering in earnest, and yet we must be in earnest about them—a sad necessity constrains us. And having got thus far, there will be a fitness in our completing the matter, if we can only find some suitable method of doing so. But what do I mean? Someone may ask this very question, and quite rightly, too.

CLE. Certainly.

ATH. I say that about serious matters a man should be serious, and about a matter which is not serious he should not be serious; and that God is the natural and worthy object of our most serious and blessed endeavors, for man, as I said before,[6] is made to be the plaything of God, and this, truly considered, is the best of him; wherefore also every man and woman should walk seriously, and pass life in the noblest of pastimes, and be of another mind from what they are at present.

CLE. In what respect?

ATH. At present they think that their serious pursuits should be for the sake of their sports, for they deem war a serious pursuit, which must be managed well for the sake of peace; but the truth is, that there neither is, nor has been, nor ever will be, either amusement or instruction in any degree worth speaking of in war, which is nevertheless deemed by us to be the most serious of our pursuits. And therefore, as we say, every one of us should live the life of peace as long and as well as he can.[7] And what is the right way of living? Are we to live in sports always? If so, in what kind of sports? We ought to live sacrificing, and singing, and dancing, and then a man will be able to propitiate the gods, and to defend himself against his enemies and conquer them in battle. The type of song or dance by which he will propitiate them has been described, and the paths along which he is to proceed have been cut for him. (804) He will go forward in the spirit of the poet: "Telemachus, some things thou wilt thyself find in thy heart, but other things God will suggest; for I deem that thou wast not born or brought up without the will of the gods."[8] And this ought to be the view of our alumni; they ought to think that what has been said is enough for them, and that any other things their genius and god will suggest to them—he will tell them to whom, and when, and to what gods severally they are to sacrifice and perform dances, and how they may propitiate the deities, and live according to the appointment of nature; being for the most part puppets, but having some little share of reality.

.   .   .   .   .   .

(810) ATH. That is quite true; and you mean to imply that the road which we are taking may be disagreeable to some but is agreeable to as many others, or if not to as many, at any rate to persons not inferior to the others, and in company with them you bid me, at whatever risk, to proceed along the path of legislation which has opened out of our present discourse, and to be of good cheer, and not to faint.

CLE. Certainly.

ATH. And I do not faint; I say, indeed, that we have a great many poets writing in hexameter, trimeter, and all sorts of measures—some who are serious, others who aim only at raising a laugh—and all mankind declare that the youth who are rightly educated should be brought up in them and saturated with them; some insist that they should be constantly hearing them read aloud, and always learning them, so as to get by heart entire poets; (811) while others select choice passages and long speeches, and make compendiums of them, saying that these ought to be committed to memory, if a man is to be made good and wise by experience and learning of many things. And you want me now to tell them plainly in what they are right and in what they are wrong.

CLE. Yes, I do.

ATH. But how can I in one word rightly comprehend all of them? I am of opinion, and, if I am not mistaken, there is a general agreement, that every one of these poets has said many things well and many things the reverse of well; and if this be true, than I do affirm that much learning is dangerous to youth.

CLE. How would you advise the guardian of the law to act?

ATH. In what respect?

CLE. I mean to what pattern should he look as his guide in permitting the young to learn some things and forbidding them to learn others. Do not shrink from answering.

ATH. My good Cleinias, I rather think that I am fortunate.

CLE. How so?

ATH. I think that I am not wholly in want of a pattern, for when I consider the words which we have spoken from early dawn until now, and which, as I believe, have been inspired by heaven, they appear to me to be quite like a poem. When I reflected upon all these words of ours, I naturally felt pleasure, for of all the discourses which I have ever learnt or heard, either in poetry or prose, this seemed to me to be the justest, and most suitable for young men to hear; I cannot imagine any better pattern than this which the guardian of the law who is also the director of education can have. He cannot do better than advise the teachers to teach the young these words and any which are of a like nature, if he should happen to find them, either in poetry or prose, or if he come across unwritten discourses akin to ours, he should certainly preserve them, and commit them to writing. And, first of all, he shall constrain the teachers themselves to learn and approve them, and any of them who will not, shall not be employed by him, but those whom he finds agreeing in his judgment, he shall make use of and shall commit to them the instruction and education of youth. (812) And here and on this wise let my fanciful tale about letters and teachers of letters come to an end.

.   .   .   .   .   .

(814) ATH. Enough of wrestling; we will now proceed to speak of other movements of the body. Such motion may be in general called dancing, and is of two kinds: one of nobler figures, imitating the honorable, the other of the more ignoble figures, imitating the mean; and of both these there are two further subdivisions. Of the serious, one kind is of those engaged in war and vehement action, and is the exercise of a noble person and a manly heart; the other exhibits a temperate soul in the enjoyment of prosperity and modest pleasures, and may be truly called and is the dance of peace. (815) The warrior dance is different from the peaceful one, and may be rightly termed pyrrhic[9]; this imitates the modes of avoiding blows and missiles by dropping or giving way, or springing aside, or rising up or falling down; also the opposite postures which are those of action, as, for example, the imitation of archery and the hurling of javelins, and of all sorts of blows. And when the imitation is of brave bodies and souls, and the action is direct and muscular, giving for the most part a straight movement to the limbs of the body—that, I say, is the true sort; but the opposite is not right. In the dance of peace what we have to consider is whether a man bears himself naturally and gracefully, and after the manner of men who duly conform to the law. But before proceeding I must distinguish the dancing about which there is any doubt, from that about which there is no doubt. Which is the doubtful kind, and how are the two to be distinguished? There are dances of the Bacchic sort, both those in which, as they say, they imitate drunken men, and which are named after the nymphs, and Pan, and Silenuses, and satyrs; and also those in which purifications are made or mysteries celebrated—all this sort of dancing cannot be rightly defined as having either a peaceful or a warlike character, or indeed as having any meaning whatever, and may, I think, be most truly described as distinct from the warlike dance, and distinct from the peaceful, and not suited for a city at all. There let it lie; and so leaving it to lie, we will proceed to the dances of war and peace, for with these we are undoubtedly concerned. Now the unwarlike muse, which honors in dance the gods and the sons of the

gods, is entirely associated with the consciousness of prosperity; this class may be subdivided into two lesser classes, of which one is expressive of an escape from some labor or danger into good, and has greater pleasures, the other expressive of preservation and increase of former good, in which the pleasure is less exciting—in all these cases, every man when the pleasure is greater, moves his body more, and less when the pleasure is less; and, again, if he be more orderly and has learned courage from discipline he moves less, (816) but if he be a coward, and has no training or self-control, he makes greater and more violent movements, and in general when he is speaking or singing he is not altogether able to keep his body still; and so out of the imitation of words in gestures the whole art of dancing has arisen. And in these various kinds of imitation one man moves in an orderly, another in a disorderly manner; and as the ancients may be observed to have given many names which are according to nature and deserving of praise, so there is an excellent one which they have given to the dances of men who in their times of prosperity are moderate in their pleasures—the giver of names, whoever he was, assigned to them a very true, and poetical, and rational name, when he called them Emmeleiai, or dances of order, thus establishing two kinds of dances of the nobler sort, the dance of war which he called the pyrrhic, and the dance of peace which he called Emmeleia,[10] or the dance of order; giving to each their appropriate and becoming name. These things the legislator should indicate in general outline, and the guardian of the law should inquire into them and search them out, combining dancing with music, and assigning to the several sacrificial feasts that which is suitable to them; and when he has consecrated all of them in due order, he shall for the future change nothing, whether of dance or song. Thenceforward the city and the citizens shall continue to have the same pleasures, themselves being as far as possible alike, and shall live well and happily.

I have described the dances which are appropriate to noble bodies and generous souls. But it is necessary also to consider and know uncomely persons and thoughts, and those which are intended to produce laughter in comedy, and have a comic character in respect of style, song, and dance, and of the imitations which these afford. For serious things cannot be understood without laughable things, nor opposites at all without opposites, if a man is really to have intelligence of either; but he cannot carry out both in action, if he is to have any degree of virtue. And for this very reason he should learn them both, in order that he may not in ignorance do or say anything which is ridiculous and out of place—he should command slaves and hired strangers to imitate such things, but he should never take any serious interest in them himself, nor should any freeman or freewoman be discovered taking pains to learn them; and there should always be some element of novelty in the imitation. Let these then be laid down, both in law and in our discourse, as the regulations of laughable amusements which are generally called comedy. (817) And, if any of the serious poets, as they are termed, who write tragedy, come to us and say: "O strangers, may we go to your city and country or may we not, and shall we bring with us our poetry—what is your will about these matters?" How shall we answer the divine men? I think that our answer should be as follows:[11] Best of strangers, we will say to them, we also according to our ability are tragic poets, and our tragedy is the best and noblest; for our whole state is an imitation of the best and noblest life, which we affirm to be indeed the very truth of tragedy. You are poets and we are poets, both makers of the same strains, rivals and antagonists in the noblest of dramas, which true law can alone perfect, as our hope is. Do not then suppose that we shall all in a moment allow you to erect your stage in the agora,[12] or introduce the fair voices of your actors, speaking above our own, and permit you to harangue our women and children, and the common people, about our institutions, in language other than our own, and very often the opposite of our own. For a state would be mad which gave you this license, until the magistrates had determined whether your poetry might be recited, and was fit for publication or not. Wherefore, O ye sons and scions of the softer Muses, first of all show your songs to the magistrates, and let them compare them with our own, and if they are the same or better we will give you a chorus; but if not, then, my friends, we cannot. Let these, then, be the customs ordained by law about all dances and the teaching of them, and let matters relating to slaves be separated from those relating to masters, if you do not object.

ARISTOTLE

(384–322 B.C.)

INTRODUCTION

The *Poetics* of Aristotle is widely recognized as the most influential document in the history of literary criticism. Its major concepts have become standard points of departure for subsequent discussions of the general nature of literature and the particular structure and function of tragedy. The reasons for the long-standing and widespread popularity of this work are not hard to discern. The *Poetics* not only embodies brilliant, verifiable insights into the nature of the artistic experience; it also links these insights together in a tightly-knit, deductively rigorous argument that further illuminates important aesthetic problems.

A survey of the structure of the *Poetics* clearly reveals its tightly-knit argument. Aristotle begins his discussion with a reference to "first principles," pointing out the essential character of poetry as *mimesis* (imitation). In Chapters 1–3 he introduces the "co-ordinates" of imitation—means, object, and manner—by which all of the various arts can be compared and contrasted. Even at this early point in the *Poetics,* it is obvious that Aristotle wishes to elevate tragedy as the literary form which "imitates" in the fullest, most complex way.

After pointing out the natural origin of poetry in Chapter 4, Aristotle provides a brief sketch of the history of the major literary forms. In Chapters 4 and 5 he is once again focusing on tragedy as the fullest realization of the possibilities of imitation, the highest "evolutionary" development of mimetic form. This emphasis is so pronounced, in fact, that it makes Aristotle's brief history less an empirical survey than a deductive schema.

Chapter 6 opens with a lengthy definition of tragedy which sums up the preceding material: tragedy is categorized in terms of its means, manner, and purpose of imitation. Aristotle then begins a lengthy inquiry (Chapters 6–22) into the six qualitative parts of tragedy: plot, character, thought, diction, melody, and spectacle. As its placement in this sequence suggests, "plot" (*mythos*) is to Aristotle the most important element (the "soul") of a tragedy.

Understood in its fullest sense, plot is what best objectifies the thematic logic of a play, what most fully engages the audience's emotions, and what most directly determines the author's other choices in the act of poetic composition.

In Chapters 7–11 Aristotle discusses specific criteria for plots. A plot must have the proper magnitude, encompassing neither too many nor too few incidents. It must manifest unity of action (the only "unity" Aristotle insists upon), creating a "meaning" of its own by selecting, condensing, shaping, and arranging the materials of real life, rather than trying to present the whole life span of its protagonist. It must, in other words, represent a "universal" action (what a certain type of individual might do) rather than a particular chronicle of events (what a specific, historical individual actually did). In Chapters 10 and 11 Aristotle divides plots into the "simple" and the "complex," the latter involving the elements of Reversal (a change of fortune to the exact opposite state of affairs) and Recognition (a change from ignorance to knowledge). Aristotle's emphasis once again elevates *complexity* as an aesthetic norm.

After a listing of the quantitative parts of drama in Chapter 12, Aristotle begins to shift his attention to "character" (*ethos*), the second qualitative element. The problem he confronts in Chapter 13 is the question of *hamartia*: how can the dramatist portray his tragic protagonist so as to guide the audience's emotional response, generating pity and fear while avoiding a reaction of disgust or pure shock? The logic of Aristotle's answer (discussed below) depends in part on his definitions of pity (aroused by the perception of *undeserved* misfortune) and fear (evoked by the realization that the sufferer is a man *like ourselves*)—but it depends even more on his understanding of "character" as manifesting moral choice (*proairesis*). This premise, in fact, accounts for most of Aristotle's general remarks in Chapter 15 on how the dramatist can develop character effectively.

Chapters 16–18 are difficult to fit into the logical sequence of Aristotle's argument; Chapter 18, for example, offers a somewhat puzzling classification of kinds of tragedies which seems unconnected to Aristotle's earlier comments.[1] In Chapter 19, however, Aristotle returns to a consideration of qualitative parts. "Thought" (*dianoia*) refers to the intellectual content of the speeches, and is related to the art of rhetoric. "Diction" (*lexis*) is treated in Chapters 19–22; Aristotle's discussion moves from the simplest elements of language (letters and syllables) to complexities of poetic metaphor.

Aristotle seems to have felt that the last two qualitative parts of drama, "melody" (*melos*) and "spectacle" (*opsis*) were accidental rather than essential elements of dramatic art, belonging more to the exigencies of stage production than to the craft of composition. In Chapter 23, then, he turns to the genre of epic, the literary form most closely related to tragedy, a form understandable in terms of the four primary qualitative parts. Chapters 23–24 stress that epic aspires to a "dramatic" ideal: unity of action.

The *Poetics* concludes with a consideration of certain technical and critical problems, and a final comparison and contrast of epic and tragedy. These last two chapters not only complete the logic of Aristotle's argument; they also reaffirm his aesthetic orientation. Poetry, in his view, has its own ontology. In the "world" or "whole" (*holos*) of a literary work, internal coherence or "probability" (*to eikos*) takes precedence over verisimilitude. One of the most significant comments in the *Poetics* (in Chapter 25) asserts that "the criticism that a work of art is not a truthful representation can be met by the argument that it represents the situation as it should be."

The original Greek text of the *Poetics* is not extant, but there are three fundamentally important witnesses for it. The most important of these is an eleventh-century manuscript (Paris 1741) which is the primary source for nearly all contemporary texts of the *Poetics*. This is supplemented by an inferior but still quite useful manuscript (Riccardianus 46) of the thirteenth or fourteenth centuries, and, less significantly, by an Arabic translation of the *Poetics* dating from the tenth century and based on a Syriac translation of a seventh-century Greek manuscript. Because difficulties exist in interpreting a number of passages in all three manuscripts, editors have been forced, in varying degrees, to amend the text of the *Poetics*. There has also been considerable speculation in recent years that some sections of the *Poetics* were not written by Aristotle, but were added by later interpolators. For the most part, textual problems do not affect our understanding of the major concepts and themes of the *Poetics*. Still, readers of Aristotle's treatise should be aware of the unsettled and disputed nature of parts of the text they are reading, and that there are differences of judgment, occasionally severe, among editors and translators of the Greek text.

Stylistically, the *Poetics* also offers problems for its readers, translators, and interpreters. The original Greek is extremely terse, sometimes to the point of obscurity, and many passages require "expansion" before they can be made meaningful. Scholars have offered two hypotheses for the special stylistic character of the *Poetics* and some of Aristotle's other works. It has been suggested that these works are really lecture notes, made either by Aristotle or his students, rather than fully developed treatises. An alternative suggestion is based on the distinction between "esoteric" and "exoteric" works. Under this view the *Poetics* would be an esoteric work—i.e., a work meant to be circulated among those already familiar with Aristotle's doctrines, and thus not in need of the complete and detailed account that would be circulated as an exoteric work among those without a specialized knowledge of the subject.

Both for textual and stylistic reasons, therefore, all interpreters of the *Poetics* must provide some expansion of the literal text in order to make the work comprehensible. The most important problem facing the student of the *Poetics*, however, does not result from difficulties in text or style. The wide influence of the *Poetics* is based on the major critical concepts it offers; but while nearly all critics agree on the importance of these major concepts, there exists wide disagreement on the full meaning and scope of a number of them. It is difficult to disentangle any of Aristotle's concepts from the rigorous argument that controls the *Poetics* as a whole, but four key terms seem to stand out from the others and demand special consideration. These terms, all of the highest significance for Aristotle's critical position, are (I) *mimesis* ("imitation"), (II) *katharsis*, (III) *hamartia* ("tragic error"), and (IV) *spoudaios* ("noble" character).

(I) *Mimesis.*   The concept of art as imitation is as central to the Aristotelian view as it is to the Platonic, but Aristotle's application of the term *mimesis* is far different from that customarily attributed to Plato.[2] In Book X of the *Republic* Plato regarded poetic imitation as "copying," and on this basis asserted that it is essentially trivial—even less significant than the "copying" of ideas which is embodied in the work of craftsmen. The *Poetics* constitutes an emphatic rejection of the view. Aristotle emphasizes the dynamic, conscious "craft" (*technê*) of art, recognizing the artist's *creativity*. The artist is not a copier, but a "maker" whose products can best be understood as imitations of human action, character, and emotion.

Aristotle's concept of imitation is very much in keeping with the main thrust of modern aesthetic criticism.[3] In his seminal work on the *Poetics*, S. H. Butcher recognized the essential modernity of Aristotle's argument. Butcher pointed out that Aristotle's statement that the artists "may imitate things as they ought to be" is evidence of a very sophisticated concept, far beyond the notion of "copying." Aristotle's phrase "ought to be" implies the existence of an *aesthetic* judgment, and suggests that art is a free activity of the human mind, independent of utilitarian consideration.[4] In effect, the concept of imitation distinguishes between "fine art" and the useful crafts (e.g., carpentry, ship-building); the product of a useful craft is not, strictly speaking, an "imitation" of anything. As John Crowe Ransom has observed, the very term "imitation" implies a variation of the art-for-art's sake position: "not being actual," an imitation "cannot be used; it can only be known."[5]

Aristotle relates imitation to learning. In Chapter 4 he notes that we enjoy seeing artistic representations of even the most disgusting and unpleasant objects, objects we would be repelled by if we saw them in reality. Tragedy, for example, deals with horrible and depressing events, but its representation of these events is itself aesthetically enjoyable. Aristotle's explanation is that in such cases the imitation results in a kind of learning, culminating in an insight that is a source of pleasure for the audience. Here and elsewhere in the *Poetics* Aristotle seems to be arguing that the process of imitation leads from the particular represented in the work of art to a universal which subsumes it, and that this movement from particular to universal is a learning experience which clarifies the particular

representation by expressing its essential nature. The act of learning or clarification is specifically identified with the essential human pleasure offered by all
forms of imitation. Understood in this way, Aristotle's *mimesis* is generically
related to the aesthetic concept of art as a source of insight.

The aesthetic implications of imitation have been analyzed further by O. B.
Hardison, who emphasizes that Aristotle's term carries an *active* meaning.
Mimesis can refer to the actual process of composition. In the writing of a
tragedy, "imitation" would involve the construction and articulation of the six
component elements enumerated in Chapter 6: plot, character, thought, diction,
melody, and spectacle. When this process. is carried out according to the laws
of probability and necessity (i.e., internal coherence), a universal form is
achieved which imparts intelligibility to the particular actions represented by the
poet.[6]

(II) *Katharsis.* *Katharsis* is a rare word in the Aristotelian critical
vocabulary. It appears twice in the *Poetics*, once in a routine technical sense to
describe Orestes' purification from madness and once at the climax of Aristotle's
definition of tragedy in Chapter 6, where its appearance has made it the most
famous term in Aristotle's impressive critical system. The essential meaning of
the concept is still much disputed, despite the interpretative labors of innumerable
scholars. Four major theories have been offered to explain catharsis. These may
be generally designated as (1) medical or therapeutic, (2) moral, (3) structural,
and (4) intellectual.

The medical or therapeutic interpretation relates the term to the ancient
theory of homeopathic medicine, which asserted that an illness should be treated
by the administration of agents similar to the illness itself (e.g., the application
of heat to expel fever). This interpretation is suggested in Milton's preface to
Samson Agonistes, and was developed into a full-scale theory by H. Weil and
J. Bernays in the nineteenth century. Critics who hold this view usually translate
katharsis as "purgation," and interpret it as a process of purging pity and fear
from an audience by exposing that audience to a representation of pitiable and
fearful events in tragedy. This theory assumes that all men are subject in varying
degrees to excesses of pity and fear, and that the essential pleasure of tragedy is
the therapeutic pleasure of removing these excesses.

Those who subscribe to the medical theory of catharsis usually support it
by citing a passage from the *Politics* (1341 B 37–42 A 17): Aristotle's reference
to the therapeutic use of certain musical melodies to purge the emotional frenzy
of some participants in religious observances. Aristotle uses the term *katharsis* to
describe this purging, indicating that he will discuss the concept in more detail in
his *Poetics.* Many scholars believe that this more explicit treatment of catharsis
was presented in a lost second book of the *Poetics.*

From Bernays' time to our own, the medical theory of catharsis has been
dominant. Its principal advantage has been that it relates an enigmatic passage

in the *Poetics* to a passage in the *Politics* where the relatively rare term *katharsis* appears in the explicit sense of "purgation." But the medical theory has failed to win universal acceptance: many critics and scholars dispute the thesis that Aristotle conceived of art as essentially and regularly a form of therapy directed at relieving audiences of psychic excesses. Such scholars question the validity of applying a discussion in the *Politics* about music as an instrument of education to a sustained argument in a different treatise about the fundamental nature of poetry.[7]

The moral interpretation of catharsis renders the term as "purification." It asserts that the principal goal of a tragedy is to purify the audience's pity and fear of any excess or deficiency, or to correct any misdirection of these emotions with respect to the persons, places, or circumstances toward which they are displayed. The moral interpretation of catharsis is didactic: it sees catharsis as a means of *disciplining* the audience's attitudes toward life in general. The principle evidence for such an interpretation is a passage from the *Nicomachean Ethics* (1106 B 8–23). Here Aristotle explicitly mentions pity among the emotions that must be felt neither in an excessive nor a deficient way, but according to a proper mean. Most interpreters have felt that this evidence is very tenuous, and they have been generally unable to accept the argument that Aristotle saw the primary purpose of art as the moral conditioning of the audience. Lessing is the most significant critic to advocate the moral view of catharsis.[8]

A form of the structural interpretation of catharsis was developed early in the twentieth century by H. Otte, but its most famous and influential formulation is in the work of Gerald Else.[9] Else argues that catharsis is not a major critical concept at all. Instead, he claims, it is a limited, although quite necessary, element in the structure of a tragedy. Else interprets catharsis as a process carried on by the plot, through which the protagonist's tragic deed is shown to be *katharmos*, free from pollution. The protagonist demonstrates to the audience that he did not intend the evils he has caused, or that he wishes to provide expiation for his crime; the audience is then able to respond with the emotions of pity and fear appropriate to a tragedy.

Else's interpretation has the advantage of linking catharsis with other concepts in the *Poetics*, especially *hamartia* and "recognition," and of avoiding vague speculation about the psychological and moral conditioning of the audience. But an important problem in Else's theory is that it removes *katharsis* from its central position of importance as a critical term without adequately explaining the appearance of this term at the climax of Aristotle's definition of tragedy.

This very problem is dealt with directly in the intellectual interpretation of catharsis, an interpretation that renders the term as "intellectual clarification." S. O. Haupt presented a version of this position early in the twentieth century.[10] Haupt's arguments, however, were only partially demonstrable on philological grounds, and his work was soon rejected and forgotten. In 1962 Leon Golden published an article in which the intellectual interpretation was given an independent defense, and he placed special emphasis on the functional role that catharsis (as "intellectual clarification") plays in the total argument of the *Poetics*.[11] In 1966 H. D. F. Kitto published another independent paper confirming a number of the positions taken by Haupt and Golden.[12]

The intellectual interpretation of catharsis rests on three main lines of argument. First, it is in accord with Aristotle's procedure, throughout his total philosophy, of attaching greatest significance to the intellectual value of any activity; his *Nicomachean Ethics*, for example, defines the contemplative mode as the highest form of human life, and his *Metaphysics* defines God as *Nous* ("Mind"). Second, the term *katharsis* was occasionally used in Greek by such authors as Plato, Epicurus, and Philodemus to mean intellectual clarification. Third, and most important, this interpretation stresses the logical coherence of the *Poetics*. The word *katharsis* appears in Chapter 6 of the *Poetics*, in a definition of tragedy prefaced by Aristotle's claim that he is "summing up" what has been said so far. *Katharsis* appears at the climax of the definition, in a position which indicates that it is the goal or final cause of tragedy. But in Chapter 4 Aristotle has already identified the ultimate goal of all artistic imitation (and specifically the representation of "horrible" events) as a learning experience. Learning, Aristotle says, is a source of pleasure for all men. This point also gains support from Aristotle's statement in Chapter 9 that poetry is more philosophical and significant than history: poetry aims at the universal while history deals with the particular.

Whatever theory of catharsis one adopts, it is clear that Aristotle's concept answers Plato's charge, in Book III of the *Republic*, that art is morally harmful. The *Poetics* was probably not written as a direct refutation of Plato, but Aristotle and Plato are at opposite poles on the question of the moral effect of art. For Aristotle the effect is catharsis, and catharsis is beneficial—a form of therapy, a morally refining experience, a release from guilt, or a kind of learning.

(III) *Hamartia*. This important term has most commonly been rendered into English as "tragic flaw," although this translation fails to convey the real nature and full scope of the concept. It was once general practice for interpreters to emphasize the moral overtones of *hamartia*, sometimes by relating the term to its usage in traditional Christian writings; in the Gospel of St. John, for example, *hamartia* means "sin." Under this theory the tragic hero commits a serious moral error and receives condign punishment for it. This line of interpretation has been challenged, however, by a number of scholars who have intensively examined the use of the term *hamartia* by Aristotle and the Greek tragedians. Their investigations, conducted independently over several decades, indicate that *hamartia* should be interpreted primarily as an intellectual error rather than a moral flaw.[13]

Aristotle's analysis of tragedy is based on *Oedipus Rex*. Both in this play and its sequel, *Oedipus at Colonus*, there is strong evidence that Sophocles thought of Oedipus' error as more intellectual than moral; indeed, in *Oedipus at Colonus* Sophocles has Oedipus make the explicit defense that he was ignorant of what he was doing in committing parricide and incest, and that he would never have performed these crimes knowingly. At the very least, Sophocles seems to show that Oedipus' punishment is *in excess* of his crime.

This point may be clarified if *hamartia* is interpreted primarily as an intellectual error. Such an interpretation deemphasizes the notion of "poetic justice," suggesting that Aristotle holds a sophisticated concept of tragedy. Aristotle's argument in Chapter 13 indicates that if a play shows that the protagonist's destruction is exactly what he deserves, there is no true pity and fear; the play is essentially *melodramatic*. In these terms tragedy can be more easily understood as a literary form which avoids demonstrating a perfect justice in this world, a literary form capable of posing such philosophical questions as the meaning of life itself.

In whatever way *hamartia* is interpreted, it must be related to the general line of inquiry in Chapter 13. Aristotle is concerned with the dynamics of audience-response. Given the essential dialectic of tragedy—the passage of a basically good man from happiness to misery—it is necessary for the dramatist to guide the reaction of the audience, preventing a response of revulsion or pure shock at the sight of totally innocent suffering. Thus, the general notion of *hamartia* means that the dramatist must assign *some* responsibility, but not a total responsibility, to the protagonist.

(IV) *Spoudaios* ("Noble" Character). Aristotle defines "character" (*ethos*) as that element in speech or action which manifests a moral choice. He uses this principle as one of the co-ordinates by which genres may be defined: in Chapter 2 he declares that the essential difference between tragedy and comedy is that the former imitates "noble" (*spoudaios*) character while the latter imitates "base" (*phaulos*) character, and in Chapter 5 he finds an essential similarity between tragedy and epic in that both imitate "noble" character.

Aristotle's description of tragic character has often been popularly construed (especially by neoclassical critics) as a social proscription: the tragic hero must be a member of "the nobility," or at least a political or military leader. Arthur Miller has attributed this view to Aristotle himself, attacking it as a social blind spot, an implicit snobbery, in the *Poetics*. According to Miller, a "common man" (such as Willy Loman in *Death of a Salesman*) is as potentially tragic as any protagonist in the works of Sophocles or Shakespeare.[14]

It would appear that Aristotle's position is not antithetical to Miller's, because the "nobility" referred to in the *Poetics* is more moral than social. The adjective *spoudaios* can also be rendered as "serious," "good," or "weighty." Aristotle's tragic protagonist might be defined as a man "weighty" enough to demand the audience's *moral attention*. To put it another way: if the action of a tragedy is viewed as a kind of ritualistic sacrifice, Aristotle's requirement would mean that the protagonist must somehow be made to seem *worth* sacrificing. It may be easier to grant such moral attention to a king or a general (especially because their actions are fraught with consequences for other people), but this is not essential; in our own age, at least, the intensity and cultural relevance of a Willy Loman can make him truly *spoudaios*.

The important point here is that Aristotle is not, as is so often thought, a *soi-disant* maker of prohibitive "rules" (e.g., the non-existent "three unities"). Such a spirit is really more typical of the conservative sensibility of Horace's *Ars Poetica*. By contrast, Aristotle's remarks on tragic character, like his other observations on poetry, are in the nature of a philosophical investigation into the entelechial "perfection" of literary form—and the spirit of this investigation is affirmative rather than negative, comprehensive rather than judicial.

In addition to the four concepts discussed above, there are many other terms and ideas in the *Poetics* which are of great significance to the critic and historian of literature. Fortunately, many of these are not controversial and are clearly defined and explained in the *Poetics*. In this category are such widely used critical concepts as "recognition" (*anagnorisis*), "reversal" (*peripeteia*), "complication" (*desis*), and "resolution" (*lysis*)—as well as such important theoretical discussions as the analysis of the six qualitative parts of tragedy. A few other concepts, however, deserve brief explanation here because of their relevance to the major ideas discussed above. The most noteworthy of these are the role of pity and fear in tragedy, the comparison of a work of art to an organism, and the primacy of plot over the other elements in drama.

One of Aristotle's major contributions to the theory of tragedy is his insistence that the genre is concerned with the representation of the pitiable and fearful rather than with other emotions or experiences. Aristotle defines pity and fear in his *Rhetoric* (Book II, Chapter 5) as well as in the *Poetics* (Chapter 13): fear is an emotion caused by the presence of whatever threatens our own selves with harm or destruction; pity is a variant of the same emotion, directed at the fate of *others* who suffer undeserved misfortune. In Chapter 6 of the *Poetics* Aristotle introduces the concepts of pity and fear in his famous definition of tragedy, and in Chapter 14 he enters into a detailed discussion of the best ways for the tragic dramatist to achieve pity and fear in his work. Aristotle's argument for the essential relation of pity and fear to tragedy is important because it unites with the other aspects of his analysis to form a persuasive and coherent theory of tragedy. For example, the emphasis on pity and fear in tragedy illuminates the need for the tragic hero to be *spoudaios*; only when a "noble" hero falls from happiness to misery, enduring a punishment in excess of his moral offense, can the properly "tragic" emotions be called forth. Thus, this line of thought in the *Poetics* unites the concepts of *katharsis*, *hamartia*, and "noble" character.

In Chapter 7 Aristotle introduces the notion that a work of art should resemble a living organism (*zoön*). His emphasis here differs from the doctrine of "organicism" in many romantic aesthetic theories. Coleridge, for example, posits an "indwelling power" which shapes the work into a living unit, a Platonic whole so perfect that no *word* in a true poem can be changed without damage. By contrast, Aristotle is more functional: he is thinking primarily of *structural* cohesiveness, emphasizing the dramatist's conscious construction of episodes. Most important, Aristotle's concept is related to audience response, and it may support the interpretation of *katharsis* as intellectual clarification: the audience must be able to perceive the coherence of the work of art. Thus, the dramatist's work must be a true "whole"—i.e., with articulated principles of beginning, middle, and end. In order to be aesthetically perceivable, the work must also possess the proper "magnitude"—being neither too large nor too small, neither too simple nor too complex. The relationship between this organic concept and the principle of audience effect is perhaps clearest in Chapter 23: discussing the epic genre, Aristotle argues that the action of the work must be unified "so that, like a single integrated organism, it achieves the pleasure natural to it." Aristotle's meaning might be clarified by a passage from his treatise on the *Parts of Animals* (Book I, Chapter 5): all living creatures, "by disclosing to intellectual perception the artistic spirit that designed them, give immense pleasure to all who can trace links of causation and are inclined to philosophy."

Aristotle's organic analogy is also operative in his attempt to elevate the concept of "plot" (*mythos*). In Chapter 6 Aristotle calls plot the "first principle" or "soul" (*psyche*) of tragedy. Plot is what makes a tragedy dynamic, and it is functionally related to audience response. Moreover, it is on the basis of plot-considerations that the dramatist must manage his characterization, writing of speeches, choice of diction, and so on. In the chapters which follow Aristotle again insists on the crucial importance of structural coherence or logical "universality" (the essential difference between poetry and history) and he demonstrates his aesthetic preference for complex plots (those involving reversal and recognition) and unhappy (i.e., pitiable and fearful) tragic endings.

Aristotle's emphasis on plot leads him to reject the idea that the difference between poetry and non-poetry is the use of verse. For him poetry is the art of fiction rather than the art of writing in verse. According to the standards of the *Poetics*, a novel would be as truly a poem as would *Paradise Lost*. L. J. Potts has stressed this in his translation of the *Poetics* by giving it the title *Aristotle on the Art of Fiction*.

In spite of the seminal quality of Aristotle's ideas, the *Poetics* exerted little influence for approximately 1800 years after its first transcription; it was largely unknown to Horace, Longinus, Plutarch, Augustine, Aquinas, Dante, and Boccaccio. Following the recovery of the *Poetics* by Renaissance scholars, the treatise entered its first period of major popularity: as a core document in the syntheses of neoclassical criticism. For Scaliger, Castelvetro, Sidney, Ben Jonson, Boileau, Pope, and Samuel Johnson, the *Poetics* was valuable as an "authoritative" work which complemented Horace's *Ars Poetica*, thus confirming a generally rhetorical view of literature.

Neoclassical critics tended to ignore Aristotle's argumentative rigor and to narrow the meanings of his major terms—e.g., by construing "probability" in terms of "verisimilitude." The nineteenth century was a period of eclipse for the *Poetics*: romantic critics, operating under new premises—a theory of the poetic imagination rather than a theory based on the materials of poetry—reacted sharply against Aristotle, or at least against the Aristotle of neoclassicism. Their doctrines are often antithetical to the *Poetics*: the exaltation of lyric over drama, of character over plot, of "genius" over "rules," and most importantly, of expression over imitation.

It has remained for twentieth-century scholars and critics to bring the *Poetics* into its second phase of major influence. S. H. Butcher's *Aristotle's Theory of Poetry and Fine Art* (1895) demonstrated the essential kinship between Aristotle and the major romantic theorists—emphasizing that the methodology of the *Poetics* is neither positivistic nor moralistic, but aesthetic. Subsequent adaptations of the *Poetics* support this view, especially in the work of Thomists (Jacques Maritain), phenomenological critics (Roman Ingarden), eclectic critics (Francis Fergusson), "new critics" (John Crowe Ransom), and the "Chicago Neo-Aristotelians" (R. S. Crane). On the other hand, Aristotle's treatise has also remained a source of evidence and insight for psychological and sociological critics (Kenneth Burke), anthropological critics (Gilbert Murray), Marxists (George Thomson), and humanists (Irving Babbitt).

That so many modern theorists, of such differing critical persuasions, have found inspiration and guidance in the *Poetics* suggests that Aristotle's insights have lost none of their vitality after two millennia. There can be little doubt that the *Poetics* will continue to exert a significant influence on the future theory and practice of literature.

The translation is my own and is reprinted from Leon Golden and O. B. Hardison, Jr., *Aristotle's Poetics: A Translation and Commentary for Students of Literature* (Englewood Cliffs: Prentice-Hall, 1968) by permission of the publisher. The numbers inserted in the translation are the page numbers of the Berlin edition of Aristotle by Immanuel Bekker. In the following English version, these numbers, which are used by scholars in the citation of passages from Aristotle's text, appear in the approximate location they occupy in the original. However, Bekker's subdivisions (a and b) have been omitted.

POETICS

I

(1447) Let us discuss the art of poetry, itself, and its species, describing the character of each of them, and how it is necessary to construct plots if the poetic composition is to be successful and, furthermore, the number and kind of parts to be found in the poetic work, and as many other matters as are relevant. Let us follow the order of nature, beginning with first principles.

Now epic poetry, tragedy, comedy, dithyrambic poetry,[1] and most forms of flute and lyre playing all happen to be, in general, imitations, but they differ from each other in three ways: either because the imitation is carried on by different means or because it is concerned with different kinds of objects or because it is presented, not in the same, but in a different manner.

For just as some artists imitate many different objects by using color and form to represent them (some through art, others only through habit), other artists imitate through sound, as indeed, in the arts mentioned above; for all these accomplish imitation through rhythm and speech and harmony, making use of these elements separately or in combination. Flute playing and lyre playing, for example, use harmony and rhythm alone; and this would also be true of any other arts (for example, the art of playing the shepherd's pipe) that are similar in character to these. Dancers imitate by using rhythm without harmony, since they imitate characters, emotions, and actions by rhythms that are arranged into dance-figures.

The art that imitates by words alone, in prose and in verse, and in the latter case, either combines various meters or makes use of only one, has been nameless up to the present time. (1447) For we cannot assign a common name to the mimes[2] of Sophron and Xenarchus and the Socratic dialogues; nor would we have a name for such an imitation if someone should accomplish it through trimeters or elegiacs or some other such meter, except that the public at large by joining the term "poet" to a meter gives writers such names as "elegiac poets" and "epic poets." Here the public classifies all those who write in meter as poets and completely misses the point that the capacity to produce an imitation is the essential characteristic of the poet. The public is even accustomed to apply the name "poet" to those who publish a medical or scientific treatise in verse, although Homer has nothing at all in common with Empedocles except the meter. It is just to call Homer a poet, but we must consider Empedocles a physicist rather than a poet.

And in the same way, if anyone should create an imitation by combining all the meters as Chairemon did when he wrote *The Centaur*, a rhapsody composed by the use of all the meters, he must also be designated a poet. Concerning these matters let us accept the distinctions we have just made.

There are some arts that use all the means that have been discussed, namely, rhythm and song and meter, as in the writing of dithyrambs and nomic poetry[3] and in tragedy and comedy. A difference is apparent here in that some arts use all the various elements at the same time, whereas others use them separately. These, then, are what I call the differences in the artistic means through which the imitation is accomplished.

II

(1448) Artists imitate men involved in action and these must either be noble or base since human character regularly conforms to these distinctions, all of us being different in character because of some quality of goodness or evil. From this it follows that the objects imitated are either better than or worse than or like the norm. We find confirmation of this observation in the practice of our painters. For Polygnotus represents men as better, Pauson as worse, and Dionysius as like the norm. It is clear that each of the above-mentioned forms of imitation will manifest differences of this type and will be different through its choosing, in this way, a different kind of object to imitate. Even in dancing, flute-playing, and lyre-playing it is possible for these differences to exist, and they are seen also in prose, and in verse that does not make use of musical accompaniment, as is shown by the fact that Cleophon represents men like the norm, Homer as better, and both Hegemon the Thasian (who was the first writer of parodies) and Nicochares, the author of the *Deiliad*, as worse. The same situation is found in dithyrambic and nomic poetry,[4] as we see in the way Timotheus and Philoxenus handled the Cyclops theme. It is through the same distinction in objects that we differentiate comedy from tragedy, for the former takes as its goal the representation of men as worse, the latter as better, than the norm.

III

There is, finally, a third factor by which we distinguish imitations, and that is the manner in which the artist represents the various types of object. For, using the same means and imitating the same kinds of object, it is possible for the poet on different occasions to narrate the story (either speaking in the person of one of his characters as Homer does or in his own person without changing roles) or to have the imitators performing and acting out the entire story.

As we said at the beginning, imitations are to be distinguished under these three headings: means, object, and manner. Thus, in one way, Sophocles is the same kind of imitative artist as Homer, since they both imitate noble men; but in another sense, he resembles Aristophanes, since they both imitate characters as acting and dramatizing the incidents of the story. It is from this, some tell us, that these latter kinds of imitations are called "dramas" because they present characters who "dramatize" the incidents of the plot.

By the way, it is also for this reason that the Dorians claim to be the originators of both tragedy and comedy. The Megarians—both those in Megara itself, who assert that comedy arose when democracy was established among them, and those Megarians in Sicily, who point out that their poet Epicharmus far antedates Chionides and Magnes—claim to have originated comedy; in addition, some of the Dorians in the Peloponnesus claim to be the originators of tragedy. As proof of their contentions, they cite the technical terms they use for these art forms; for they say that they call the towns around their city *komai*, but that the Athenians call their towns *demoi*. By this they argue that the root of the name "comedian" is not derived from *komazein* [the word for "reveling"] but from *komai* [their word for the towns] that the comic artists visited in their wanderings after they had been driven in disgrace from the city. (1448) In support of their claim to be the originators of "drama," they point out that the word for "doing" is *dran* in their dialect, whereas Athenians use the word *prattein* for this concept.

Concerning the number and kind of distinctions that characterize "imitations," let us accept what has been said above.

IV

Speaking generally, the origin of the art of poetry is to be found in two natural causes. For the process of imitation is natural to mankind from childhood on: Man is differentiated from other animals because he is the most imitative of them, and he learns his first lessons through imitation, and we observe that all men find pleasure in imitations. The proof of this point is what actually happens in life. For there are some things that distress us when we see them in reality, but the most accurate representations of these same things we view with pleasure—as, for example, the forms of the most despised animals and of corpses. The cause of this is that the act of learning is not only most pleasant to philosophers but, in a similar way, to other men as well, only they have an abbreviated share in this pleasure. Thus men find pleasure in viewing representations because it turns out that they learn and infer what each thing is—for example, that this particular object is that kind of object; since if one has not happened to see the object previously, he will not find any pleasure in the imitation *qua* imitation but rather in the workmanship or coloring or something similar.

Since imitation is given to us by nature, as are harmony and rhythm (for it is apparent that meters are parts of the rhythms), men, having been naturally endowed with these gifts from the beginning and then developing them gradually, for the most part, finally created the art of poetry from their early improvisations.

Poetry then diverged in the directions of the natural dispositions of the poets. Writers of greater dignity imitated the noble actions of noble heroes; the less dignified sort of writers imitated the actions of inferior men, at first writing invectives as the former writers wrote hymns and encomia. We know of no "invective" by poets before Homer, although it is probable that there were many who wrote such poems; but it is possible to attribute them to authors who came after Homer—for example, the *Margites*[5] of Homer himself, and other such poems. In these poems, the fitting meter came to light, the one that now bears the name "iambic" [i.e., invective] because it was originally used by men to satirize each other. Thus, of our earliest writers, some were heroic and some iambic poets. And just as Homer was especially the poet of noble actions (for he not only handled these well but he also made his imitations dramatic), so also he first traced out the form of comedy by dramatically presenting not invective but the ridiculous. For his *Margites* has the same relation to comedy as the *Iliad* and *Odyssey* have to tragedy. (1449) But when tragedy and comedy began to appear, poets were attracted to each type of poetry according to their individual natures, one group becoming writers of comedies in place of iambics, and the other, writers of tragedies instead of epics because these genres were of greater importance and more admired than the others.

Now then, the consideration of whether or not tragedy is by now sufficiently developed in its formal elements, judged both in regard to its essential nature and in regard to its public performances, belongs to another discussion. What is relevant is that it arose, at first, as an improvisation (both tragedy and comedy are similar in this respect) on the part of those who led the dithyrambs, just as comedy arose from those who led the phallic songs that even now are still customary in many of our cities. Tragedy, undergoing many changes (since our poets were developing aspects of it as they emerged), gradually progressed until it attained the fulfillment of its own nature. Aeschylus was the first to increase the number of actors from one to two; he also reduced the role of the chorus and made the dialogue the major element in the play. Sophocles increased the number of actors to three and introduced scene painting. Then tragedy acquired its magnitude. Thus by developing away from a satyr-play[6] of short plots and absurd diction, tragedy achieved, late in its history, a dignified level. Then the iambic meter took the place of the tetrameter. For the poets first used the trochaic tetrameter because their poetry was satyric and very closely associated with dance; but when dialogue was introduced, nature itself discovered the appropriate meter. For the iambic is the most conversational of the meters—as we see from the fact that we speak many iambs when talking to each other, but few [dactylic] hexameters, and only when departing from conversational tone. Moreover, the number of episodes was increased. As to the other elements by which, we are told, tragedy was embellished, we must consider them as having been mentioned by us. For it would probably be an enormous task to go through each of these elements one by one.

V

As we have said, comedy is an imitation of baser men. These are characterized not by every kind of vice but specifically by "the ridiculous," which is a subdivision of the category of "deformity." What we mean by "the ridiculous" is some error or ugliness that is painless and has no harmful effects. The example that comes immediately to mind is the comic mask, which is ugly and distorted but causes no pain.

Now then, the successive changes in the history of tragedy and the men who brought them about have been recorded; but the analogous information about the history of comedy is lacking because the genre was not treated, at the beginning, as a serious art form. (1449) It was only recently that the archons[7] began to grant choruses to the comic poets; until then, the performers were all volunteers. And it was only after comedy had attained some recognizable form that we began to have a record of those designated as "comic poets." Who introduced masks or prologues, who established the number of actors, and many other matters of this type, are unknown. The creation of plots came first from Sicily, where it is attributed to Epicharmus and Phormis; and it was the first Crates among the Athenian poets who departed from iambic [or invective] poetry and began to write speeches and plots of a more universal nature.

Now epic poetry follows the same pattern as tragedy insofar as it is the imitation of noble subjects presented in an elevated meter. But epic differs from tragedy in that it uses a single meter, and its manner of presentation is narrative. And further, there is a difference in length. For tragedy attempts, as far as possible, to remain within one circuit of the sun or, at least, not depart from this by much. Epic poetry, however, has no limit in regard to time, and differs from tragedy in this respect; although at first the poets proceeded in tragedy in the same way as they did in epic. Some of the parts of a poem are common to both tragedy and epic, and some belong to tragedy alone. Therefore, whoever can judge what is good and bad in tragedy can also do this in regard to epic. For whatever parts epic poetry has, these are also found in tragedy; but, as we have said, not all of the parts of tragedy are found in epic poetry.

VI

We shall speak about the form of imitation that is associated with hexameter verse and about comedy later. Let us now discuss tragedy, bringing together the definition of its essence that has emerged from what we have already said. Tragedy is, then, an imitation of a noble and complete action, having the proper magnitude;[8] it employs language that has been artistically enhanced by each of the kinds of linguistic adornment, applied separately in the various parts of the play; it is presented in dramatic, not narrative form, and achieves, through the representation of pitiable and fearful incidents, the catharsis of such pitiable and fearful incidents. I mean by "language that has been artistically enhanced," that which is accompanied by rhythm and harmony and song; and by the phrase "each of the kinds of linguistic adornment applied separately in the various parts of the play," I mean that some parts are accomplished by meter alone and others, in turn, through song.

And since [in drama] agents accomplish the imitation by acting the story out, it follows, first of all, that the arrangement of the spectacle should be, of necessity, some part of the tragedy as would be melody and diction, also; for these are the means through which the agents accomplish the imitation. I mean by diction the act, itself, of making metrical compositions, and by melody, what is completely obvious. Since the imitation is of an action and is accomplished by certain agents, the sort of men these agents are is necessarily dependent upon their "character" and "thought." It is, indeed, on the basis of these two considerations that we designate the quality of actions, (1450) because the two natural causes of human action are thought and character. It is also in regard to these that the lives of all turn out well or poorly. For this reason we say that tragic plot is an imitation of action.

Now I mean by the plot the arrangement of the incidents, and by character that element in accordance with which we say that agents are of a certain type; and by thought I mean that which is found in whatever things men say when they prove a point or, it may be, express a general truth. It is necessary, therefore, that tragedy as a whole have six parts in accordance with which, as a genre, it achieves its particular quality. These parts are plot, character, diction, thought, spectacle, and melody. Two of these parts come from the means by which the imitation is carried out; one from the manner of its presentation, and three from the objects of the imitation. Beyond these parts there is nothing left to mention. Not a few poets, so to speak, employ these parts; for indeed, every drama [theoretically] has spectacle, character, plot, diction, song, and thought.

The most important of these parts is the arrangement of the incidents; for tragedy is not an imitation of men, *per se,* but of human action and life and happiness and misery. Both happiness and misery consist in a kind of action; and the end of life is some action, not some quality.[9] Now according to their characters men have certain qualities; but according to their actions they are happy or the opposite. Poets do not, therefore, create action in order to imitate character; but character is included on account of the action. Thus the end of tragedy is the presentation of the individual incidents and of the plot; and the end is, of course, the most significant thing of all. Furthermore, without action tragedy would be impossible, but without character it would still be possible. This point is illustrated both by the fact that the tragedies of many of our modern poets are characterless, and by the fact that many poets, in general, experience this difficulty. Also, to take an example from our painters, Zeuxis illustrates the point when compared to Polygnotus; for Polygnotus is good at incorporating character into his painting, but the work of Zeuxis shows no real characterization at all. Furthermore, if someone arranges a series of speeches that show character and are well-constructed in diction and thought, he will not, by this alone, achieve the end of tragedy; but far more will this be accomplished by the tragedy that employs these elements rather inadequately but, nevertheless, has a satisfactory plot and arrangement of incidents. In addition to the arguments already given, the most important factors by means of which tragedy exerts an influence on the soul are parts of the plot, the reversal, and the recognition. We have further proof of our view of the importance of plot in the fact that those who attempt to write tragedies are able to perfect diction and character before the construction of the incidents, as we see, for example, in nearly all our early poets.

The first principle, then, and to speak figuratively, the soul of tragedy, is the plot; and second in importance is character. A closely corresponding situation exists in painting. (1450) For if someone should paint by applying the most beautiful colors, but without reference to an over-all plan, he would not please us as much as if he had outlined the figure in black and white. Tragedy, then, is an imitation of an action; and it is, on account of this, an imitation of men acting.

Thought is the third part of tragedy and is the ability to say whatever is pertinent and fitting to the occasion, which, in reference to the composition of speeches, is the essential function of the arts of politics and rhetoric. As proof of this we point out that our earlier poets made their characters speak like statesmen, and our contemporary poets make them speak like rhetoricians. Now character is that part of tragedy which shows an individual's purpose by indicating, in circumstances where it is not clear, what sort of things he chooses or rejects. Therefore those speeches do not manifest character in which there is absolutely nothing that the speaker chooses or rejects. Thought we find in those speeches in which men show that something is or is not, or utter some universal proposition.

The fourth literary part is diction, and I mean by diction, as has already been said, the expression of thoughts through language which, indeed, is the same whether in verse or prose.

Of the remaining parts, melody is the greatest of the linguistic adornments; and spectacle, to be sure, attracts our attention but is the least artistic and least essential part of the art of poetry. For the power of tragedy is felt even without a dramatic performance and actors. Furthermore, for the realization of spectacle, the art of the costume designer is more effective than that of the poet.

VII

Now that we have defined these terms, let us discuss what kind of process the arrangement of incidents must be, since this is the first and most important element of tragedy. We have posited that tragedy is the imitation of a complete and whole action having a proper magnitude. For it is possible for something to be a whole and yet not have any considerable magnitude. To be a whole is to have a beginning and a middle and an end. By a "beginning" I mean that which is itself not, by necessity, after anything else but after which something naturally is or develops. By an "end" I mean exactly the opposite: that which is naturally after something else, either necessarily or customarily, but after which there is nothing else. By a "middle" I mean that which is itself after something else and which has something else after it. It is necessary, therefore, that well-constructed plots not begin by chance, anywhere, nor end anywhere, but that they conform to the distinctions that have been made above.

Furthermore, for beauty to exist, both in regard to a living being and in regard to any object that is composed of separate parts, not only must there be a proper arrangement of the component elements, but the object must also be of a magnitude that is not fortuitous. For beauty is determined by magnitude and order; therefore, neither would a very small animal be beautiful (for one's view of the animal is not clear, taking place, as it does, in an almost unperceived length of time), nor is a very large animal beautiful (1451) (for then one's view does not occur all at once, but, rather, the unity and wholeness of the animal are lost to the viewer's sight as would happen, for example, if we should come across an animal a thousand miles in length). So that just as it is necessary in regard to bodies and animals for there to be a proper magnitude—and this is the length that can easily be perceived at a glance—thus, also, there must be a proper length in regard to plots, and this is one that can be easily taken in by the memory. The limit of length in regard to the dramatic contests and in terms of the physical viewing of the performance is not a matter related to the art of poetry. For if it were necessary for a hundred tragedies to be played, they would be presented by timing them with water clocks as we are told happened on some occasions in the past. The limit, however, that is set in regard to magnitude by the very nature of the subject itself is that whatever is longer (provided it remains quite clear) is always more beautiful. To give a general rule, we say that whatever length is required for a change to occur from bad fortune to good or from good fortune to bad through a series of incidents that are in accordance with probability or necessity, is a sufficient limit of magnitude.

VIII

A plot is a unity not, as some think, merely if it is concerned with one individual, for in some of the many and infinitely varied things that happen to any one person, there is no unity. Thus, we must assert, there are many actions in the life of a single person from which no over-all unity of action emerges. For this reason all those poets seem to have erred who have written a *Heracleid* and a *Theseid* and other poems of this type; for they think that since Heracles was one person it is appropriate for his story to be one story. But Homer, just as he was superior in other respects, also seems to have seen this point well, whether through his technical skill or his native talent, since in making the *Odyssey* he did not include all the things that ever happened to Odysseus. (For example, it happened that Odysseus was wounded on Parnassus and that he feigned madness at the time of the call to arms; but between these two events there is no necessary or probable relation.) Homer, rather, organized the *Odyssey* around one action of the type we have been speaking about and did the same with the *Iliad.* Necessarily, then, just as in other forms of imitation, one imitation is of one thing, so also, a plot, since it is an imitation of an action, must be an imitation of an action that is one and whole. Moreover, it is necessary that the parts of the action be put together in such a way that if any one part is transposed or removed, the whole will be disordered and disunified. For that whose presence or absence has no evident effect is no part of the whole.

IX

It is apparent from what we have said that it is not the function of the poet to narrate events that have actually happened, but rather, events such as might occur and have the capability of occurring in accordance with the laws of probability or necessity. (1451) For the historian and the poet do not differ by their writing in prose or verse (the works of Herodotus might be put into verse but they would, nonetheless, remain a form of history both in their metrical and prose versions). The difference, rather, lies in the fact that the historian narrates events that have actually happened, whereas the poet writes about things as they might possibly occur. Poetry, therefore, is more philosophical and more significant than history, for poetry is more concerned with the universal, and history more with the individual. By the universal I mean what sort of man turns out to say or do what sort of thing according to probability or necessity— this being the goal poetry aims at, although it gives individual names to the characters whose actions are imitated. By the individual I mean a statement telling, for example, "what Alcibiades did or experienced."

Now then, this point has already been made clear in regard to comedy; for the comic poets, once they have constructed the plot through probable incidents, assign any names that happen to occur to them, and they do not follow the procedure of the iambic poets who write about specific individuals. In regard to tragedy, however, our poets cling to the names of the heroes of the past on the principle that whatever is clearly capable of happening is readily believable. We cannot be sure that whatever has not yet happened is possible; but it is apparent that whatever has happened is also capable of happening for, if it were not, it could not have occurred. Nevertheless in some tragedies one or two of the names are well known and the rest have been invented for the occasion; in others not even one is well-known, for example, Agathon's *Antheus,* since in this play both the incidents and the names have been invented, and nonetheless they please us. Thus we must not seek to cling exclusively to the stories that have been handed down and about which our tragedies are usually written. It would be absurd, indeed, to do this since the well-known plots are known only to a few, but nevertheless please everyone. It is clear then from these considerations that it is necessary for the poet to be more the poet of his plots than of his meters, insofar as he is a poet because he is an imitator and imitates human actions. If the poet happens to write about things that have actually occurred, he is no less the poet for that. For nothing prevents some of the things that have actually occurred from belonging to the class of the probable or possible, and it is in regard to this aspect that he is the poet of them.

Of the simple plots and actions the episodic are the worst; and I mean by episodic a plot in which the episodes follow each other without regard for the laws of probability or necessity. Such plots are constructed by the inferior poets because of their own inadequacies, and by the good poets because of the actors. For since they are writing plays that are to be entered in contests (and so stretch the plot beyond its capacity) they are frequently forced to distort the sequence of action. (1452)

Since the imitation is not only a complete action but is also of fearful and pitiable incidents, we must note that these are intensified when they occur unexpectedly, yet because of one another. For there is more of the marvelous in them if they occur this way than if they occurred spontaneously and by chance. Even in regard to coincidences, those seem to be most astonishing that appear to have some design associated with them. We have an example of this in the story of the statue of Mitys in Argos killing the man who caused Mitys' death by falling upon him as he was a spectator at a festival. The occurrence of such an event, we feel, is not without meaning and thus we must consider plots that incorporate incidents of this type to be superior ones.

X

Plots are divided into the simple and the complex, for the actions of which the plots are imitations are naturally of this character. An action that is, as has been defined, continuous and unified I call simple when its change of fortune arises without reversal and recognition, and complex when its change of fortune arises through recognition or reversal or both. Now these aspects of the plot must develop directly from the construction of the plot, itself, so that they occur from prior events either out of necessity or according to the laws of probability. For it makes quite a difference whether they occur *because* of those events or merely *after* them.

XI

Reversal is the change of fortune in the action of the play to the opposite state of affairs, just as has been said; and this change, we argue, should be in accordance with probability and necessity. Thus, in the *Oedipus* the messenger comes to cheer Oedipus and to remove his fears in regard to his mother; but by showing him who he actually is he accomplishes the very opposite effect. And in *Lynceus,*[10] Lynceus is being led away to die and Danaus is following to kill him; but it turns out, because of the action that has taken place, that Danaus dies and Lynceus is saved. Recognition, as the name indicates, is a change from ignorance to knowledge, bringing about either a state of friendship or one of hostility on the part of those who have been marked out for good fortune or bad. The most effective recognition is one that occurs together with reversal, for example, as in the *Oedipus.* There are also other kinds of recognition for, indeed, what we have said happens, in a way, in regard to inanimate things, even things of a very casual kind; and it is possible, further, to "recognize" whether someone has or has not done something. But the type of recognition that is especially a part of the plot and the action is the one that has been mentioned. For such a recognition and reversal will evoke pity or fear, and we have defined tragedy as an imitation of actions of this type; (1452) and furthermore, happiness and misery will appear in circumstances of this type. Since this kind of recognition is of persons, some recognitions that belong to this class will merely involve the identification of one person by another when the identity of the second person is clear; on other occasions it will be necessary for there to be a recognition on the part of both parties: for example, Iphigenia is recognized by Orestes from her sending of the letter; but it is necessary that there be another recognition of him on her part.

Now then, these are two parts of the plot, reversal and recognition, and there is also a third part, suffering. Of these, reversal and recognition have been discussed; the incident of suffering results from destructive or painful action such as death on the stage, scenes of very great pain, the infliction of wounds, and the like.

XII

The parts of tragedy that we must view as formal elements we have discussed previously; looking at the quantitative aspect of tragedy and the parts into which it is divided in this regard, the following are the distinctions to be made: prologue, episode, exode, and the choral part, which is divided into parode and stasimon. These are commonly found in all plays, but only in a few are found songs from the stage and *kommoi*. The prologue is the complete section of a tragedy before the parode of the chorus; an episode is the complete section of a tragedy between complete choric songs; the exode is the complete section of a tragedy after which there is no song of the chorus. Of the choral part, the parode is the entire first speech of the chorus, the stasimon is a song of the chorus without anapests and trochees, and a *kommos* is a lament sung in common by the chorus and the actors. The parts of tragedy that we must view as formal elements we have discussed previously; the above distinctions have been made concerning the quantitative aspect of tragedy, and the parts into which it is divided in this regard.

XIII

What goals poets must aim at, what difficulties they must be wary of when constructing their plots, and how the proper function of tragedy is accomplished are matters we should discuss after the remarks that have just been made.

Since the plots of the best tragedies must be complex, not simple, and the plot of a tragedy must be an imitation of pitiable and fearful incidents (for this is the specific nature of the imitation under discussion), it is clear, first of all, that unqualifiedly good human beings must not appear to fall from good fortune to bad; for that is neither pitiable nor fearful; it is, rather, repellent. Nor must an extremely evil man appear to move from bad fortune to good fortune for that is the most untragic situation of all because it has none of the necessary requirements of tragedy; it both violates our human sympathy and contains nothing of the pitiable or fearful in it. (1453) Furthermore, a villainous man should not appear to fall from good fortune to bad. For, although such a plot would be in accordance with our human sympathy, it would not contain the necessary elements of pity and fear; for pity is aroused by someone who undeservedly falls into misfortune, and fear is evoked by our recognizing that it is someone like ourselves who encounters this misfortune (pity, as I say, arising for the former reason, fear for the latter). Therefore the emotional effect of the situation just mentioned will be neither pitiable nor fearful. What is left, after our considerations, is someone in between these extremes. This would be a person who is neither perfect in virtue and justice, nor one who falls into misfortune through vice and depravity; but rather, one who succumbs through some miscalculation. He must also be a person who enjoys great reputation and good fortune, such as Oedipus, Thyestes, and other illustrious men from similar families. It is necessary, furthermore, for the well-constructed plot to have a single rather than a double construction, as some urge, and to illustrate a change of fortune not from bad fortune to good but, rather, the very opposite, from good fortune to bad, and for this to take place not because of depravity but through some great miscalculation on the part of the type of person we have described (or a better rather than a worse one).

A sign of our point is found in what actually happens in the theater. For initially, our poets accepted any chance plots; but now the best tragedies are constructed about a few families, for example, about Alcmaeon, Oedipus, Orestes, Meleager, Thyestes, Telephon, and any others who were destined to experience, or to commit, terrifying acts. For as we have indicated, artistically considered, the best tragedy arises from this kind of plot. Therefore, those critics make the very mistake that we have been discussing who blame Euripides because he handles the material in his tragedies in this way, and because many of his plots end in misfortune. For this is, indeed, the correct procedure, as we have said. The very great proof of this is that on the stage and in the dramatic contests such plays appear to be the most tragic, if they are properly worked out; and Euripides, even if, in other matters he does not manage things well, nevertheless appears to be the most tragic of the poets. The second ranking plot, one that is called first by some, has a double structure of events, as in the *Odyssey*, ending in opposite ways for the better and worse characters. It seems to be first on account of the inadequacy of the audience. For our poets trail along writing to please the tastes of the audience. But this double structure of events involves a pleasure that is not an appropriate pleasure of tragedy but

rather of comedy. For in comedy, whoever are the greatest enemies in the story
—for example, Orestes and Aegisthus—becoming friends at the end, go off
together, and no one is killed by anyone.

XIV

(1453) Pity and fear can arise from the spectacle and also from the very
structure of the plot, which is the superior way and shows the better poet. The
poet should construct the plot so that even if the action is not performed before
spectators, one who merely hears the incidents that have occurred both shudders
and feels pity from the way they turn out. That is what anyone who hears the
plot of the *Oedipus* would experience. The achievement of this effect through
the spectacle does not have much to do with poetic art and really belongs to the
business of producing the play. Those who use the spectacle to create not the
fearful but only the monstrous have no share in the creation of tragedy; for we
should not seek every pleasure from tragedy but only the one proper to it.

Since the poet should provide pleasure from pity and fear through
imitation, it is apparent that this function must be worked into the incidents.
Let us try to understand what type of occurrences appear to be terrifying and
pitiable. It is, indeed, necessary that any such action occur either between
those who are friends or enemies to each other, or between those who have no
relationship, whatsoever, to each other. If an enemy takes such an action against
an enemy, there is nothing pitiable in the performance of the act or in the intention to perform it, except the suffering itself. Nor would there be anything
pitiable if neither party had any relationship with the other. But whenever the
tragic incidents occur in situations involving strong ties of affection—for example, if a brother kills or intends to kill a brother or a son a father or a
mother a son or a son a mother or commits some equally terrible act—there will
be something pitiable. These situations, then, are the ones to be sought. Now,
it is not possible for a poet to alter completely the traditional stories. I mean,
for example, the given fact that Clytemnestra dies at the hands of Orestes, and
Eriphyle at the hands of Alcmaeon; but it is necessary for the poet to be inventive
and skillful in adapting the stories that have been handed down. Let us define
more clearly what we mean by the skillful adaptation of a story. It is possible
for the action to occur, as our early poets handled it, with the characters knowing
and understanding what they are doing, as indeed Euripides makes Medea kill
her children. It is also possible to have the deed done with those who accomplish the terrible deed in ignorance of the identity of their victim, only later
recognizing the relationship as in Sophocles' *Oedipus*. The incident, here, is
outside the plot, but we find an example of such an incident in the play itself,
in the action of Astydamas' *Alcmaeon* or of Telegonus in the *Wounded Odys-*

seus;[11] and there is further a third type in addition to these that involves some-one who intends to commit some fatal act through ignorance of his relationship to another person but recognizes this relationship before doing it. Beyond these possibilities, there is no other way to have an action take place. For it is necessary either to do the deed or not and either knowingly or in ignorance.

Of these possibilities, the case in which one knowingly is about to do the deed and does not is the worst; for it is repellent and not tragic because it lacks the element of suffering. (1454) Therefore, no one handles a situation this way, except rarely; for example, in the *Antigone,* Haemon is made to act in this way toward Creon. To do the deed knowingly is the next best way. Better than this is the case where one does the deed in ignorance and after he has done it recognizes his relationship to the other person. For the repellent aspect is not present, and the recognition is startling. But the most effective is the final type, for example, in the *Cresphontes,* where Merope is going to kill her son and does not, but, on the contrary, recognizes him, and in the *Iphigenia,* where a sister is involved in a similar situation with a brother, and in the *Helle,* where a son who is about to surrender his mother recognizes her.[12]

It is for this reason that, as we have said previously, tragedies are con-cerned with a few families. For proceeding not by art, but by trial and error, poets learned how to produce the appropriate effect in their plots. They are compelled, therefore, to return time and again to that number of families in which these terrifying events have occurred. We have now spoken sufficiently about the construction of the incidents and of what type the plot must be.

XV

In regard to character, there are four points to be aimed at. First and foremost, character should be good. If a speech or action has some choice con-nected with it, it will manifest character, as has been said, and the character will be good if the choice is good. Goodness is possible for each class of in-dividuals. For, both a woman and a slave have their particular virtues even though the former of these is inferior to a man, and the latter is completely ignoble. Second, character must be appropriate. For it is possible for a person to be manly in terms of character, but it is not appropriate for a woman to exhibit either this quality or the intellectual cleverness that is associated with men. The third point about character is that it should be like reality, for this is different from making character virtuous and making it appropriate, as we have defined these terms. The fourth aspect of character is consistency. For even if it is an inconsistent character who is the subject of the imitation (I refer to the model that suggested the kind of character being imitated), it is nevertheless necessary for him to be consistently inconsistent. We have an example of

unnecessarily debased character in the figure of Menelaus in the *Orestes,* of
unsuitable and inappropriate character in the lament of Odysseus in the *Scylla*[13]
and the speech of Melanippe,[14] and of inconsistency of character in *Iphigenia
at Aulis* where the heroine's role as a suppliant does not fit in with her character
as it develops later in the play.

In character, as in the construction of the incidents, we must always
seek for either the necessary or the probable, so that a given type of person says
or does certain kinds of things, and one event follows another according to
necessity or probability. (1454) Thus, it is apparent that the resolutions of
the plots should also occur through the plot itself and not by means of the
deus ex machina,[15] as in the *Medea,* and also in regard to the events surrounding
the departure of the fleet in the *Iliad.* The *deus ex machina* must be reserved for
the events that lie outside the plot, either those that happened before it that
are not capable of being known by men, or those that occur after that need to
be announced and spoken of beforehand. For we grant to the gods the power
of seeing all things. There should, then, be nothing improbable in the action;
but if this is impossible, it should be outside the plot as, for example, in
Sophocles' *Oedipus.*

Because tragedy is an imitation of the nobler sort of men it is necessary
for poets to imitate the good portrait painters. For even though they reproduce
the specific characteristics of their subjects and represent them faithfully, they
also paint them better than they are. Thus, also, the poet imitating men who are
prone to anger or who are indifferent or who are disposed in other such ways in
regard to character makes them good as well, even though they have such characteristics, just as Agathon and Homer portray Achilles.

It is necessary to pay close attention to these matters and, in addition, to
those that pertain to the effects upon an audience that follow necessarily from
the nature of the art of poetry. For, indeed, it is possible frequently to make
mistakes in regard to these. We have spoken sufficiently about these matters in
our published works.

XVI

What we mean by "recognition" we have indicated previously. Of the
kinds of recognition that occur, there is one, first of all, that is least artistic,
which poets mainly use through the poverty of their inspiration. This is the form
of recognition that is achieved through external signs; some of these are birth-
marks, for example, "the spearhead which the Earth-born are accustomed to
bear,"[16] or the "stars" such as Carcinus wrote about in his *Thyestes.* Then there
are characteristics that we acquire after birth. Of these some are found on the
body, for example, scars; and others are external to the body, such as necklaces,

and as another example, the ark through which the recognition is accomplished in the *Tyro*.[17] It is also possible to employ these recognitions in better and worse ways; for example, Odysseus was recognized through his scar in one way by the nurse and in another way by the swineherds. Now those recognitions are less artistic that depend on signs as proof, as well as all that are similar to these; but those that derive from the reversal of action, as in the Bath Scene of the *Odyssey,* are better.

In second place come those recognitions that have been contrived for the occasion by the poet and are therefore inartistic. For example, the way Orestes in the *Iphigenia* makes known that he is Orestes; for Iphigenia made herself known through the letter, but he himself says what the poet wishes him to say but not what the plot requires. Therefore this type of recognition is rather close to the error that has already been mentioned; for it would have been just as possible for him to carry tokens with him. Another example of this type of recognition is the use of the "voice of the shuttle"[18] in the *Tereus* of Sophocles.

The third type arises from our being stimulated by something that we see to remember an event that has an emotional significance for us. (1455) This type of recognition occurs in the *Cyprioe* of Dicaeogenes where the sight of the painting brings forth tears, and also in the story of Alcinous where Odysseus hears the lyre player and, reminded of his past fortunes, weeps; in both instances, it was by their emotional reactions that the characters were recognized.

The fourth type of recognition occurs through reasoning, for example, in the *Choëphoroe*[19] it is achieved by the deduction: Someone like me has come; there is no one resembling me except Orestes; he, therefore, has come. Another recognition of this type was suggested by Polyidus the Sophist in regard to Iphigenia; for it was reasonable for Orestes to infer that, since his sister was sacrificed, he was also going to be sacrificed. Again, in the *Tydeus* of Theodectes, the deduction is made that he who had come to find a son was, himself, to perish. Another example is in the *Phinidae*[20] where the women, when they had seen the place, inferred their destiny: that since they had been exposed there, they were fated to die there.

There is also a type of composite recognition from false reasoning on the part of another character, for example, in the story of Odysseus, the False Messenger; for he said that he would know the bow that he had not seen, but it is false reasoning to suppose through this that he *would* recognize it again (as if he had seen it before).

The best recognition is the one that arises from the incidents themselves, striking us, as they do, with astonishment through the very probability of their occurrence as, for example, in the action of the *Oedipus* of Sophocles and in the *Iphigenia*, where it is reasonable for the heroine to wish to dispatch a letter. Such recognitions, alone, are accomplished without contrived signs and necklaces. The second best type of recognition is the one that is achieved by reasoning.

XVII

In constructing plots and working them out with diction, the poet must keep the action as much as possible before his eyes. For by visualizing the events as distinctly as he can, just as if he were present at their actual occurrence, he will discover what is fitting for his purpose, and there will be the least chance of incongruities escaping his notice. A sign of this is found in the criticism that is made of Carcinus. For Amphiarus is coming back from the temple, a point that would have escaped the audience's notice if it had not actually seen it; and on the stage, the play failed because the audience was annoyed at this incongruity.

As much as is possible the poet should also work out the action with gestures. For, given poets of the same natural abilities, those are most persuasive who are involved in the emotions they imitate; for example, one who is distressed conveys distress, and one who is enraged conveys anger most truly. Therefore, the art of poetry is more a matter for the well-endowed poet than for the frenzied one. For poets marked by the former characteristic can easily change character, whereas those of the latter type are possessed.

In regard to arguments, both those that already are in existence and those he himself invents, the poet should first put them down in universal form and then extend them by adding episodes. (1455) I mean that the poet should take a general view of the action of the play, like, for example, the following general view of the *Iphigenia*: A young girl had been sacrificed and had disappeared in a way that was obscure to the sacrificers. She settled in another country in which it was the custom to sacrifice strangers to the goddess, and she came to hold the priesthood for this sacrifice. Later, it turned out that the brother of the priestess came to this country (the fact that the god, for some reason, commanded him to come is outside the argument; the purpose of his coming is outside of the plot). When he came he was seized, and on the point of being sacrificed he made himself known, either as Euripides handled the situation or as Polyidus arranged it, by his saying, in a very reasonable way, that not only had it been necessary for his sister to be sacrificed but also for him; and from this came his deliverance. After this, when the names have already been assigned, it is necessary to complete the episodes. The episodes must be appropriate, as, for example, the madness of Orestes through which he was captured and his deliverance through purification.

In drama, the episodes are short, but epic achieves its length by means of them. For the argument of the *Odyssey* is not long: A certain man is away from home for many years, closely watched by Poseidon but otherwise completely alone. His family at home continually faces a situation where his possessions are being squandered by the suitors who plot against his son. Storm-driven, he arrives home and, having made certain people acquainted with him, he attacks the suitors and, while destroying his enemies, is himself saved. This is the essence of the story; everything else is episode.

XVIII

In every tragedy, we find both the complication and the resolution of the action. Frequently some matters outside the action together with some within it comprise the complication, and the rest of the play consists of the resolution. By complication I mean that part of the play from the beginning up to the first point at which the change occurs to good or to bad fortune. By resolution I mean the part of the play from the beginning of the change in fortune to the end of the play. For example, in the *Lynceus* of Theodectes, the complication comprises everything done before the action of the play begins and the seizing of the child, and, in turn, of the parents; the resolution comprises all that happens from the accusation of murder to the end of the play.[21]

There are four kinds of tragedy (for that number of parts has been mentioned): the complex, which consists wholly in reversal and recognition; the tragedies of suffering, for example, the *Ajaxes* and *Ixions* that have been written; (1456) the tragedies of character, for example, the *Phthiotian Women* and the *Peleus*.[22] And a fourth type [the tragedy of spectacle], for example, is *The Daughters of Phorcis* and *Prometheus*[23] and those plays that take place in Hades. Now it is necessary to attempt, as much as possible, to include all elements in the play, but if that is not possible, then as many as possible and certainly the most important ones. This is especially so now, indeed, when the public unjustly criticizes our poets. For although there have been poets who were outstanding in regard to each kind of tragedy, the public now demands that one man be superior to the particular virtue of each of his predecessors.

It is correct to speak of a tragedy as different from or similar to another one on the basis of its plot more than anything else: that is, in regard to an action having the same complication and resolution. Many poets are skillful in constructing their complications, but their resolutions are poor. It is, however, necessary for both elements to be mastered.

The poet, as has frequently been said, must remember not to make a tragedy out of an epic body of incidents (by which I mean a multiple plot), [as would be the case], for example, if someone should construct a plot out of the entire *Iliad*. For, there, because of the length, the parts take on the appropriate magnitude, but the same plot used in the drama turns out quite contrary to one's expectations. A sign of this is that so many as have written about the entire destruction of Troy (and not of sections of it, as Euripides) or about the entire story of Niobe (and not just a part, as Aeschylus) either completely fail on stage or do badly, since even Agathon failed for this reason alone. But in their reversals and in their simple plots, these poets aim with marvelous accuracy at the effects that they wish for: that is, whatever is tragic and touches our human sympathy. This occurs whenever a clever but evil person is deceived, as Sisyphus, or a brave but unjust man is defeated. Such an event is probable, as Agathon says, because it is probable for many things to occur contrary to probability.

It is necessary to consider the chorus as one of the actors and as an integral part of the drama; its involvement in the action should not be in Euripides' manner but in Sophocles'. In the hands of our later poets, the songs included in the play are no more a part of that particular plot than they are of any other tragedy. They have been sung, therefore, as inserted pieces from the time Agathon first introduced this practice. And yet what difference does it make whether one sings an inserted song or adopts a speech or a whole episode from one play into another?

XIX

We have already spoken about other matters; it remains for us to discuss diction and thought. Concerning thought, let it be taken as given what we have written in the *Rhetoric,* for this is more appropriately a subject of that discipline. All those matters pertain to thought that must be presented through speech; and they may be subdivided into proof and refutation and the production of emotional effects, for example, pity or fear or anger or other similar emotions. (1456) Indications of the importance or insignificance of anything also fall under this heading. It is clear that we must employ thought also in actions in the same ways [as in speech] whenever we aim at the representation of the pitiable, the terrible, the significant, or the probable, with the exception of this one difference —that the effects arise in the case of the incidents without verbal explanation, whereas in the speech they are produced by the speaker and arise because of the speech. For what would be the function of the speaker if something should appear in the way that is required without being dependent on the speech?

Concerning diction one kind of study involves the forms of diction that are investigated by the art of elocution and are the concern of the individual who considers this his guiding art, for example, what a command is and what a prayer is, what a statement is, and threat and question and answer and any other such matters. For in regard to the knowledge or ignorance of these matters, no censure worth taking seriously can be made against the art of poetry. Why should any one accept as an error Protagoras' censure of Homer on the grounds that when he said, "Sing, O goddess, of the wrath . . ."[24] he gave a command, although he really wished to utter a prayer. For Protagoras says to order someone to do something or not is a command. Let us, therefore, disregard such a consideration as being a principle of some other art, not the art of poetry.

XX

The following parts comprise the entire scope of diction: letter, syllable, connective, noun, verb, inflection and sentence. A letter is an indivisible sound; not every such sound is a letter, however, but only one from which a compound sound can be constructed. For I would call none of the individual sounds uttered by wild animals letters. The subdivisions of this category of "letter" are vowel, semivowel, and mute. A vowel is a sound that is audible without the contact of any of the physical structures of the mouth, a semivowel is a sound that is audible with the contact of some of the physical structures of the mouth, for example, the *S* and *R* sounds; and a mute is a letter produced by the contact of the physical structures of the mouth, but inaudible in itself, although it becomes audible when it is accompanied by letters that are sounded, for example, the *G* and *D* sounds. These letters differ in the positions taken by the mouth to produce them, in the places in the mouth where they are produced, in aspiration and smoothness, in being long or short and, furthermore, in having an acute, grave, or middle [circumflex] pitch accent. The detailed investigation concerning these matters belongs to the study of metrics.

A syllable is a nonsignificant sound constructed from a mute and a vowel. For, indeed, *GR* without an *A* is a syllable and also with it, for example, *GRA*. However, it is the business of the art of metrics also to investigate distinctions in this area.[25]

(1457) A connective is a nonsignificant sound that neither hinders nor promotes the creation of one significant sound from many sounds and that it is not appropriate to place at the beginning of a speech that stands independently, for example, *men, dē, toi, de.* Or it is a nonsignificant sound that is naturally able to make one significant sound from a number of sounds, for example, *amphi, peri,* and others like them. There is also a kind of connective that is a nonsignificant sound that shows the beginning, end, or division of a sentence and that may naturally be placed at either end or in the middle of a sentence.

A noun is a compound significant sound, not indicating time, no part of which is significant by itself. For in compound nouns we do not consider each part of the compound as being significant in itself; for example, in the name "Theodore" the root *dor* [gift] has no significance.

A verb is a compound significant sound indicating time, no part of which is significant by itself in the same way as has been indicated in regard to nouns. For "man" or "white" do not tell us anything about "when"; but "He goes" or "He has gone" indicate the present and the past.

Inflection is a characteristic of a noun or verb signifying the genitive or dative relation, or other similar ones, or indicating the singular or plural, that is, man or men, or is concerned with matters that fall under the art of elocution, for example, questions and commands; for the phrases, "Did he go?" or "Go!" involve inflections of the verb in regard to these categories.

A speech is a compound, significant sound some of whose parts are significant by themselves. For not every speech is composed of verbs and nouns but it is possible to have a speech without verbs (for example, the definition of man). However, part of the speech will always have some significance, for example, "Cleon" in the phrase "Cleon walks." A speech is a unity in two ways. Either it signifies one thing or it is a unity through the joining together of many speeches. For example, the *Iliad* is a unity by the process of joining together many speeches, and the definition of man by signifying one thing.

XXI

Nouns are either simple, by which I mean constructed solely from non-significant elements, for example *gē* [earth], or compound. This latter category is divided into nouns that are constructed from both significant and nonsignificant elements (except that neither element is significant within the compound word itself) and nouns that are composed solely out of significant elements. Nouns may also be made up of three, four, or more parts, for example, many of the words in the Massilian vocabulary, such as Hermocaicoxanthus. . . .[26]

(1457) Every word is either standard, or is a strange word, or is a metaphor, or is ornamental, or is a coined word, or is lengthened, or contracted, or is altered in some way. I mean by standard, words that everyone uses, and by a strange word, one that foreigners use. Thus, it is apparent, the same word can be both strange and ordinary but not, of course, to the same persons. The word *sigunon* [spear] is ordinary for the Cyprians and strange to us.

Metaphor is the transference of a name from the object to which it has a natural application; this transference can take place from genus to species or species to genus or from species to species or by analogy. I mean by from genus to species, for example, "This ship of mine stands there." For to lie at anchor is a species of standing. An example of the transference from species to genus, "Odysseus has truly accomplished a myriad of noble deeds." For a myriad is the equivalent of "many," for which the poet now substitutes this term. An example of the transference from species to species is "having drawn off life with a sword" and also "having cut with unyielding bronze." For here to draw off is to cut and to cut is called to draw off, for both are subdivisions of "taking away."

I mean by transference by analogy the situation that occurs whenever a second element is related to a first as a fourth is to a third. For the poet will then use the fourth in place of the second or the second in place of the fourth, and sometimes poets add the reference to which the transferred term applies. I mean, for example, that a cup is related to Dionysus as a shield is to Ares. The poet will, therefore, speak of the cup as the shield of Dionysus and the shield as the cup of Ares. The same situation occurs in regard to the relation of old age to life and evening to day. A poet will say that evening is the old age of day, or however Empedocles expressed it, and that old age is the evening of life or the sunset of life. In some situations, there is no regular name in use to cover the analogous relation, but nevertheless the related elements will be spoken of by analogy; for example, to scatter seed is to sow, but the scattering of the sun's rays has no name. But the act of sowing in regard to grain bears an analogous relation to the sun's dispersing of its rays, and so we have the phrase "sowing the god-created fire."

It is also possible to use metaphor in a different way by applying the transferred epithet and then denying some aspect that is proper to it—for example, if one should call the shield not the cup of Ares but the wineless cup. A coined word is one that is not in use among foreigners but is the invention of the poet. There seem to be some words of this type, for example, horns [*kerata*] called "sprouters" [*ernuges*], and a priest [*iereus*] called "supplicator" [*arētēr*].

A word may be lengthened or contracted. (1458) It is lengthened if it makes use of a longer vowel than is usual for it, or a syllable is inserted in it; and it is contracted if any element is removed from it. An example of lengthening is *poleōs* to *polēos* and *Pēleidou* to *Pēlēiadeō*: an example of contraction is *krī* and *dō* and *ops* in *"mia ginetai amphoterōn ops."*

A word is altered whenever a poet utilizes part of the regular name for the object he is describing and invents part anew, for example, in the phrase *"deksiteron kata mazon"* the use of *deksiteron* in place of *deksion*.[27]

Nouns are subdivided into masculine, feminine, and neuter. Those are masculine that end in nu, rho, and sigma and in the two letters psi and ksi that are constructed in combination with sigma. Those nouns are feminine that end in the vowels that are always long, the eta and omega, and that end (in regard to the vowels subject to lengthening) in the lengthened alpha. Thus it turns out that there are an equal number of terminations for masculine and feminine nouns since psi and ksi are subdivisions of sigma. No noun ends in a mute nor in a short vowel. Only three end in iota, *meli, kommi, peperi,* and five end in upsilon. Neuter nouns end in these vowels and in nu and sigma.

XXII

Diction achieves its characteristic virtue in being clear but not mean. The clearest style results from the use of standard words; but it is also mean, as can be seen in the poetry of Cleophon and Sthenelus. A really distinguished style varies ordinary diction through the employment of unusual words. By un-

usual I mean strange words and metaphor and lengthened words and everything that goes beyond ordinary diction. But if someone should write exclusively
in such forms the result would either be a riddle or a barbarism. A riddle will
result if someone writes exclusively in metaphor; and a barbarism will result
if there is an exclusive use of strange words. For it is in the nature of a riddle
for one to speak of a situation that actually exists in an impossible way. Now it is
not possible to do this by the combination of strange words; but it can be done
by metaphor, for example, "I saw a man who welded bronze on another man
by fire," and other metaphors like this. A statement constructed exclusively
from strange words is a barbarism.

It is therefore necessary to use a combination of all these forms. The
employment of strange words and metaphor and ornamental words and the
other forms of speech that have been mentioned will prevent the diction from
being ordinary and mean; and the use of normal speech will keep the diction
clear. (1458) The lengthening and contraction of words and alterations in them
contribute in no small measure to the diction's clarity and its elevation above
ordinary diction. For because such words are different they will prevent the
diction from being ordinary through their contrast with the ordinary expression;
and because they have a share in the customary word, they will keep the diction
clear.

Thus, the criticism is not well-taken on the part of those who censure
this way of using language and who mock the poet, as the elder Euclid did, on
the grounds that it is easy to write poetry if you are allowed to lengthen forms
as much as you want; Euclid composed a satiric verse in the very words he used,
Epicharēn eidon Marathōnade badizonta and *ouk an g'eramenos ton ekeinou
elleboron.*[28]

Now then, the employment of the technique of lengthening in excess is
ridiculous, and moderation is a quality that is commonly needed in all aspects of
diction. For, indeed, if one employs metaphors and strange words and other forms
in an inappropriate way and with intended absurdity, he can also accomplish the
same effect. When the ordinary words are inserted in the verse, it can be seen how
great a difference the appropriate use of lengthening makes in epic poetry. If
someone should also change the strange words and metaphors and other forms to
ordinary words, he would see the truth of what we have said. For example,
Aeschylus and Euripides wrote the same iambic line, but Euripides changed one
word and instead of using a standard one employed a strange one; his line thus
has an elegance to it, whereas the other is mean. For Aeschylus wrote in his
Philoctetes:[29] *"phagedaina hē mou sarkas esthiei podos"* [this cancerous sore eats
the flesh of my leg]. Euripides in place of "eats" substitutes *thoinatai* [feasts
upon]. A similar situation would occur in the line *"nun de m'eōn oligos te kai
outidanos kai aeikēs"*[30] if someone should substitute the ordinary words *"nun de
m'eōn mikros te kai asthenikos kai aeidēs"* or if we changed the line *"diphron*

aeikelion katatheis oligēn te trapezan''[31] to *"diphron moxthēron katatheis mikran te trapezan"* or for *ēiones booōsin,* we substituted *ēiones krazousin.*[32] Furthermore, Ariphrades mocked the tragedians because no one would use their style in conversation; for example, the word order *dōmatōn apo* in place of *apo dōmatōn,* and the word *sethen,* and the phrase *egō de nin,* and the word order *Achilleōs peri* in place of *peri Achilleōs,* and many other similar expressions. (1459) For he missed the point that the virtue of all these expressions is that they create an unusual element in the diction by their not being in ordinary speech.

It is a matter of great importance to use each of the forms mentioned in a fitting way, as well as compound words and strange ones, but by far the most important matter is to have skill in the use of metaphor. The skill alone it is not possible to obtain from another; and it is, in itself, a sign of genius. For the ability to construct good metaphors implies the ability to see essential similarities.

In regard to words, compounds are especially suitable for dithyrambs, strange words for heroic verse, and metaphors for iambic verse; in heroic verse all the forms mentioned are serviceable; but in iambic verse, because as much as possible it imitates conversation, only those words are appropriate that might be used in prose. Of this nature are standard words, metaphors, and ornamental words.

Now, then, concerning tragedy and the imitation that is carried out in action, let what has been said suffice.

XXIII

Concerning that form of verse imitation that is narrative, it is necessary to construct the plot as in tragedy in a dramatic fashion, and concerning a single action that is whole and complete (having a beginning, middle, and end) so that, like a single integrated organism, it achieves the pleasure natural to it.

The composition of incidents should not be similar to that found in our histories, in which it is necessary to show not one action but one period of time and as many things as happened in this time, whether they concern one man or many, and whether or not each of these things is related to the others. For just as there occurred in the same period of time a sea battle at Salamis and a battle with the Carthaginians in Sicily, but these did not at all lead to a common goal, thus also in the sequence of time, occasionally one event happens after another without there being a common goal to join them.

However, almost all the poets commit this error. Also in this, then, Homer would appear to be of exceptional skill in relation to other poets, as we have already said, since he did not attempt to write about the complete war, although it had a beginning and end; for that would have been a very large subject and could not have been taken in easily in a single view; or even if its magnitude were moderate, the story still would be tangled because of the diversity of incidents. But note how although treating only one part of the war, he also introduces many of the other episodes in the war, for example, the catalogue of ships and others, by which he gives variety to his poem. (1459) Others write about one man and about one period and one action with diverse parts, for example, the poet who wrote the *Cypria*[33] and the *Little Iliad*.[34] Therefore from the *Iliad* and *Odyssey* one or two tragedies apiece are constructed; but from the *Cypria* many tragedies are constructed and from the *Little Iliad* eight, for example, *The Award of the Arms, Philoctetes, Neoptolemus*,[35] *Eurypylus, The Beggar, The Laconian Woman, The Sack of Troy, The Return Voyage,* and a *Sinon,* and a *Women of Troy*.[36]

XXIV

Moreover, it is necessary for epic poetry to exhibit the same characteristic forms as tragedy; for it is either simple or complex, displays character or suffering, and is composed of the same parts, with the exception of song and spectacle. In epic, there is also a necessity for reversals, recognitions, and the depiction of suffering. Here too, thought and diction must be handled with skill. Homer used all these elements first and in a proper way. For each of his poems is well-constructed; the *Iliad* is simple and exhibits suffering, whereas the *Odyssey* is complex (for there is recognition throughout) and shows character. In addition to these matters, Homer outstrips all others in diction and thought.

Epic differs from tragedy in regard to the length of the plot, and the meter. The sufficient limit of length has been mentioned, for we have noted that it must be possible to take in the plot's beginning and end in one view. This would occur if the plots were shorter than those of the old epics but would extend to the length of the number of tragedies that are designated for one performance. For the purpose of extending its length, epic poetry has a very great capacity that is specifically its own, since it is not possible in tragedy to imitate many simultaneous lines of action but only that performed by the actors on the stage. But because of the narrative quality of epic it is possible to depict many simultaneous lines of action that, if appropriate, become the means of increasing the poem's scope. This has an advantage in regard to the elegance of the poem and in regard to varying the interest of the audience and for constructing a diverse sequence of episodes. For the rapid overloading of tragedies with the same kind of incident is what makes tragedies fail.

The heroic meter[37] has been found appropriate to epic through practical experience. If someone should write a narrative imitation in another meter, or in a combination of meters, we would feel it to be inappropriate. For the heroic is the stateliest and most dignified meter, and therefore it is especially receptive to strange words and metaphors, for narrative poetry in this regard is exceptional among the forms of imitation; the iambic and the trochaic tetrameter are expressive of motion, the latter being a dance meter and the former displaying the quality of action. (1460) Furthermore, it makes a very strange impression if someone combines these meters as Chairemon did. Therefore no one has written a long poem in a meter other than the heroic; but, as we said, nature herself teaches us to choose the appropriate meter.

Homer deserves praise for many qualities and, especially, because alone of the poets he is not ignorant of the requirements of his craft. For it is necessary for the poet himself to speak in his own person in the poem as little as possible, because he is not fulfilling his function as an imitator when he appears in this way. Now the other poets are themselves active performers throughout the poem, and they perform their imitative function infrequently and in regard to only a few objects. Homer, on the other hand, when he has made a brief prelude immediately brings in a man or woman or some other character; and all his figures are expressive of character, and none lacks it.

Now then, it is necessary in tragedy to create the marvelous, but the epic admits, even more, of the irrational, on which the marvelous especially depends, because the audience does not see the person acting. The whole business of the pursuit of Hector would appear ridiculous on the stage with some men standing about and not pursuing and Achilles nodding at them to keep them back; but in the narrative description of epic, this absurdity escapes notice.

The marvelous is pleasant, and the proof of this is that everyone embellishes the stories he tells as if he were adding something pleasant to his narration. Homer has especially taught others how it is necessary to lie, and this is through the employment of false reasoning. For whenever one event occurs or comes into existence and is naturally accompanied by a second event, men think that whenever this second event is present the first one must also have occurred or have come into existence. This, however, is a fallacy. Therefore, if the first event mentioned is false but there is another event that must occur or come into existence when the first event occurs, we feel compelled to join the two events in our thought. For our mind, through knowing that the second event is true, falsely reasons that the first event must have occurred or have come into existence also. There is an example of this type of fallacy in the Bath Scene in the *Odyssey*.

The use of impossible probabilities is preferable to that of unpersuasive possibilities. We must not construct plots from irrational elements, and we should especially attempt not to have anything irrational at all in them; but if this is not possible, the irrational should be outside the plot (as in Oedipus' ignorance of how Laius died); it should not be in the drama itself, as occurs in the *Electra* concerning those who bring news of the Pythian games,[38] or in the *Mysians*,[39] concerning the man who has come from Tegea to Mysia without speaking. To say that without the use of such incidents the plot would have been ruined is ridiculous. For it is necessary, right from the beginning, not to construct such plots.

If the poet takes such a plot and if it appears to admit of a more probable treatment, the situation is also absurd, since it is clear that even the improbable elements in the *Odyssey* concerning the casting ashore of Odysseus would not be bearable if a poor poet had written them. (1460) Here the poet conceals the absurdity by making it pleasing through his other skillful techniques. It is necessary to intensify the diction only in those parts of the poem that lack action and are unexpressive of character and thought. For too brilliant a diction conceals character and thought.

XXV

Concerning the number and character of the problems that lead to censure in poetry and the ways in which this censure must be met, the following considerations would be apparent to those who study the question. Since the poet is an imitator, like a painter or any maker of likenesses, he must carry out his imitations on all occasions in one of three possible ways. Thus, he must imitate the things that were in the past, or are now, or that people say and think to be or those things that ought to be. The poet presents his imitation in standard diction, as well as in strange words and metaphors and in many variations of diction, for we grant this license to poets. In addition to this, there is not the same standard of correctness for politics and poetry, nor for any other art and poetry. In regard to poetry itself, two categories of error are possible, one essential, and one accidental. For if the poet chose to imitate but imitated incorrectly, through lack of ability[40] the error is an essential one; but if he erred by choosing an incorrect representation of the object (for example, representing a horse putting forward both right hooves) or made a technical error, for example, in regard to medicine or any other art, or introduced impossibilities of any sort, the mistake is an accidental, not an essential, one.

As a result, we must meet the criticisms of the problems encountered in poetry by taking these points into consideration. First, in regard to the problems that are related to the essential nature of art: if impossibilities have been represented, an error has been made; but it may be permissible to do this if the representation supports the goal of the imitation (for the goal of an imitation has been discussed) and if it makes the section in which it occurs, or another part of the poem, more striking. An example of such a situation is the pursuit of Hector in the *Iliad*. If, indeed, the goal of the imitation admits of attainment as well, or better, when sought in accordance with technical requirements, then it is incorrect to introduce the impossible. For, if it is at all feasible, no error should be committed at all. Further, we must ascertain whether an error originates from an essential or an accidental aspect of the art. For it is a less important matter if the artist does not know that a hind does not have horns than if he is unskillful in imitating one. In addition, the criticism that a work of art is not a truthful representation can be met by the argument that it represents the situation as it should be. For example, Sophocles said that he himself created characters such as should exist, whereas Euripides created ones such as actually do exist. If neither of the above is the case, the criticism must be met by reference to men's opinions, for example, in the myths that are told about the gods. For, perhaps, they do not describe a situation that is better than actuality, nor a true one, but they are what Xenophanes said of them—in accordance, at any rate, with men's opinions. (1461) Perhaps the situation described by the artist is not better than actuality but was one that actually existed in the past, for example, the description of the arms that goes, "The spears were standing upright on their butt spikes"; for once this was customary, as it is now among the Illyrians. Now to judge the nobility or ignobility of any statement made or act performed by anyone, we must not only make an investigation into the thing itself that has been said or done, considering whether it is noble or ignoble, but we must also consider the one who does the act or says the words in regard to whom, when, by what means, and for what purpose he speaks or acts—for example, whether the object is to achieve a greater good or to avoid a greater evil.

We must meet some kinds of criticism by considering the diction, for example, by reference to the use of a strange word, as in the phrase, *ouréas men próton*.[41] The word oureas here could cause some difficulty because perhaps the poet does not mean mules but guards. Dolon's statement, "I who was badly formed,"[42] has a similar difficulty involved in it; for he does not mean that he was misshapen in body but that he was ugly, because the Cretans use *eueidēs* [of fair form] to denote "handsome." A difficulty might arise in the phrase "mix the drink purer,"[43] which does not mean stronger, as if for drunkards, but faster. Difficulties arise in thoughts that are expressed in metaphors, for example, "All the gods and men slept the entire night through," which is said at the same time as "When truly he turned his gaze upon the Trojan plain, and heard the sound of flutes and pipes." "All" is used here metaphorically in place of "many," since "all" is some division of "many." The phrase "alone, she has no share"[44] shows a similar use of metaphor, since the best known one is "alone." A problem may arise from the use of accent; Hippias the Thasian solved such a problem in the phrase, *didomen de oi* and similarly, in the phrase, *to men hoi katapythetai ombrō*.[45] Some difficulties are solved through punctuation, for example, in Empedocles' statement that "Suddenly things became mortal that had previously learned to be immortal and things unmixed before mixed."[46] Some problems are solved by reference to ambiguities, for example, "more than two thirds of night has departed" because "more" is ambiguous here.[47] Some difficulties are met by reference to customary usages in our language. Thus, we call "wine" the mixture of water and wine; and it is with the same justification that the poet writes of "a greave of newly wrought tin"; and iron workers are called *chalkeas*, literally, copper smiths; and it is for this reason that Ganymede is called the wine pourer of Zeus, although the gods do not drink wine. This would also be justified through metaphor.

Whenever a word seems to signify something contradictory, we must consider how many different meanings it might have in the passage quoted; for example, in the phrase "the bronze spear was held there," we must consider how many different senses of "to be held" are possible, whether by taking it in this way or that one might best understand it. The procedure is opposite to the one that Glaucon mentions in which people make an unreasonable prior assumption and, (1461) having themselves made their decree, they draw their conclusions, and then criticize the poet as if he had said whatever they think he has said if it is opposed to their thoughts. We have had this experience in regard to discussions of the character Icarius.[48] People assume that he was a Spartan; but then it appears ridiculous that Telemachus did not meet him in Sparta when he visited there. Perhaps the situation is as the Cephallenians would have it, for they say that Odysseus married amongst them and that there was an Icadius involved, but no Icarius. Thus, it is probable that the difficulty has arisen through a mistake.

Speaking generally, the impossible must be justified in regard to the requirements of poetry, or in regard to what is better than actuality, or what, in the opinion of men, is held to be true. In regard to the art of poetry, we must prefer a persuasive impossibility to an unpersuasive possibility. Perhaps it is impossible[49] for the kind of men Zeuxis painted to exist; but they illustrate what is better than the actual. For whatever is a model must express superior qualities. The irrational must be justified in regard to what men say and also on the grounds that it is, sometimes, not at all irrational. For it is reasonable that some things occur contrary to reason.

We must consider contradictions in the same way as the refutation of arguments is carried on: that is, with reference to whether the same object is involved, and in the same relationship, and in the same sense, so that the poet, indeed, has contradicted himself in regard to what he himself says or what a sensible person might assume. There is justifiable censure for the presence of irrationality and depravity where, there being no necessity for them, the poet makes no use of them, as Euripides' handling of Aegeus in the *Medea* (in regard to the irrational) or in the same poet's treatment of the character of Menelaus in the *Orestes* (in regard to depravity). Criticisms of poetry, then, derive from five sources: either that the action is impossible or that it is irrational or that it is morally harmful or that it is contradictory or that it contains technical errors. The answers to these criticisms must be sought from the solutions, twelve in number, that we have discussed.

XXVI

The problem of whether epic or tragedy is the better type of imitation might be raised. For if whatever is less common is better, that art would be superior that is directed at the more discriminating audience; and it is very clear that the art that imitates every detail is common. For on the grounds that the audience does not see the point unless they themselves add something, the actors make quite a commotion; for example, the poorer sort of flute players roll about the stage if they must imitate a discus throw and drag their leader about if they are playing the *Scylla*. Now tragedy is considered to be of the same character that our older actors attribute to their successors; for, indeed, Mynescus called Callippides an ape on the grounds of overacting, and such an opinion was also held about Pindarus. (1462) As these two types of actor are related to each other, so the whole art of tragedy is thought to be related to epic by some people, who then conclude that epic is oriented toward a reasonable audience that does not at all require gestures, but that tragedy is disposed toward a less sophisticated audience. If, then, tragedy is directed toward a more common audience, it would be clear that it is the inferior art form.

Now then, first, this accusation is made against the art of acting, not poetry, since it is possible to overdo gestures both in epic recitations as Sosistratus did, and in song competitions as Mnasitheus the Opuntian did. Then, too, not every movement is to be rejected, if dancing indeed is not to be condemned, but only the movements of the ignoble, a point that was criticized in Callippides and now in others, since, it was charged, they were not representing free-born women. Further, tragedy even without action achieves its function just as epic does; for its character is apparent simply through reading. If, then, tragedy is better in other respects, this defect is not essential to it. We argue, next, that it is better since it contains all of the elements that epic has (for it is even possible to use epic meter in tragedy) and, further, it has no small share in music and in spectacle, through which pleasure is very distinctly evoked. Tragedy also provides a vivid experience in reading as well as in actual performance. Further, in tragedy the goal of the imitation is achieved in a shorter length of time (for a more compact action is more pleasant than one that is much diluted). (1462) I mean, for example, the situation that would occur if someone should put Sophocles' *Oedipus* into an epic as long as the *Iliad*. Further, the imitation of an epic story is less unified than that of tragedy (a proof of this is that a number of tragedies can be derived from any one epic). So that if epic poets write a story with a single plot, that plot is either presented briefly and appears to lack full development, or, if it follows the accustomed length of epic, it has a watered-down quality (I mean, for example, if the epic should be composed of very many actions in the same way as the *Iliad* and *Odyssey* have many such elements that also have magnitude in themselves). And yet these poems are constructed in the best possible way and are, as much as possible, the imitations of a single action.

If, then, tragedy is superior in all these areas and, further, in accomplishing its artistic effect (for it is necessary that these genres create not any chance pleasure, but the one that has been discussed as proper to them), it is apparent that tragedy, since it is better at attaining its end, is superior to epic.

Now then, we have expressed our view of tragedy and epic, both in general, and in their various species, and of the number and differences in their parts, as well as of some of the causes of their effectiveness or ineffectiveness, and the criticisms that can be directed against them, and the ways in which these criticisms must be answered. . . .

DEMETRIUS

(1st century B.C.?)

INTRODUCTION

The actual date and authorship of *On Style* are in doubt. The work was originally attributed, on significant manuscript authority, to Demetrius of Phalerum, a student of Theophrastus, who died in 283 B.C. This attribution has been questioned for a variety of reasons. First, Demetrius of Phalerum is himself mentioned in the text in a way that would appear strange if he is the author of it. Second, Demetrius of Phalerum is known to have favored a florid style of rhetoric, and many scholars feel that a critic with such a tendency would not have been capable of writing the eminently fair and balanced treatment of the various rhetorical styles which we have in this treatise. Third, the treatment of rhetoric according to classes or types of style which characterizes this work is a practice which began much later than the third century B.C. Finally, the language of the treatise offers many examples of post-classical forms and there are a number of details of grammar and syntax that indicate composition at a later date than the third century B.C.

Although there are still important scholarly views to the contrary, the current consensus is that this work was probably written in the first century B.C. by a critic named Demetrius. The work itself shows that this Demetrius was greatly influenced by Aristotle and Theophrastus, but we are unable to identify him further, although a number of possible candidates have been suggested.

The treatise *On Style* begins with an introductory section on clauses and periods and then systematically treats the four principal rhetorical styles: the elevated, the elegant, the plain, and the forceful. In each case the qualities of diction, composition, and subject matter that produce the various styles are discussed, as are the faults to which each style is liable.

As a representative example of Demetrius' method, the section of his treatise dealing with the elevated style is included in this collection. Demetrius' procedure is to survey all of the means by which elevation can be achieved in style. He points out that certain types of rhythmic clauses can add dignity to expression, and he cites the initial and final paeon (—ᴜᴜᴜ and ᴜᴜᴜ—) as accomplishing this purpose. Lengthened clauses and periodic sentence structure are seen as further ways of enhancing the grandeur of the elevated style. Demetrius recommends that the arrangement of words in this style be from least vivid to most vivid and that connectives and expletives be mixed to intensify the elevation of the style.

The elevated style requires that a dignified and impressive subject matter be chosen and that it be framed in impressive diction. Among figures of speech, metaphors contribute most of all to the elevation of style. Demetrius also recommends the use of allegory, statements added at the end of the work, and poetic language as means of achieving the goals of the elevated style.

The stylistic fault which corresponds to the stylistic excellence of the elevated style is that of frigidity, which arises whenever the legitimately elevated style is distorted by the expression of what is exaggerated or impossible. This may occur when an excessively unrealistic thought is expressed or when the literary style is characterized by a very inappropriate use of elevated diction, rhythm, and meter.

Demetrius' treatment of the "high style" might be compared with "Longinus'" *Peri Hypsous,* especially since both critics consider stylistic questions as pertaining equally to literary and rhetorical works. Unlike "Longinus," Demetrius does not probe into the philosophical basis of art; his concern does not transcend the stylistic phenomena of artistic expression. Nevertheless, in this area he provides some of the best classical analyses of how diction, rhythm, and figures of speech can be used.

The translation here used (and most of the notes) are taken from G. M. A. Grube, *A Greek Critic: Demetrius on Style* (Toronto, University of Toronto Press, 1961) and reprinted by permission of the publisher.

from ON STYLE

36. There are four simple types of style: the plain, the grand, the elegant, and the forceful. The rest are combinations of these, but not all combinations are possible: the elegant can be combined with both the plain and the grand, and so can the forceful; the grand alone does not mix with the plain; these two face one another as opposite extremes. That is why some critics recognize only these last two as styles, and the other two as intermediate. They class the elegant rather with the plain, because the elegant is somewhat slight and subtle; while the forceful, which has weight and dignity, is classed with the grand.

37. Such a theory is absurd. With the exception of the two opposite extremes mentioned (the plain and the grand), we find combinations of all these types in the Homeric epic, in the works of Plato, Xenophon, Herodotus, and many other writers who display a frequent mixture of grandeur, forcefulness, and charm, so that the number of types is such as we have indicated, and the manner of expression appropriate to each will be seen in what follows.

IMPRESSIVE WORD-ARRANGEMENT

38. I shall begin with the grand or impressive manner which is today called eloquence. Grandeur resides in three things: the content, the diction, and the appropriate arrangement of words. This last is impressive, as Aristotle says, if it is paeonic in rhythm.[1] There are two kinds of paeon: the initial paeon which consists of one long followed by three shorts, for example

ērxătŏ dĕ

and the final paeon, its opposite, in which three shorts are followed by one long, for example

Ărăbĭā

39. In impressive speech, the clauses should begin with the initial paeon and the final paeon comes later. We may take an example from Thucydides:

ērxătŏ dĕ to kakon ex Aithĭŏpĭās (the evil began in Ethiopia).[2]

Why did Aristotle advise this? Because the start and opening of a clause should impress at once, and so should the end. We will achieve this by using a long syllable in both places. A long syllable has a natural dignity; it impresses at the start and leaves a strong impression at the end. All of us particularly remember the initial and final words and are affected by them but what comes in between has less effect on us, as if it were hidden and obscured.

40. This is obvious in Thucydides. In almost every instance, his impressiveness is wholly due to long-syllable rhythms. The grandeur of the man is many-sided, but it is this kind of word-arrangement which is the sole, or at any rate the main, factor in his greatest effects.

41. We should realize, however, that if we cannot have a paeon exactly at the beginning and at the end of each clause, we can still make our arrangement generally paeonic by at least beginning and ending with long syllables. This would seem to be what Aristotle advises us to do but he goes into details about the two kinds of paeon for no purpose except greater accuracy. Hence Theophrastus gives as an example of the grand manner a clause[3] of which the rhythm does not consist of exact paeons, yet it is paeonic in its general effect. We should therefore incorporate paeons into our prose; it is a measure mixing

long and short, and less risky than others. The long syllables give dignity, while the shorts preserve the character of prose.

42. As for the other meters, the heroic is stately but unsuited to prose; it resounds too much. It is not a good rhythm, indeed it is not a rhythm at all when it becomes a mere succession of long syllables,[4] for the number of longs is far too great for prose rhythm.

43. The iambus ($\cup$—) is commonplace and like the rhythm of ordinary speech. Many people converse in iambics without knowing it. The paeon is a mean between the heroic and the iambic and is a mixture of the two. One should use the paeonic rhythm in impressive passages in some such way as we have indicated.

44. Lengthy clauses also make for grandeur, as in "Thucydides of Athens wrote this account of the war between the Peloponnesians and the Athenians,"[5] and "The history of Herodotus the Halicarnassian is here set forth." To end quickly with a short clause lowers the dignity of the sentence even if there is grandeur in the thought or in the words.

45. A rounded sentence-structure also contributes to grandeur, as in Thucydides': "After flowing from Mount Pindus through Dolopia and the land of the Agrianians and Amphilochians, and passing inland by Stratus, the river Achelous, as it makes its way to the sea near Oeniadae, surrounds that city with a marsh, thus making a winter attack on it impossible because of the water."[6] All the grandeur of this sentence is due to its periodic structure, and to the fact that Thucydides never allows himself or his reader to pause.

46. Now break up the sentence and say: "The river Achelous flows from Mount Pindus; it runs into the sea near Oeniadae; it turns the nearby plain of Oeniadae into a marsh; the water forms a natural protection against winter attacks." Written like this, there are many pauses, but the grandeur has vanished.

47. Long journeys seem shorter if one stops frequently at an inn; on the other hand, a deserted road makes even a short journey seem long. The same is true of clauses.

48. A harsh joining of sounds often makes for impressiveness, as in: "Aias the massive aimed always at Hector's bronze casque."[7] The clash of sounds is not in other ways euphonious but its very exaggeration suggests the greatness of the hero. Smoothness and euphony have no place in the grand style, except occasionally. Thucydides almost always avoids what is smooth and even; his word-order stumbles like men walking along a rough path. For example: "from other outbreaks of disease the year, it was agreed, was free."[8] This could have been put more easily and pleasingly, as "all agreed that the year was free from other diseases," but it is no longer impressive.

49. Harsh-sounding words make for grandeur, as does the juxtaposition of harsh sounds in the arrangement of words. "Shrieking" (*kekragōs*) has a harsher sound than "calling" (*boōn*), and "bursting" (*rhēgnumenon*) than

"going" (*pheromenon*). Thucydides uses all these harsh words; he chooses his words to fit his arrangement of them, and *vice versa.*

50. We should also arrange our words in the following manner: those that are not very vivid should come first, and the more vivid second and last. The sense of vividness then increases from one word to the next. The opposite order gives a feeling of weakness, of lapsing, as it were, from the stronger word to the weaker.

51. Plato has the following example: "When a man allows music to play upon him, and to flood through his ears into his soul," where the second verb is much more vivid than the first. He then goes on: "when the flood does not cease but puts a spell upon him, it weakens and melts his spirit."[9] Here "melts" is a stronger word than "weakens" and closer to poetry. If the second word had been first, the addition of "weakens" would have seemed rather feeble.

52. Homer too, in his description of the Cyclops, continually increases the hyperbole and seems to rise higher and higher with it: "He was not like a mortal man but like a wooded hilltop,"[10] and he goes on to speak of a high mountain towering over its fellows. The things mentioned first are big, but they seem small as bigger things follow.

53. Connectives should not correspond exactly, a *de* after a *men*, for instance, for there is something petty in precise writing. Impressiveness requires a certain disorder, as in a passage of Antiphon[11] where we have *men* used three times before one answering *de* occurs.

54. However, it often happens that a succession of connectives magnifies even trifling things. Homer joins together the names of the Boeotian cities, in themselves ordinary and unimportant, by a string of connectives and this gives them a certain weight and impressiveness: "And Schoinos and Scolos and many-topped Eteonos. . . ."[12]

55. Expletive connectives should not be used as mere empty fillers, like superfluities or excrescences, as some writers use *dē* (then, indeed) without reason, and *nu* (now), and *pote* (ever), but only when they contribute to the impressiveness of what is said.

56. So in Plato's "And in the heavens then (*dē*) the great Zeus,"[13] and Homer's "when they came then (*dē*) to the ford of the wide-flowing river."[14] Thus placed near the beginning of the clause the connective separates it from what precedes and adds a certain impressiveness. To amplify the beginnings of sentences lends dignity. If Homer had merely said: "When they came to the ford of the river" this would have seemed but a trivial description of one particular event.

57. The particle *dē* is also frequently used to express strong emotion, as in Calypso's words to Odysseus, "God-born son of Laertes, wily Odysseus, do you then (*dē*) long so much for your beloved land?"[15] If you remove the expletive, you will destroy the emotional tone. Altogether, as Praxiphanes says,

such particles were employed instead of groans and lamentations, like *ai ai* (Ah! Ah!) or *pheu* (Alas) or *poion ti esti* (what is it?). And he points out too that the connective *kai nu ke* in Homer's line[16] is appropriate to lamentation and has the same effect as a word expressing sorrow.

58. Praxiphanes says that those who use expletive as mere fillers are like actors who add a word here and there without reason, as if one said:

> This country, Calydon, of Pelops' land
> Alas!
> The opposite shore, fertile and happy plains
> Ah me! Ah me!

Just as here "Alas" and "Ah me" only distract the audience's attention, so connectives scattered everywhere without reason have the same effect.

FIGURES OF SPEECH

59. Connectives then can make the word-arrangement impressive, as we said. Figures of speech are themselves a kind of word-arrangement. For to say the same thing twice by repetition, by *epanaphora* or by *anthypallagē*, is to order and arrange the words in a different way. We must assign to each style the figures that are appropriate to it. The following are appropriate to the grand style which is our present concern. ,

60. First there is anthypallagē (the substitution of one case for another). When Homer says: "The two rocks, one reaching to the sky . . ."[17] he uses a much more impressive construction than if he had used the usual genitive: "Of the two rocks, one reaching to the sky . . . ," for what is customary is trivial and fails to arouse wonder.

61. Nireus is not himself important in the *Iliad*, and his contribution is even less so, three ships and a few men, but Homer makes him appear important and his contribution great instead of small by using and combining two figures, epanaphora and *dialysis*. "Nireus brought three ships," he says, "Nireus, son of Aglaïa," "Nireus, who was the most beautiful man."[18] The epanaphora as a figure of speech in connection with the same name, and the dialysis give an impression of abundant possessions, even though it is only two or three ships.

62. Although Nireus is mentioned only once in the action, we remember him as well as Achilles and Odysseus who are talked about in almost every line. This is due to the effectiveness of the figure of speech. If Homer had said: "Nireus, the son of Aglaïa brought three ships from Syme," he might as well not have mentioned him. At banquets a few well-arranged dishes give an impression of plenty; the same is true in discourse.

63. Frequently, however, impressiveness can be achieved by the opposite

of lack of connectives, namely by *synapheia*, as in: "On this campaign went the Greeks and the Carians and the Lycians and the Pamphilians and the Phrygians."[19] Here it is the repetition of the same connective which gives the impression of large numbers.

64. In such a phrase as "high-arched, white-crested"[20] on the other hand, it is the absence of the connective "and" which makes for greater impressiveness than if he had said "high-arched and white-crested."

65. Impressiveness by means of figures is also attained by varying the case, as in Thucydides: "First to step on the gangway to land he fainted, and as he fell among the oars . . ."[21] This is much more impressive than if he had retained the same case and said: "he fell among the oars and lost his shield."

66. *Anadiplōsis* also heightens the effect, as when Herodotus says: "The serpents in the Caucasus are large, large and numerous."[22] The repetition of "large" gives weight to the style.

67. One should avoid crowding the figures, for this argues a lack of taste and indicates an uneven style. It is true that the old writers use many figures; but because they use them skillfully, their style is more natural than that of those who do not use figures at all.

68. Opinions vary about the clashing of vowels (in hiatus). Isocrates[23] and his school took care to avoid it; others have paid no heed to it at all. We should neither arrange our words so that they ring in our ears through haphazard collisions, for these interrupt our flow with stops and jerks, nor altogether avoid such collisions. Total avoidance of hiatus would, it is true, make our words flow more smoothly, but the result would be flat and unmusical, without the euphony which often results from a clash of vowels.

69. We should in the first place note that customary speech, which certainly favors euphony, itself does bring vowels together within such words as *Aiakos* and *chiōn* (snow); indeed there are words which consist entirely of vowel sounds, for example, *Aiaiē* and *Euios*.[24] These words are no harsher than others; indeed they are perhaps more musical.

70. Poetic forms such as *ēelios* (sun) and *oreōn* (of mountains) with their deliberate lengthening of the words and the resulting clash of vowels, are more euphonious than the shorter forms *hēlios* and *orōn*. The resolving of one syllable into two clashing vowels introduces an added effect not unlike singing.[25] There are many other words which, when run together by elision or contraction, are less harmonious and, when resolved with resulting hiatus, they are more euphonious. Running the sounds together is both harsher in sound and more commonplace.

71. The priests of Egypt, when singing hymns to their gods, utter the seven vowels[26] in succession and men listen to the singing sound of these vowels instead of to the flute or the lyre, because it is so euphonious. It follows that to remove the hiatus is to deprive language of its song and its music. But this is perhaps not the time to pursue the subject further.

72. The grand style favors the clash of long vowels. This is obvious in Homer's *lāan anō ōtheske* (he pushed the stone uphill).[27] The line acquires length through the juxtaposition of long vowels; it imitates the violent straining of the stone uphill. The same is true in the phrase of Thucydides *to mē ēpeiros einai* (not being the mainland),[28] and you will find clashing diphthongs in that sentence of his which describes the founding of Epidamnus by the Corcyraeans.[29]

73. As the clash of the same long vowels or diphthongs makes for impressiveness, the clash of different sounds may have the same result, and it provides variety as well—as in *ēōs* (dawn) or *hoiēn* (such). Not only are the sounds different, but the breathings also, one being rough and the other smooth, so that there is much variety.

74. In songs too there can be musical variations on the same long vowel, like song upon song, so that the clash of similar vowels can be regarded as part of a song or a musical variation. This is enough about the clash of vowels and about the impressive kind of word-arrangement.

IMPRESSIVE SUBJECT MATTER

75. The grandeur may lie also in the subject matter—a great and notable battle on land or sea, or when there is talk of the heavens, or of the earth. When one hears a person discoursing on an impressive subject one is at once apt to think his style impressive even when it is not. One should consider the manner of his discourse, rather than the matter, for an important subject may be dealt with in a trifling and quite unsuitable manner. Some authors, like Theopompus, are considered forceful when in fact it is their subject, not their style, that is forceful.

76. Nicias, the painter, used to say that to choose a great subject is in itself no small part of the painter's art and that he should not fritter away his talent on trifling themes like birds or flowers. Rather he should choose cavalry charges or naval battles as his subjects, where he could introduce many horses galloping, rearing or crouching, many bowmen shooting, many riders falling from their chargers. Nicias considered the choice of theme to be itself a part of the art of painting just as it is of the poet's art. We should therefore not be surprised if, even in prose, great subjects have their own impressiveness.

IMPRESSIVE DICTION

77. The grand style requires the diction to be distinguished, out of the ordinary, unusual. It will then have weight, whereas current and customary language makes for clarity, but it is also commonplace.

METAPHORS

78. In the first place, we should use metaphors. They contribute more than anything else to delight and impressiveness of style. They should not be too numerous, however, or our prose will turn into dithyramb, nor too far-fetched, but arise spontaneously from a true likeness in things. For example, a general, a pilot, and a charioteer all rule over something; one can therefore safely call the general the pilot of his city, or again the pilot the ruler of his ship.

79. Not all metaphors, however, are interchangeable like those just mentioned. The poet (Homer) could call the lower slopes of Ida its foot, but he could not call a man's foot his slope.[30]

80. Whenever a metaphor seems too bold, we can change it into a simile, which is safer. A simile is an extended metaphor, as when instead of: "then the orator Python, rushing upon us, a torrent of words"[31] you add to it and say: "then *like a* torrent of words, the orator Python. . . ." Now you have a simile which is a safer method of expression, while the first is a metaphor which is more chancy. Plato is thought to take more chances because he uses metaphors more freely than similes, while Xenophon makes greater use of similes.

81. Aristotle thought that the best type of metaphor is the so-called active metaphor,[32] by which inanimate things are represented as acting like living things, as in Homer's reference to the arrow as "sharp-pointed, eager to fly into the throng," and to the waves as "high-arched, foam-crested," for these epithets imply the actions of living creatures.

82. Some things are expressed more clearly and properly by a metaphor than by the proper terms themselves, as, for example: "the battle shivered." The meaning could not be more truly or lucidly expressed by changing the phrase and using the proper terms. The confused motion of spears and their continuous subdued sound are rendered by "the shivering battle."[33] At the same time the poet is using the active type of metaphor just described, for he says that the battle shivers like a living creature.

83. We should not forget, however, that the effect of certain metaphors is paltry rather than impressive, even though the metaphor is intended to achieve grandeur, as when Homer says that "the wide sky trumpeted about them."[34] A noise ringing through the high heavens should not be compared to the sound of a trumpet, unless indeed one were to defend Homer by saying that the high heavens resounded as if the whole sky were trumpeting.

84. Let us then consider this other kind of metaphor which makes for triviality instead of grandeur. Metaphors should be transferred from the greater

to the smaller and not *vice versa*. Xenophon says, for example: "On the march a part of the line surged out"[35] and compares the disorder in the line to the surge of the sea. But if one were to reverse this and say that the sea swerved, the metaphor would be inappropriate and certainly trivial.

85. When they consider metaphors too bold, some writers try to make them more acceptable by adding an epithet, as Theognis speaks of the bow of an archer in the act of shooting as "a tuneless lyre."[36] To call a bow a lyre is a bold metaphor, and it is softened by the adjective "tuneless."

86. Common usage is a good teacher in all things, but especially in the use of metaphor. We do not notice that it expresses almost everything by metaphors because they are inoffensive, like "a clear voice," "a sharp man," "a rough character," "a lengthy speaker," and so on. These metaphors are so appropriate that they seem like proper terms.

87. I make the art—or is it the naturalness?—of common usage the criterion of a good metaphor in prose. For usage has produced some metaphors so successfully that we no longer need the proper term and the metaphor has usurped its place, as in "the eye of the vine"[37] and other such expressions.

88. Certain parts of the body[38] derive their names not from a metaphorical usage but from their physical resemblance to other objects.

89. When we turn a metaphor into a simile, as mentioned above, we should aim at brevity, and add only the word "like" (*hōsper*) before it. Otherwise it will not be a simile but a poetic comparison. When Xenophon says: "As a noble hound leaps at a boar without caution," or again: "Like a horse let loose, kicking and prancing in a meadow"[39] he is no longer using similes but poetic comparisons.

90. Such poetic comparisons should not be freely used in prose, but with the greatest caution. And this is a sufficient outline on the subject of metaphors.

COMPOUND WORDS

91. We should also use compound words but we should avoid dithyrambic formations such as "the heaven-portented wanderings" and "the fiery-lanced host of stars." Our compounds should be like those which are formed by usage, for in usage I see the universal criterion of good diction. It forms without challenge such words as lawgiver,[40] and the like.

92. A compound word, because of its composite nature, will also provide a certain ornamental variety and dignity, as well as brevity. One word will take the place of a whole phrase, "corn-supply,"[41] for example, instead of "the supplying of corn," and this is much more impressive. Sometimes, however, this greater effect is better obtained by resolving one word into a phrase, for example, by saying "the supply of corn" instead of "the corn-supply."

93. A word replaces a whole phrase, for example, when Xenophon says: "it was impossible to catch a wild ass unless the hunters took up positions at intervals and hunted in relays."[42] By the word "relays" he means that some riders pursued the animal from behind, while others met it head on so that the wild ass was caught between them.

We should be careful not to combine words already compound. Such double combinations are not suitable in prose.

NEW WORDS

94. Newly-coined words are usually defined as words used to imitate some emotion or action like "sizzled" and "lapping."[43]

95. These words are impressive because they imitate noises, and mostly because they are strange. The poet is not using existing words, for this is their first occurrence. Making a new word is thought to be a clever thing, as if one were creating a usage of one's own. For by creating new words one seems to act in the same way as the originators of language.

96. When coining a new word we should aim at clarity and remain within the bounds of usage. The new coinage should be analogous to existing words, for one should not appear to use Scythian or Phrygian expressions when writing Greek.

97. We should make new words where no existing names are available, as when someone called the kettledrums and other instruments used in effeminate ritual "lewderies" or when Aristotle spoke of an elephant-driver as an "elephanteer."[44] Or we may make new derivatives from existing forms, as someone called a man who rows a boat a "rowman," and Aristotle spoke of a man who dwelt alone as "selfsome."

98. We read in Xenophon: "The army battle-shouted." He makes a kindred verb from the battle-shout the army was raising continually. As I said, this is a risky business, even for a poet. Any compound word, however, is a sort of coined word, for what is composite must have been built from its parts.

99. *Allēgoria* (hidden meaning) is also impressive, especially in threats such as that of Dionysius: "Their grasshoppers will sing to them from the ground."[45]

100. If he had simply said that he would ravage the country of Locris, he would have sounded angrier but more commonplace. As it is, he uses allēgoria to camouflage his meaning. What is implied is always more frightening, for different interpretations are possible. What is clear and obvious is likely to be considered commonplace, like men without their clothes.

101. That is why mystic formulae are expressed by means of allēgoria, to frighten people and make them shudder as they do in the dark and at night. Allēgoria is not unlike darkness and night.

102. A succession of such veiled expressions should, however, be avoided, for then we would be writing riddles like that of the doctor's cupping-glass, "I saw a man who had welded bronze upon another man."[46] The Spartans too used many veiled threats, as when they said to Philip: "Dionysius [is] in Corinth,"[47] and on many other occasions.

103. Sometimes it is impressive to express a thought briefly, and most impressive not to express it at all, for there are things which increase in importance by not being spoken but implied.[48]

At other times, however, to be brief is to be trivial, and grandeur is found in repetition, as when Xenophon says: "The chariots drove on; some drove through the lines of their friends, others through the lines of their foes,"[49] which is much more impressive than if he had said: "The chariots drove on through the lines of friend and foe."

104. An oblique construction is frequently more impressive than a straightforward one: "The decision was of charging the Greek lines and breaking through them,"[50] instead of "They decided to charge and break through."

105. Words similar in sound and an apparent lack of euphony may also contribute to impressiveness. For what is not euphonious often gives an impression of weight. In the line which describes the attack of Ajax upon Hector[51] the combination of these two factors makes us realize the greatness of Ajax better than his shield of seven layers of ox-hide.

106. The so-called *epiphōnēma* might be described as an added ornamentation. It is most impressive in prose. One part of a passage serves to express the thought, the other part is added to embellish it. In the following lines of Sappho the thought is expressed in these words: "The mountain-hyacinths are trodden down/By shepherds' boots" and then comes the epiphōnēma: "and on the ground/The purple blooms lie bleeding." This has obviously been added to what precedes, as a beautiful ornament.

107. Homer's poetry is full of these ornamental additions. For example:

> I've put the arms away, out of the smoke.
> They are already quite unlike the armor
> Odysseus left when he set out for Troy.
> And I bethought me of a graver matter:
> I feared that, flushed with wine and prone to quarrel,
> You wound each other.

Then comes the added phrase: "Steel makes men reckless."[52]

108. Altogether, the epiphōnēma may be compared to those external displays of riches: cornices, triglyphs, and broad purples.[53] The epiphōnēma too is a sign of riches, verbal riches.

109. The enthymeme might be thought to be a kind of epiphōnēma, but it is not. It is added in order to prove something, not to embellish. However it may be added at the end, like the epiphōnēma.

110. The maxim too is an addition like the epiphōnēma, but it is not an

epiphōnēma. It often stands at the beginning, although at times it fills the place of an epiphōnēma.

111. A line like: "Fool! He was not to escape his evil doom"[54] is not an epiphōnēma either. It does not come at the end and it does not beautify. Indeed, it is quite unlike an epiphōnēma and more like a form of address or a rebuke.

112. Even a blind man can see, as the saying is, that poetic language gives a certain grandeur to prose, except that some writers imitate the poets quite openly, or rather they do not so much imitate them as transpose their words into their own work, as Herodotus does.

113. When Thucydides, on the other hand, takes over some expression from a poet, he uses it in his own way and makes it his own. The poet said of Crete, for example, "Crete lies in the midst of the wine-dark sea,/A land comely and fertile, ocean-bound."[55] Homer uses the word "ocean-bound" with impressive effect. Thucydides considers it a fine thing for the Sicilians to have a common policy, since they are the denizens of one land, and that ocean-bound. He uses all the same words as the poet; he says land instead of island but calls it ocean-bound in the same way. Yet one feels that he is not saying what Homer said. The reason is that he uses the word not in order to impress but to underline the need for a common policy.

So much for the grand manner.

FRIGIDITY

114. Every attractive quality has as its neighbor a specific weakness: rashness is close to bravery, and shame is close to respect; similarly, successful styles have certain faulty styles lurking nearby.

We shall deal first with the fault which borders on the grand style. We call it frigidity, and Theophrastus defined the frigid as that which overshoots its appropriate expression. For example, to say "Unbaséd goblets cannot tabled be" instead of "goblets without a base cannot be put on a table" is frigid because the trivial subject cannot carry such weighty words.

115. Frigidity, like grandeur, arises in three ways: it may be in the thought, as when a certain writer said in describing the Cyclops hurling a rock at the ship of Odysseus: "As the rock hurtled through the air, goats were grazing upon it." This is frigid because the thought is exaggerated and impossible.

116. There are, according to Aristotle, four sources of frigidity of diction. [It is due to the use of unnecessary epithets][56] as in Alcidamas' "damp sweat," or to a compound where the nature of the double word is dithyrambic, like "lone-journeyed" or some such overelaborate word; or it may be due to a metaphor such as "pallid and tremulous troubles." These then are the four kinds of frigidity of diction.

117. The arrangement of words is frigid when the rhythm is poor, as when, in a phrase, all the syllables are long.[57] This deserves censure, for it is not like prose.

118. On the other hand, a succession of metrical phrases is equally frigid. Some writers write like that, but the meters are obvious because they follow one another. Verse is out of place in prose, and therefore frigid, as is everything which is too metrical.

119. Generally speaking, pretence and frigidity are alike. The writer who deals with a trivial subject in weighty language is like a man who pretends to qualities he does not possess, undeterred by his lack of them, or like a man who boasts about trifles. To discuss trivialities in an exalted style is, as the saying is, like beautifying a pestle.

120. Yet some people say we should discourse in the grand manner on trivialities and they think that this is a proof of outstanding oratorical talent. Now I admit that Polycrates, the rhetorician, eulogized [Thersites][58] as if he were Agamemnon and in so doing used antitheses, metaphors, and every device used in encomia. But he was doing this in jest, not writing a serious eulogy, and the dignified tone of the whole work was itself a game. Let us be playful by all means, but we must also observe what is fitting in each case: that is, we must write in the appropriate manner, lightly when our subject is slight, impressively when it is impressive.

121. Xenophon says of the small, pretty river Teleboas: "This river was not large, it was pretty though."[59] The short sentence, and its ending with "though" makes us almost see the little river. But when another writer says of a similar stream "from its source in the mountains of Laurium it flows into the sea,"[60] one would think he was describing the cataracts of the Nile or the Danube pouring into the sea. All such writing is called frigid.

122. Small matters can be magnified in another way without inappropriateness, and sometimes this has to be done. We may, for example, want to exalt a general after a slight military success, or the punishment inflicted by the Spartan ephor[61] who had a man whipped for playing ball earnestly and in an un-Spartan way. One is at once struck by the trifling nature of the offence, but we can dramatize its importance by saying that to ignore the formation of bad habits in small things is to open the door to more serious crimes, and that, therefore, it is the lesser, not the graver, infractions of the law that must be punished more severely. We shall then bring in the proverb about "work begun is work half-done"[62] as applying to these trivial offences, or indeed as showing that no offence is trivial.

123. A trivial success may thus be greatly magnified without doing anything inappropriate. Just as it is often useful to minimize what is important, so the unimportant may be magnified.

124. The most frigid of all devices is the hyperbole. It is of three kinds; one thing is said to be like another, as in "they run like the wind"; or one thing

may be made superior to another, for example, "whiter than snow"[63]; or, thirdly, what is said is impossible: "her head reached unto heaven."

125. Every hyperbole is really impossible.[64] Nothing is whiter than snow, no horse can run like the wind, but the type mentioned just now is especially called so. It is precisely because every hyperbole states an impossibility that every hyperbole is thought to be frigid.

126. Hence comic poets use hyperbole very freely, and they make the impossibility a source of laughter, as when someone said hyperbolically, in connection with the insatiability of the Persians: "their excrements covered the plains," and again "they carry oxen between their jaws."[65]

127. Of the same type are the well-known "balder than a cloudless sky" and "healthier than a pumpkin." As for Sappho's phrase "more golden than gold," although it is expressed as a hyperbole and is indeed an impossibility, it is the more charming because impossible. Indeed it is a most admirable feature of the divine Sappho's art, that she extracts great charm from devices which are in themselves questionable and difficult.

So much for frigidity and hyperbole, and we now turn to the elegant style.

HORACE

(65–8 B.C.)

INTRODUCTION

In form the *Ars Poetica* of Horace is a letter of advice to young acquaintances who are contemplating a career as poets. It thus has a more informal tone than most other works of literary criticism, but it also represents an extremely serious statement of a major poet's aesthetic theory. Scholars have observed underneath the relaxed surface of the poem a firm structure that is modeled on the traditional Hellenistic form for a treatise on literary criticism. This structure requires a discussion of *poiesis* or poetic subject matter, *poema* or poetic form, and *poeta* or the nature of the poet himself. As we shall see, each one of these themes is treated by Horace.

Scholars have identified Neoptolemus of Parium as the Hellenistic critic who, in a work now lost to us, exerted the major positive influence on Horace. Another important Hellenistic critic, Philodemus, is known to have been Horace's teacher for a time, but there are major differences between Horace's critical principles and those of his teacher.

Horace is not a critic in the mold of a Plato or an Aristotle intent on searching out the essential nature of art and its relationship to all other human activities. He is, rather, a practical poet-critic concerned with finding ways of improving the artistic efforts of his contemporaries. His most basic norm is one of "sensibility"—a disciplined and civilized, yet flexible, "taste." Although Horace's methodology is far removed from Aristotle's kind of rigorous theoretical analysis, the *Ars Poetica* does contain judgments of universal value which have been highly influential in the subsequent history of literary criticism. Especially noteworthy are Horace's many admiring references to the great achievements of Greek civilization. Throughout the *Ars Poetica* examples from Greek literature are cited as models worthy of Roman imitation although Horace is, of course, aware that even great Homer nods (*bonus dormitat Homerus*).

Horace begins his study with a discussion of poetic subject matter (*poiesis*). The large concept of "appropriateness"—the idea of decorum which was to become an important principle in literary criticism—is used as the standard against which all aspects of the treatment of subject matter are judged. Horace demands that a poet choose a subject appropriate to his abilities and experience and that he include in his work only elements that make an appropriate contribution to the subject. Once the subject has been chosen the poet must then use the specific meter that is appropriate for heroic, tragic, comic, or lyric content.

One important way to achieve appropriateness in the handling of subject matter is to aim at realism, and Horace strongly recommends that if a poet or actor wants his audience to feel a strong emotion he must first experience that emotion himself. The poet must also be careful to see that the emotions expressed by a character are appropriate to his traditional status, age, and station in life. If a poet is to present traditional stories successfully, therefore, he must portray Achilles as implacable in his anger, Medea as fierce in her pursuit of vengeance, and Orestes as strongly grieved by his father's murder and the matricide it necessitates. It is in judgments such as these that Horace's norm of verisimilitude seems to replace Aristotle's concern with "probability" (*internal* coherence). The *Ars Poetica* has a strong rhetorical orientation, generally based on a sense of what the audience will accept.

This same orientation is evident in Horace's discussion of appropriate narrative technique. Here, as in so much of the *Ars Poetica,* Homer serves as the model. According to Horace, the proper way to begin a poem is exemplified in the technique of the *Odyssey*: Homer starts in a minor key and then rushes *in medias res* (into the midst of things) to the presentation of the great events of the story. This method permits the appropriate development of poetic intensity, and avoids the diminution of interest that would result from a movement from more significant to less significant action.

After a discussion of poetic subject matter (*poiesis*), Hellenistic literary criticism regularly required a treatment of poetic form (*poema*). Horace discusses several poetic forms, but gives his most detailed treatment to drama. Here, too, appropriateness is the standard against which dramatic techniques and procedures are judged. Horace's first prescription is that nothing excessively violent or monstrous can be presented on stage. In regard to the formal structure of tragedy Horace argues that appropriate practice requires that a play consist of five acts, that a *deus ex machina* not be employed unless absolutely necessary, and that the chorus should be directly involved in the action of the drama and should be a spokesman for what is morally right. These strictures are more extreme than Aristotle's, precisely because they derive from a concept of "sensibility" rather than from an aesthetic argument. Exemplifying the quality of "classical restraint," the *Ars Poetica* encourages a notion of poetry as a discipline and of the poem as a finished product. In this regard, Horace enunciates the doctrine of *ut pictura poesis*: a poem should be a kind of static beauty analogous to that of a painting.

These premises also control the third part of Horace's treatise, the consideration of the character of the poet (*poeta*). Horace discusses the sources of poetic achievement, concluding that it is necessary for the successful poet to possess both natural genius and a capacity for diligent practice. Throughout the *Ars Poetica* as a whole, however, Horace is primarily concerned with giving advice to prospective poets, and thus he tends to place more emphasis on the second quality: mastery of artistic techniques. Discussing pitfalls the poet faces, he mentions, among others, the incongruous use of purple patches (*purpureus pannus*), the tendency to become obscure when trying to be brief (*brevis esse laboro, obscurus fio*), and to forfeit punch and vitality while straining for smoothness and polish (*sectantem levia nervi deficiunt animique*). Horace also admonishes the aspiring author not to rush into print (*nonumque prematur in annum*) and encourages "imitation"—which is not the *mimesis* propounded by either Plato or Aristotle, but rather the young poet's attempt to emulate the spirit of great models.[1]

One of the most important passages in the *Ars Poetica* is Horace's discussion of the ultimate goal of poetry: *aut prodesse volunt aut delectare poetae*. Almost all modern commentators interpret this as an either/or judgment; the successful poet aims *either* at being useful (communicating philosophical or moral teachings beneficial to the audience) *or* at producing pleasure. Such a view directly conflicts with Horace's statement: *omne tulit punctum qui miscuit utile dulci, lectorem delectando pariterque monendo* (that poet carries every vote who mixes the useful with the pleasant, equally delighting and teaching the reader). For Horace the ideal poet is one who can combine both aims, and the major tradition of Western criticism has taken Horace's dictum as an inclusive judgment. An excellent example of this is Sir Philip Sidney's quasi-Aristotelian argument in his *Defence of Poesie*: "Poetry, therefore, is an art of imitation, for so Aristotle termeth it in the word *Mimesis,* that is to say, a representing, counterfeiting, or figuring forth: to speak metaphorically, a speaking picture, with this end, to teach and delight."[2]

As Sidney's comment indicates, Renaissance critics tended to use the *Ars Poetica* as a "key" to the recently-rediscovered *Poetics*.[3] Horace's sensibility matched their own, and the civilized restraint preached in the *Ars Poetica* also helped to make it the core document of neo-classical syntheses from Ben Jonson to the late Augustans. To Pope in *An Essay on Criticism* (653–60),

> Horace still charms with graceful negligence,
> And without method talks us into sense;
> Will, like a friend, familiarly convey
> The truest notions in the easiest way.
> He who supreme in judgment, as in wit,
> Might boldly censure, as he boldly writ,
> Yet judged with coolness, though he sung with fire;
> His precepts teach but what his works inspire.

Horace's sensibility was naturally at odds with that of most romantic critics, especially in their emphasis on expression, spontaneity, and genius. And the temper of most modern criticism exalts "delight," but not "utility," as the ultimate goal of poetry. To modern humanists, however, the *Ars Poetica* has retained much of its original viability. In the writings of Matthew Arnold, Irving Babbitt, and T. S. Eliot, Horace is frequently echoed; and his sensibility is re-embodied.

The translation which follows is by Norman DeWitt. It appeared first in *Drama Survey,* October, 1961 and is reprinted here with the permission of Mrs. Lois DeWitt and Professor John D. Hurrell, the former editor of *Drama Survey.*

The numbers inserted in the translation give the approximate location of every tenth line in the Latin text.

ARS POETICA

Suppose a painter meant to attach a horse's neck to the head of a man, and to put fancy-work of many-colored feathers on limbs of creatures picked at random; the kind of thing where the torso of a shapely maiden merges into the dark rear half of a fish; would you smother your amusement, my friends, if you were let in to see the result?

Believe me, Pisones,[1] a book will be very much like that painting if the meaningless images are put together like the dreams of a man in a fever, to the end that the head and the foot do not match the one body.

"Poets and painters have always enjoyed this fair privilege, of experimenting however they will." (10)

I know it; and I claim that privilege as a poet and, as a poet, I grant it to the painter; but not to the extent that vicious creatures mate with gentle ones, that snakes are paired with birds, lambs with tigers.

When a poem has a pretentious introduction, promising great themes, a bright red patch or two is usually stitched on, to achieve an expansive, colorful effect, as when a sacred grove and an altar of Diana are described, or a hurrying rivulet of water wandering through the lovely meadows, or the river Rhine, or a rainbow. All very well; but there was no place for these scenes at this point in the poem.

And perhaps you know how to represent a cypress tree: what good is this when the client who has paid your fee in advance is swimming for his life in the picture from the wreckage of his ship?[2] (20) I have started to mould a two-handled jar to hold wine: why does a pitcher come off the potter's turning wheel? What I am getting at is this: let the work of art be whatever you want, as long as it is simple and has unity.

To you, Piso senior, and to you sons worthy of your father, I admit that the majority of us poets are tricked by our own standards. I work hard to be brief; I turn out to be obscure. When I try to achieve smoothness and polish, I lose punch, the work lacks life; the poet who proposes grandeur is merely pompous; the poet who tries to be too conservative creeps on the ground, afraid of gusts of wind; if he is anxious to lend marvellous variety to a single subject, he paints a dolphin in the forest, a boar in the breakers. (30) The avoidance of mistakes leads to serious defects if one is lacking in artistic sense. The sculptor in the last studio around the [gladiatorial] school of Aemilius will mould finger-nails and imitate wavy hair in bronze, but the net effect of the work will be unfortunate because he will not know how to represent the whole. If I wanted to make a comparison, I would not care to be like him any more than to go through life with an ugly nose but good-looking otherwise, with dark eyes and dark hair.

If you plan to write, adopt material to match your talents, and think over carefully what burdens your shoulders will not carry and how strong they really are. When a writer's chosen material matches his powers, the flow of words will not fail nor will clarity and orderly arrangement. (40) This is the virtue and charm of such arrangement, unless I am mistaken: that one says now what ought to be said and puts off for later and leaves out a great deal for the present. The author of a poem that has been [asked for and] promised likes one thing and rejects another, is sensitive and careful in putting words together.

Again, you will have expressed yourself with distinction if a clever association gives an old word new meaning. If it turns out to be necessary to explain recent discoveries with new terms, you will be allowed to invent words never heard by the Cethegi[3] in their loin-cloths; (50) and license will be given if you exercise it with due restraint; and new words, recently invented, will win acceptance if they spring from a Greek source with a minor twist in meaning. For that matter, what will a Roman grant to Caecilius and Plautus that he takes away from Vergil and Varius? As for me, why should I be criticized if I add a few words to my vocabulary, when the language of Cato and Ennius enriched the speech of our fathers and produced new names for things? It has always been permissible, and always will be, to mint words stamped with the mark of contemporary coinage. (60)

As the forests change their foliage in the headlong flight of years, as the first leaves fall, so does the old crop of words pass away, and the newly born, like men in the bloom of their youth, come then to the prime of their vigor. We and our works are mortgaged to die. It may be that the land embraces Neptune and diverts the north wind from our navy, the engineering of a king;[4] or a swamp, long unproductive, and good only for boating, now feeds nearby towns and feels the heavy burden of the plow;[5] or it may be that a river, a ravager of fruitful fields, has changed its course, has been taught to follow a better channel:[6] no matter, human accomplishments will pass away, much less does the status of speech endure and popular favor persist. Many things are resurrected which once had passed away, and expressions which are now respected in turn will pass, (70) if usage so decrees—the usage over which the authority and norm of daily speech have final jurisdiction.

The careers of kings and leaders, and sorrow-bringing battles: the meter[7] in which to compose these, Homer has shown us. Laments were first expressed in couplets of unequal lines;[8] later, sentiments of vows fulfilled were included [in this verse] as well. However, what author first published dainty elegiacs, the philologists are arguing, and up to now the dispute rests unresolved. A nasty temper armed Archilochus with his specialty, iambic lines;[9] the sock [10] of comedy and the elevated boot[11] of tragedy took on this meter, (80) just the thing for on-stage conversation, to rise above the noisy audience and quite natural for relations of events. The Muse gave men of wealth and sons of gods, and the victor in the boxing ring and the horse first in the contest, and the heartaches of youth and relaxing wine, to lyric poetry to sing about.

The standard distinctions and overtones of poetic forms: why should I be addressed as a poet if I cannot observe and know nothing about them? Why should I, with a feeble sense of shame, prefer to be ignorant rather than learn them? A comic situation does not want to be treated in tragic verse forms; in the same way, the banquet of Thyestes repudiates a telling in the lines of every-day affairs, close to the level of comedy. (90)

Let each form of poetry occupy the proper place allotted to it.

There are times, however, when comedy raises its voice and an angry Chremes scolds in fury with his swollen cheeks; and, in tragedy, Telephus and Peleus[12] very often express their pain in prose, when the penniless hero and the exile both project inflated lines and complicated compound words, if they are anxious to touch the hearts of the audience with their complaints of deep distress.

It is not enough for poems to be pretty; they must have charm and they must take the heart of the hearer wheresoever they will. (100) Just as the faces of men smile back at those who smile at them, so they join with those who weep. If you want me to weep, you must first feel sorrows yourself; then your mis-fortunes, Telephus or Peleus, hurt me, too. If you speak your lines badly, I'll go to sleep—or laugh out loud. Sad words fit a mournful face, words full of threats an angry face, playful words a face in fun, words seriously expressed, a sober face. I mean that Nature has already shaped us inwardly for every phase of fortune: fortune makes us happy, or drives us into anger or brings us down to earth with a burden of grief and then torments us. (110) Afterwards it brings out our emotions and our tongue acts as interpreter. If the lines do not correspond to the emotional state of the speaker, the members of the Roman audience will burst out laughing, regardless of their income bracket.

It will make a great deal of difference whether a comedy slave or a tragic hero is speaking, or a man of ripe old age, or a hothead in the flower of youth, or a great lady, or a worrying nursemaid, or a traveling merchant or the farmer of a few flourishing acres, a character from Colchis or an Assyrian, a native of Thebes or of Argos.

You have two choices: either follow the conventions of the stage or invent materials that are self-consistent.

If, as a writer, you happen to bring back on the stage an Achilles (120) whose honor has been satisfied, energetic, hotheaded, ruthless, eager, let him claim that laws were not made for him, that there is nothing not subject to possession by force. Let Medea be wild and untamed, Ino an object of pity and tears, Ixion treacherous, Io a wanderer, Orestes depressed.

If you risk anything new and original on the stage and have the courage to invent a new character, let it maintain to the very end the qualities with which it first appeared—and let it be self-consistent.

It is difficult to develop everyday themes in an original way, and you would do better to present the *Iliad* in dramatic form than if you were the first to produce unknown materials never used before on stage. Material in the public domain will become your private property if you do not waste your time going around in worn-out circles, and do not be a literal translator, faithfully rendering word for word from Greek, and do not be merely an imitator, thereby getting yourself into a hole from which either good conscience, or the laws of the work itself, will forbid you to climb out.

And do not start off like this, the way a cyclic[13] poet once did: "I shall sing of the fate of Priam and a war of renown." What did this promise produce to match such a wide open mouth? The mountains will go into labor and deliver a silly mouse! How much more properly this poet began who undertook nothing in poor taste: (140) "Sing to me, Muse, of the man who, after the time of the capture of Troy, saw the ways of numbers of men and their cities."[14] He gives thought to producing a light from the smoke, not smoke from the gleam of the firelight, so that he may bring forth beauty thereafter, and wonder, Antiphates and Scylla and with the Cyclops, Charybdis; nor does he in detail relate the return of Diomedes after the passing of Meleager, or the story of the Trojan War, starting with the twin eggs.[15] He speeds always on to the outcome, and rushes his hearer into the midst of the action just as if the setting were known, and the events that he cannot hope to treat with brilliance, he omits. (150) And then, too, his inventions are such that fiction is mingled with fact to the end that the middle may match with the start and the end with the middle.

Listen to me: here is what I look for in a play, and with me, the public.

If you want a fan in the audience who waits for the final curtain and stays in his seat to the very end, when the singer says, "Give us a hand," you must observe the habits and manners of each period in men's lives, and the proper treatment must be given to their quickly changing characters and their years. The little boy who already knows how to talk plants his feet firmly on the ground, and is eager to play with boys of his own age, and loses his temper and for no good reason gets it back, and changes his disposition every hour. (160)

The adolescent boy with no beard as yet, when [to his relief] he at last is on his own, has fun with hounds and horses and the turf of the sunny Campus,[16] soft as wax to be moulded to folly, resentful of advice, slow to anticipate what is good for him, throwing his money around, high-spirited and eager, quick to change his interests.

The age of maturity brings a change of interests, and the manly character seeks influence and friends, becomes a slave to ambition and is wary of commitments that he will soon have to break off with great difficulty.

Many disagreeable circumstances surround the old man; for example, he still seeks for wealth and, poor fellow, shrinks from spending it. (170) or, again, his management of everything is over-cautious and without any fire, he is indecisive, hopeful without reason, slow to act, grasping for time, hard to get along with, always complaining, always praising the way things were when he was a boy, scolding and correcting the young generation. The years as they come bring with them many advantages, and as they go, take many things away.

Do not by any chance let the character of the elderly be assigned to a younger man, or a man to a boy; we shall always insist upon the qualities of character joined and fitted to the proper age of man.

An event is either acted on the stage or is reported as happening elsewhere. (180) Events arouse our thoughts more slowly when transmitted through the ears than when presented to the accuracy of the eye and reported to the spectator by himself. On the other hand, do not bring out on stage actions that should properly take place inside, and remove from view the many events which the descriptive powers of an actor present on the stage will soon relate. Do not have Medea butcher her sons before the audience, or have the ghoulish Atreus cook up human organs out in public, or Procne turn into a bird, Cadmus into a snake. If you show me anything of this kind, I will not be fooled and I shall resent it.

Do not let a play consist of less than five acts or be dragged out to more than this length, if you want it to enjoy popular demand and have a repeat performance. (190)

Do not have a god intervene unless the complication of the plot turns out to be appropriate to divine solution; and do not have a fourth leading character working hard to get in with his lines.

Have the chorus carry the part of an actor and take a manly role in the play, and do not let them sing anything between the acts which does not contribute to the plot and fit properly into it. The chorus should side with the good and give friendly advice, curb those who are angry and befriend those who fear to do wrong; the chorus should praise a dinner which has but few courses, healthy legal processes and law, and the conditions of peace when the gates of the city stand open; the chorus will keep secrets, entreat the gods and pray that good fortune will come back to the afflicted and desert the over-confident. (200)

The pipes (not, as now, displaced by the brass and their rival the trumpet, but slender in tone and simple, with only a few stops) used to be helpful in accompanying and supporting the chorus and in filling the auditorium (which was not, in those days, overcrowded) with its music—the audience in which the entire community gathered was then such as one could count, what with its small size; it was thrifty, moral and proper.

After the community began to win wars and extend its domain, and the walls of the city enclosed a wider area, and one's guardian spirit was appeased on holidays without reproach with wine in the daytime, (210) greater license in meters and modes came to the theater. This is to say: what critical sense could an ignorant community have when freed from work, the farmer mingling with the townsman, the commoner with the gentleman? And so the flute player added movement and display to the old-fashioned art and trailed his costume about on the platform. And so, again, they invented special notes for the once sober lyre, and the unrestrained speech of the chorus gave rise to a new kind of eloquence, wise in advice on matters of state, and its divine utterances of things to come were quite in the oracular manner of Delphic ambiguities.

The writer who entered the contest for a common goat[17] (220) in tragic verse soon added rustic satyrs with scanty clothing, and crudely tried his hand at humor without loss of tragic dignity, for the reason that the member of the audience had to be kept in his seat by the enticements of novelties, because after taking part in the Bacchic rituals, he was drunk and rowdy. But it is expedient, nonetheless, to sanction the merry, impudent satyrs, to turn solemnity into jest, so that whatever god, whatever hero, may have been but now presented on the stage in gold and royal purple, shall not move into the slums, use vulgar speech, or, while avoiding the ground, grasp at verbal clouds and empty words. (230)

Tragedy is above spouting frivolous lines, like a modest matron told to dance on festive days; she [tragedy]will have little to do, as a respectable woman, with the boisterous satyrs.

As a writer of satyr-plays,[18] my Pisones, I for one will not favor the commonplace and current nouns and verbs, and I shall not try to differ in vocabulary, from the speech that gives tragedy its color; it will make a difference whether Davus is speaking and the saucy Pythias who has swindled a talent out of Simo,[19] or Silenus, the guardian and attendant of a divine foster child.

I shall follow a poetic style from well-known material, just the same as anyone may expect to do himself; (240) and just the same, if he tries it, he will perspire freely and make little progress: that's how difficult the order and connections of words are: that's how much distinction is attached to our everyday vocabulary.

Fauns imported from the woodlands, in my opinion, should be careful not to carouse around in polished lines, like boys reared at the four corners and practically brought up in the Forum, nor shout out dirty words, make scandalous remarks. I mean, they will offend members of the audience who have a house, a distinguished father, and wealth, who will not accept calmly and give the prize to entertainment that pleases the purchaser of dried peas and nuts. (250)

A long syllable following a short is called "iambic," a rapid foot; for this reason, it had the name "three-measure iambic" [trimeter] applied to itself although the beat, the same from first to last, adds up to six per line. Not so very long ago, so that the line might come to the ear more slowly and with a little more weight, the iambic shared its traditional privileges with the steady spondee, accommodating and tolerant, with the reservation that the iambic foot would not, as a partner, move out of its first and fourth position. The spondee, I may add, rarely appears in Accius' "noble"[20] trimeters; and it burdens Ennius' verses, sent ponderously out on the stage, (260) with the charge of overhasty work and the lack of care and attention, or shameful neglect of the principles of art.

No critic whom you may name in Rome can see that a poem is unmusical; and Roman poets have been given unwarranted freedom. Because of that, am I to wander around and write free verse? Or am I to assume that everyone will see my mistakes and play it safe and stay cautiously within the limits of the license I may be granted? No; what I have been saying simply amounts to this: I have merely managed to escape criticism; I have not earned praise.

You—turn our Greek models in your hands at night, turn them in the daytime. But, you say, your forefathers praised the lives and jokes of Plautus; (270) they were much too tolerant of both; they admired him, if I may say so, stupidly, assuming that you and I know how to tell the difference between expressions in poor and good taste, and have had enough experience to tell, on our fingers and by ear, when a sound has been produced according to the rules of meter.

Thespis is said to have discovered the form of tragic poetry and to have hauled his plays around on carts: plays sung and acted by those who had smeared their faces with sediment from wine jars.

After Thespis: the discoverer of the mask and colorful costume, Aeschylus, also constructed the stage on a limited scale, and taught how to speak in lofty style and to walk in the high boots of tragedy. (280)

After these came old comedy, not without considerable popular approval; but its freedom of speech fell off into license and a violence that deserved restraint by law: law was acknowledged and the chorus was disgraced into silence when its right to libel was removed.

Our Roman poets have not failed to try all forms of drama; they deserve no honor whatsoever for venturing to desert the trail blazed by the Greeks and attempting to give fame to Roman events—those who presented serious history or comedies of daily life. Nor would the land of the Latins be more mighty in valor and glory in war than in words, if the toil of time and polish did not discourage our poets, every one of them. (290) As for you, who represent the bloodline of Pompilius, see that you are severe in your censure of a poem that many a day and many an erasure has not trimmed down, and not corrected ten times by the test of a newly-cut fingernail.

Because Democritus believed natural talent to contribute more to success than pitiful technical competence, he barred from Helicon all poets who were mentally well-balanced; most poets do not bother to trim their nails, their beards, they look for out-of-the-way places, steer clear of the baths. I mean, one will acquire the title of poet and the reputation, if he never entrusts his head—too crazy to be cured by medicine even from three Anticyras[21]—to Licinus the barber. (300)

Oh, how inept I am! I have myself purged of bile as the spring season comes on! Otherwise no man could write a better poem. But it isn't worth the trouble. I'll play the role of whetstone, which is good enough to put an edge on iron but is out of luck when it comes to cutting. While I write nothing myself, I'll teach the gift, the business of the poet, where he gets his material, what nourishes and forms the poet, what is appropriate, the way of right and wrong.

The origin and source of poetry is the wisdom to write according to moral principles: the Socratic dialogues will be able to clarify your philosophy, (310) and the words themselves will freely follow the philosophy, once it has been seen before you write. The man who has learned what he owes to his country, what he owes to his friends, what love is due a father, how a brother and a family friend are loved, what the duties of a senator are, what the duties of a judge, what roles a leader sent to war should play: he knows, as a matter of course, how to assign to each character what is appropriate for it.

I shall tell you to respect the examples of life and of good character— you who have learned the art of imitation—and from this source bring forth lines that live. Quite often a play which is impressive in spots and portrays good character, but with no particular charm, without real content and really good writing, (320) will give the public more pleasure and hold them better than lines without ideas and with resounding platitudes.

To the Greeks, genius, the gift of speaking in well-rounded phrases— these the Muse presented. The Greeks are greedy for nothing save acclaim. The Roman boys learn to calculate percentages of money by long division. "Let the son of Albinus tell me: if one-twelfth is taken from five-twelfths, what's the remainder? You should have been able to tell us by this time." "*One-third.*" "*Très bien!* You'll make a good businessman. Add a twelfth, what happens?" "One-half." (330) When this smut, this worrying about business arithmetic, has permeated our minds, do you think we can expect to put together poems to be treated with oil of cedar and kept in cypress-wood cases?

Poets aim either to help or to amuse the reader, or to say what is pleasant and at the same time what is suitable. Whatever you have in the way of a lesson, make it short, so that impressionable minds can quickly grasp your words and hold them faithfully: every unnecessary word spills over and is lost to a heart that is already filled up to the brim.

Whatever you invent to please, see that it is close to truth, so your play does not require belief in anything it wants; do not have it pull a living child from Lamia's[22] insides just after she has eaten lunch. (340)

The centuries[23] of elders in the audience cannot stand a play that has no moral; the noble young gentlemen ignore an austere composition; but the writer who has combined the pleasant with the useful [*miscuit utile dulci*] wins on all points, by delighting the reader while he gives advice. This kind of book makes money for the Sosii;[24] this kind of book is sold across the sea and prolongs the famous writer's age.

There are, however, faults which I should like to overlook: I mean that the string, when plucked, does not give forth the sound that heart and hand desire; it very often gives back a high note when one calls for a low; and the arrow does not always hit precisely the mark at which it aimed and threatened. (350) So, when most of the passages are brilliant, I am personally not bothered by blots, which are spattered here and there by oversight or those which human nature failed to guard against enough.

Well, what's the point?

If a library copyist keeps on making the same mistake, even though he has been warned about it, there is no excuse for him, and a lyre player who always strikes the same sour note is laughed at; so a writer who is consistently sloppy is in a class with Choerilus—you know who I mean—whom I regard with amused admiration if he happens to write two or three good passages. Similarly, I think it's too bad whenever good old Homer dozes off, as he does from time to time, but when all is said and done, it is natural enough for drowsiness to creep up on a long job of writing. (360) A poem is like a painting: you will find a picture which will attract you more if you stand up close, another if you stand farther back. This picture favors shadow, another likes to be viewed in the light—neither has apprehensions about the keen perceptions of the good critic. Here's one that pleases you only once; here's another that you'll like if you come back to it ten times.

And now to address the older of the two of you: ah, even though your tastes have been formed to appreciate the right things by your father (as well as by others), and you have much good sense of your own, acknowledge what I am going to say and remember it: perfectly proper concessions are made to second-raters in certain fields. A second-rate legal authority and member of the bar

(370) can be far from having the qualities of Messala, a very able speaker, and not be as learned as Casellius Aulus, but still he has a certain value—*a second-rate poet gets no advertising posters from either men, gods, or booksellers.*

You know how music off-key grates on your nerves at an otherwise pleasant banquet, and greasy ointment for your hair, and bitter honey from Sardinia mixed with poppy seeds, because the banquet could be carried on without them. That is how it is with poetry: created and developed to give joy to human hearts; but if it takes one step down from the very highest point of merit, it slides all the way back to the bottom.

The lad who does not know how to take part in sports keeps out of the cavalry exercises in the Campus; and if he has not learned how to work with the ball, the disc or the hoop (380) —he sits where he is because he is afraid that the spectators, jammed together, will laugh at his expense—there will be nothing he can do about it. For all of that, the man who has no notion of how to compose poetry has the nerve to go ahead anyhow. Why shouldn't he? After all, he's a free man and born free and what's more to the point, his income is in the top brackets—which puts him beyond criticism.

As for you, my boy, don't do or say anything that Minerva would not approve: that's your standard of judgment, that's your philosophy. However, if you ever do write something, see that it comes into court—to the ears of Maecius as critic, or your father's, or mine, and also see that it is weighted down in storage, put away between the leaves of parchment; you can always edit what you haven't published: the word that is uttered knows no return. (390)

Orpheus, a holy man and spokesman for the gods, forced the wild men of the woods to give up human killing and gruesome feasting; he is said, because of these powers, to soothe tigers and the raging of the lion; yes, and Amphion, the builder of the city of Thebes, is said to move rocks with his lyre and with the softness of song to lead them where he will.

I will tell you what was once the poet's wisdom: to decide what were public and what were private suits at law, to say what was sacred and what was not, to enjoin from sexual license, provide a code of conduct for marriage, to build up towns, and carve the laws on wooden tablets. This was the way honor and renown came to god-like poet-preachers and their songs. (400)

After these, Homer gained renown, and Tyrtaeus with his verses whetted the spirits of males for Mars and war; oracles were given in the form of poems and the way of life was shown; the favor of kings was sought in Pierian[25] strains; and dramatic festivals were invented and thus the end of a long task [of development]—in case the Muse in her lyric artistry and Apollo with his song embarrass you.

The question has been asked: is good poetry created by nature or by training?

Personally, I cannot see what good enthusiasm is or uncultivated talent without a rich vein of genius; (410) each requires the help of the other and forms a friendly compact. The would-be poet whose passion is to reach the hoped-for goal in this race for fame, has worked hard in boyhood and endured a great deal, has sweated and shivered, abstained from women and wine; the artist who plays the pipe at the Pythian games[26] has first learned his art and lived in terror of a teacher. Nowadays it's enough to have said, "I beat out wonderful poems; the hell with the rest of the mob; it's a dirty deal for me to be left at the starting line and admit that I obviously don't know what I never learned."

Like a huckster who collects a crowd to buy his wares, the poet with his wealth in land, with wealth resting on coin put out at interest, tells yes-men to come to his readings for gain. (430) Yes, indeed; if there is a man who can set out a really fat banquet, and co-sign notes for irresponsible paupers, and save the neck of the client tangled in a murder trial, I'll be surprised if, for all his wealth, he can tell the difference between a liar and an honest friend! Whether you have already given someone a present or only expect to do so, don't let him near your verses when he's full of joy: I mean, he'll gush "Lovely! Great! Swell!" On top of this, he'll turn pale, he'll even squeeze drops of dew from sympathetic eyes, leap to his feet and stamp on the ground. (430)

The way hired mourners wail at a funeral and—so they say—carry on more painfully than those who sorrow quite sincerely, thus the critic with his tongue in cheek is more deeply moved than the ordinary flatterer. Rich men are said to keep pushing glasses of wine at, and to torment with wine poured straight, the man whom they are trying hard to see through—to see if he is worthy of friendship. If you will put together poems, motives disguised with a foxy expression will never deceive you.

If you were to read anything to Quintilius, "Change this, please, he kept saying, "and this." If you said you couldn't do better, you'd tried twice, three times, with no success, (440) Quintilius used to say to rub it out and put back on the anvil the lines that were spoiled on the lathe. If you preferred to defend your mistake, not revise it, he would not waste another word or go to more useless trouble to keep you from being your only friend, with no competitors.

A true critic and wise one will scold you for weak lines, blame you for rough ones, he'll indicate unpolished lines with a black crossmark made with his pen, he'll cut out pretentious embellishments, make you clarify obscure phrases, remove ambiguities, mark things to be changed, he'll turn into an Aristarchus, and he will not say, "Why should I hurt the feelings of a friend over these trifles?" (450) Well, these trifles will get you into serious trouble once you have been laughed down and given a poor reception.

As in the case of a man with a bad attack of the itch or inflammation of the liver or one who's offended Diana—he's moon-struck—everyone with any sense is afraid to touch the madman and keeps out of the way of the poet; small boys pester him and don't know any better than to follow him around. If, while burping out his lines and thinking they're sublime, he goes off the roadway, falls into an excavation or a well, like a hunter intent on his blackbirds—he can yell so you can hear him a mile away, "Help! Hey, neighbors!"—no one would be worried about fishing him out. (460) If someone should get excited about rescuing him and let down a rope, I'll say, "How do you know that he didn't do it on purpose when he threw himself down there, and doesn't want to be rescued?" And I'll tell the story about the death of the Sicilian poet.

While he had a yearning to be regarded as an immortal god, Empedocles was cool enough to jump down into the red-hot crater of Aetna. Let poets have the right to perish; issue them a license! When you rescue a man against his will, you do the same as kill him. This isn't the first time he's done it, either; and if he's hauled out, he still won't behave like a human and give up his love of dying for publicity. And it isn't very clear, either, why he keeps on grinding out his verses, (470) whether he's used his father's funeral urn as a pisspot or whether he's tampered with the boundary markers of a holy plot of ground—an act of sacrilege. He's crazy, that's sure; and like a bear that's powerful enough to break the bars at the front of his cage, this dedicated elocutionist puts to flight the scholar and the layman without discrimination. Yes, and when he catches one, he'll hold on to him and recite him to death. You can be sure he won't let go of the hide of his victim until he's as full of blood as a leech.

DIONYSIUS
OF HALICARNASSUS

(1st century B.C.)

INTRODUCTION

Other than his work, most of which has fortunately survived, we have no significant biographical data about Dionysius of Halicarnassus. His most important treatise, *On Literary Composition*, is represented in this collection by the selections that follow. The complete work consists of an introduction on the nature of literary composition, a discussion of the techniques of intensifying the effect of words, an analysis of the arrangement of clauses, an important discussion of the basis of charm and beauty of expression in words, and a conclusion devoted to the relationship between poetry and prose.

The wide range of Dionysius' interests as a critic is seen in the subject matter of his other works. In his *On Ancient Orators* an account is given of earlier rhetoricians who could serve as models for the contemporary period. *On Thucydides* is a study of the subject matter and style of the historian, while *On Dinarchus* attempts to distinguish between the orator's genuine and spurious speeches. The *First Letter to Ammaeus* shows that Demosthenes' speeches preceded Aristotle's *Rhetoric* and could not have been dependent for their technical inspiration on that work; and the *Second Letter to Ammaeus* is a study of the grammatical and linguistic characteristics of Thucydides' style. The *Letter to Gnaeus Pompeius* defends Dionysius' critical attitude toward aspects of Plato's literary style; and *On Imitation*, which exists only as a fragment, originally was a study of (1) the nature of imitation in general, (2) the choice of authors for imitation, and (3) the proper method of imitation.

As in the case of other critics of this period, Dionysius' major purpose was the establishment of high standards for rhetorical and other literature. He went back to the literature of classical Greece as a model for contemporary writers and he set down as requirements for literary achievement the possession of natural talent, the capacity for careful study, and the willingness to endure the rigors of the intensive practice of one's art.

170

In the selections included in this collection Dionysius indicates that the two essential qualities of good composition are charm and beauty. These two concepts are closely related but they are not identical. Thus Dionysius is able to cite works in which both qualities are present as well as those in which only one is found. He indicates that the four most important sources of charm and beauty in literary composition are (1) melody, (2) rhythm, (3) variety, and (4) appropriateness. In terms of charm these sources result in freshness, grace, euphony, sweetness, persuasivness, and similar qualities; in terms of beauty they result in grandeur, impressiveness, solemnity, dignity, mellowness, and related qualities.

According to Dionysius, the ear of the audience is delighted first by melody, second by rhythm, third by variety, and fourth by appropriateness. These effects are found in all arts where language is used, and the difference between music and oratory, according to Dionysius, is one of degree. Dionysius then shows how the very accents of Greek words produce a verbal music insofar as the Greek accent was a pitch accent involving a change of tone for the syllable being accented.

Dionysius recognizes that some sounds are naturally beautiful and others are not, and thus there is a necessity to combine these sounds in order to obtain a pleasant effect. He also indicates the need to avoid monotony in sounds, words, and metaphors and the need to use words that are melodious, rhythmical, and euphonious. Wherever possible, words that possess these qualities should be interwoven with others which lack them. According to Dionysius, the proper use of these techniques of literary composition will create both beauty and charm, the objectives of good style.

The selections included here show Dionysius' major quality as a critic: his sensitivity to the stylistic elements that contribute significantly to the emotional effect of a work of art. Any analysis of the impact of a work of art must include a study of the qualities which Dionysius discusses so well in *On Literary Composition.*

The translation used here is by W. Rhys Roberts and reprinted from Dionysius of Halicarnassus, *On Literary Composition* (London: Macmillan, 1910).

from ON LITERARY COMPOSITION

X
Aims and Methods of Good Composition

Now that I have laid down these broad outlines, the next step will be to state what should be the aims kept in view by the man who wishes to compose well, and by what methods his object can be attained. It seems to me that the two essentials to be aimed at by those who compose in verse and prose are charm and beauty. The ear craves for both of these. It is affected in somewhat the same way as the sense of sight which, when it looks upon molded figures, pictures, carvings, or any other works of human hands, and finds both charm and beauty residing in them, is satisfied and longs for nothing more. And let not anyone be surprised at my assuming that there are two distinct objects in style, and at my separating beauty from charm; nor let him think it strange if I hold that a piece of composition may possess charm but not beauty, or beauty without charm. Such is the verdict of actual experience; I am introducing no novel axiom. The styles of Thucydides and of Antiphon of Rhamnus are surely examples of beautiful composition, if ever there were any, and are beyond all possible cavil from this point of view, but they are not remarkable for their charm. On the other hand, the style of the historian Ctesias of Cnidus, and that of Xenophon the disciple of Socrates, are charming in the highest possible degree, but not as beautiful as they should have been. I am speaking generally, not absolutely; I admit that in the former authors there are instances of charming, in the latter of beautiful arrangement. But the composition of Herodotus has both these qualities; it is at once charming and beautiful.

XI
General Discussion of the Sources of Charm and Beauty in Composition

Among the sources of charm and beauty in style there are, I conceive, four which are paramount and essential—melody, rhythm, variety, and the appropriateness demanded by these three. Under "charm" I class freshness, grace, euphony, sweetness, persuasiveness, and all similar qualities; and under "beauty" grandeur, impressiveness, solemnity, dignity, mellowness, and the like. For these seem to me the most important—the main heads, so to speak, in either case. The aims set before themselves by all serious writers in epic, dramatic, or lyric poetry, or in the so-called "language of prose," are those specified, and I think these are all. There are many excellent authors who have been distinguished in one or both of these qualities. It is not possible at present to adduce examples from the writings of each one of them; I must not waste time over such details; and besides, if it seems incumbent on me to say something about some of them individually, and to quote from them anywhere in support of my views, I shall have a more suitable opportunity for doing so, when I sketch the various types of literary arrangement. For the present, what I have said of them is quite sufficient. So I will now return to the division I made of composition into charming and beautiful, in order that my discourse may "keep to the track," as the saying is.

Well, I said that the ear delighted first of all in melody, then in rhythm, thirdly in variety, and finally in appropriateness as applied to these other qualities. As a witness to the truth of my words I will bring foward experience itself, for it cannot be challenged, confirmed as it is by the general sentiment of mankind. Who is there that is not enthralled by the spell of one melody while he remains unaffected in any such way by another,—that is not captivated by this rhythm while that does but jar upon him? Before now I myself, even in the most popular theatres, thronged by a mixed and uncultured multitude, have seemed to observe that all of us have a sort of natural appreciation for correct melody and good rhythm. I have seen an accomplished harpist, of high repute, hissed by the public because he struck a single false note and so spoilt the melody. I have seen, too, a fluteplayer, who handled his instrument with the practiced skill of a master, suffer the same fate because he blew thickly or, through not compressing his lips, produced a harsh sound or so-called "broken note" as he played. Nevertheless, if the amateur critic were summoned to take up the instrument and himself to render any of the pieces with whose performance by professionals he was just now finding fault, he would be unable to do it. Why so? Because this is an affair of technical skill, in which we are not all partakers; the other of feeling, which is nature's universal gift to man. I have noticed the same thing occur in the case of rhythms. Everybody is vexed and annoyed when a performer strikes an instrument, takes a step, or sings a note, out of time, and so destroys the rhythm.

Again, it must not be supposed that, while melody and rhythm excite pleasure, and we are all enchanted by them, variety and appropriateness have less freshness and grace, or less effect on any of their hearers. No, these too fairly enchant us all when they are really attained, just as their absence jars upon us intensely. This is surely beyond dispute. I may refer, in confirmation, to the case of instrumental music, whether it accompanies singing or dancing; if it attains grace perfectly and throughout, but fails to introduce variety in due season or deviates from what is appropriate, the effect is dull satiety and that disagreeable impression which is made by anything out of harmony with the subject. Nor is my illustration foreign to the matter in hand. The science of public oratory is, after all, a sort of musical science, differing from vocal and instrumental music in degree, not in kind. In oratory, too, the words involve melody, rhythm, variety, and appropriateness; so that, in this case also, the ear delights in the melodies, is fascinated by the rhythms, welcomes the variations, and craves always what is in keeping with the occasion. The distinction between oratory and music is simply one of degree.

Now, the melody of spoken language is measured by a single interval, which is approximately that termed a *fifth*. When the voice rises towards the acute, it does not rise more than three tones and a semitone; and, when it falls towards the grave, it does not fall more than this interval. Further, the entire utterance during one word is not delivered at the same pitch of the voice throughout, but one part of it at the acute pitch, another at the grave, another at both. Of the words that have both pitches, some have the grave fused with the acute on one and the same syllable—those which we call circumflexed; others have both pitches falling on separate syllables, each retaining its own quality. Now in disyllables there is no space intermediate between low pitch and high pitch; while in polysyllabic words, whatever their number of syllables, there is but one syllable that has the acute accent (high pitch) among the many remaining graves ones. On the other hand, instrumental and vocal music uses a great number of intervals, not the fifth only; beginning with the octave, it uses also the fifth, the fourth, the third, the tone, the semitone, and, as some think, even the quarter-tone in a distinctly perceptible way. Music, further, insists that the words should be subordinate to the tune, and not the tune to the words. Among many examples in proof of this, let me especially instance those lyrical lines which Euripides has represented Electra as addressing to the Chorus in the *Orestes* (140–42): "Hush, hush! Light be the tread / Of the sandal; not a sound! / This way, far, far from his bed." In these lines the words *sîga sîga leukón* are sung to one note; and yet each of the three words has both low pitch and high pitch. And the word *arbúles* has its third syllable sung at the same pitch as its middle syllable, although it is impossible for a single word to take two acute accents. The first syllable of *títhete* is sung to a lower note, while the two that follow it are sung to the same high note. The circumflex accent of *ktupeîte* has disappeared, for the two syllables are uttered at one and the same pitch. And the word *apopróbate* does not receive the acute accent on the middle syllable; but the pitch of the third syllable has been transferred to the fourth.

The same thing happens in rhythm. Ordinary prose speech does not violate or interchange the quantities in any noun or verb. It keeps the syllables long or short as it has received them by nature. But the arts of rhythm and music alter them by shortening or lengthening, so that often they pass into their opposites: the time of production is not regulated by the quantity of the syllables, but the quantity of the syllables is regulated by the time.

The difference between music and speech having thus been shown, some other points remain to be mentioned. If the melody of the voice—not the singing voice, I mean, but the ordinary voice—has a pleasant effect upon the ear, it will be called melodious rather than in melody. So also symmetry in the quantities of words, when it preserves a lyrical effect, is rhythmical rather than in rhythm. On the precise bearing of these distinctions I will speak at the proper time. For the present I will pass on to the next question, and try to show how a style of civil oratory can be attained which, simply by means of the composition, charms the ear with its melody of sound, its symmetry of rhythm, its elaborate variety, and its appropriateness to the subject. These are the headings which I have set before myself.

XII

How to Render Composition Charming

It is not in the nature of all the words in a sentence to affect the ear in the same way, any more than all visible objects produce the same impression on the sense of sight, things tasted on that of taste, or any other set of stimuli upon the sense to which they correspond. No, different sounds affect the ear with many different sensations of sweetness, harshness, roughness, smoothness, and so on. The reason is to be found partly in the many different qualities of the letters which make up speech, and partly in the extremely various forms in which syllables are put together. Now since words have these properties, and since it is impossible to change the fundamental nature of any single one of them, we can only mask the uncouthness which is inseparable from some of them, by means of mingling and fusion and juxtaposition—by mingling smooth with rough, soft with hard, cacophonous with melodious, easy to pronounce with hard to pronounce, long with short; and generally by happy combinations of the same kind. Many words of few syllables must not be used in succession (for this jars upon the ear), nor an excessive number of polysyllabic words; and we must avoid the monotony of setting side by side words similarly accented or agreeing in their quantities. We must quickly vary the cases of substantives (since, if continued unduly, they greatly offend the ear); and in order to guard against satiety, we must constantly break up the effect of sameness entailed by placing many nouns, or verbs, or other parts of speech, in close succession. We must not always adhere to the same figures, but change them frequently; we must not reintroduce the same metaphors, but vary them; we must not exceed due measure by beginning or ending with the same words too often.

Still, let no one think that I am proclaiming these as universal rules— that I suppose keeping them will always produce pleasure, or breaking them always produce annoyance. I am not so foolish. I know that pleasure often arises from both sources—from similarity at one time, from dissimilarity at another. In every case we must, I think, keep in view good taste, for this is the best criterion of charm and its opposite. But about good taste no rhetorician or philosopher has, so far, produced a definite treatise. The man who first under-took to write on the subject, Gorgias of Leontini, achieved nothing worth mentioning. The nature of the subject, indeed, is not such that it can fall under any comprehensive and systematic treatment, nor can good taste in general be apprehended by science, but only by personal judgment. Those who have con-tinually trained this latter faculty in many connections are more successful than others in attaining good taste, while those who leave it untrained are rarely successful, and only by a sort of lucky stroke.

To proceed. I think the following rules should be observed in composi-tion by a writer who looks to please the ear. Either he should link to one another melodious, rhythmical, euphonious words, by which the sense of hearing is touched with a feeling of sweetness and softness—those which, to put it broadly, come home to it most; or he should intertwine and interweave those which have no such natural effect with those that can so bewitch the ear that the unattractive-ness of the one set is overshadowed by the grace of the other. We may com-pare the practice of good tacticians when marshalling their armies: they mask the weak portions by means of the strong, and so no part of their force proves useless. In the same way I maintain we ought to relieve monotony by the tasteful introduction of variety, since variety is an element of pleasure in everything we do. And last, and certainly most important of all, the setting which is assigned to the subject matter must be appropriate and becoming to it. And, in my opinion, we ought not to feel shy of using any noun or verb, however hackneyed, unless it carries with it some shameful association; for I venture to assert that no part of speech which signifies a person or a thing will prove so mean, squalid, or otherwise offensive as to have no fitting place in discourse. My advice is that, trusting to the effect of the composition, we should bring out such expressions with a bold and manly confidence, following the example of Homer, in whom the most commonplace words are found, and of Demosthenes and Herodotus and others, whom I will mention a little later so far as is suitable in each case. I think I have now spoken at sufficient length on charm of style. My treatment has been but a brief survey of a wide field, but will furnish the main heads of the study.

XIII
How to Render Composition Beautiful

So far, so good. But, if some one were to ask me in what way, and by attention to what principles, literary structure can be made beautiful, I should reply: In no other way, believe me, and by no other means, than those by which it is made charming, since the same elements contribute to both, namely noble melody, stately rhythm, imposing variety, and the appropriateness which all these need. For as there is a charming diction, so there is another that is noble; as there is a polished rhythm, so also is there another that is dignified; as variety in one passage adds grace, so in another it adds mellowness; and as for appropriateness, it will prove the chief source of beauty, or else the source of nothing at all. I repeat, the study of beauty in composition should follow the same lines throughout as the study of charm. The prime cause, here as before, is to be found in the nature of the letters and the phonetic effect of the syllables, which are the raw material out of which the fabric of words is woven. The time may perhaps now have come for redeeming my promise to discuss these.

QUINTILIAN

(ca. 30/35–ca. 100 A.D.)

INTRODUCTION

From 68 to about 88 A.D. Quintilian was the leading teacher of rhetoric at Rome. On his retirement from teaching he wrote a treatise *On the Decay of Oratory,* which is no longer extant, and in 93 A.D. he wrote the *Institutio Oratoria,* a broad-ranging investigation of all phases of the training of an orator. This treatise stands as one of the most important statements of Roman rhetorical theory and practice. The work was undertaken at the behest of friends who wanted authoritative guidance in rhetoric. In addition to its vast amount of factual material, it offers an occasional insight into the personality and emotions of its author. The most moving of these occasions is found in the introduction to Book VI where Quintilian speaks somberly of the death of his son, for whom this volume was to have been a legacy, and expresses his deep despair over the previous deaths of his wife and another son. Now he faces the prospect of a lonely old age.

Central to Quintilian's theory of rhetoric is the belief he shares with Plato, Horace, "Longinus," and others that a good orator must be a good human being. The *Institutio Oratoria* indicates in its twelve books the appropriate course of technical training that would permit a good human being to achieve success as a rhetorician. Book I opens with a survey of the preliminary education a student should undergo prior to the actual study of rhetoric. Book II is devoted to an investigation of the aims and nature of rhetoric. Books III–VII are concerned with many technical features of oratory, such as the invention and arrangement of arguments, with major emphasis on forensic speeches. Books VIII–X deal with oratorical style, and Book XI is concerned with the memorization and oral delivery of speeches. The final book discusses the nature of the perfect orator.

The selections from the *Institutio Oratoria* included in this collection are taken from Book X. The first selection—from Quintilian's famous and very concise history of literature—deals with Homer. Quintilian's judgments of literary works are based principally on their value for oratorical training, and this orientation must be kept in mind when assessing them. Quintilian covers the entire field of classical literature, beginning with Homer, by providing brief critical assessments of each author discussed.

The analysis of Homer, whom Quintilian admires as a poet of supreme genius, is a good place to observe his approach to the evaluation of literature, because the discussion here is more extensive than that given to other writers. Quintilian praises Homer's ability to deal with both large and small subjects successfully, and he commends Homer's appropriateness in using a variety of styles, expansive and brief, gentle and forceful. He applauds Homer's ability to achieve both poetic and rhetorical excellence as exhibited in the laudatory, exhortatory, and consolatory speeches in his poems. Quintilian points out that Homer established the rules for proper rhetorical presentation by, first, favorably disposing his audience toward him through his invocation of the muse of poetry; second, seizing the attention of the audience by the very grandeur of his subject; and, finally, making his audience eager for further information by setting forth a concise but comprehensive view of his entire subject. Quintilian also praises Homer for his knowledge of all emotions, subtle and intense, for his great skill in all forms of establishment and refutation of proof, and for his expert use of similes, amplifications, and illustrations. As a rhetorical standard of excellence Quintilian cites Priam's speech to Achilles in which the bereaved father begs for the return of his son's body. In similar fashion, principally emphasizing the rhetorical qualities of the author under discussion, Quintilian proceeds through the history of Greek and Latin literature.

The second selection from Quintilian included here is the entire second chapter of Book X, which deals with the subject of mimesis or imitation. In this context the term is subjected to an interpretation that is quite different from those of Plato and Aristotle and comes to mean essentially "copying." Quintilian recommends that students of rhetoric imitate the virtues they find in the works of others. He rates invention as more significant than imitation, but he declares that it is important to take advantage of qualities that have already been proved successful by incorporating them into one's own style. Complete reliance on imitation is, however, rejected by Quintilian on the grounds that it would prevent (or, at least, obstruct) future progress in the field of rhetoric.

Quintilian urges that the student must imitate only what is best in the authors chosen for imitation, and that he must do this in a skillful and effective way. The student must also choose for imitation models that are naturally suited to his own natural abilities. Quintilan further recommends that the student imitate the virtues of many authors, instead of choosing to rely on only one, and that, in doing so, the student combine his own good qualities with those observed in each model. In this way Quintilian expresses the hope that every generation may be able to provide models of excellence for emulation by rhetoricians of the future.

As we have seen, Quintilian's primary interests are rhetorical, and this gives a special orientation to his use and evaluation of literature. But Quintilian's rhetorical emphasis, like that of Cicero and "Longinus," is united with a strong moral impulse. The balance between these two elements made the *Institutio Oratoria* a work of enduring popularity. Although it was known only in fragmentary versions in the Middle Ages, it still became for scholars a standard reference work in rhetoric. The *Institutio Oratoria* attained its highest critical status from the late Renaissance through the neoclassical period. (The complete text, discovered in 1417, was edited by Cardinal Campano in 1470.) Thus, for about three hundred years, Quintilian, like Aristotle, was used to supplement and enlarge an essentially Horatian poetic. And, as Pope's tribute to Quintilian indicates, the adaptation of "rules" of rhetoric became relevant to the evaluation of literary works:

> In grave Quintilian's copious work, we find
> The justest rules, and clearest method joined.
> Thus useful arms in magazines we place,
> All ranged in order, and disposed with grace;
> But less to please the eye, than arm the hand,
> Still fit for use, and ready at command.
> (*An Essay on Criticism* 669–74)

The translation which follows is by H. E. Butler and has been taken from Quintilian, *Institutio Oratoria*. 4 vols. (Cambridge: Harvard University Press, 1958–60) with the permission of the publisher.

INSTITUTIO ORATORIA

from BOOK X

(I.46.) I shall, I think, be right in following the principle laid down by Aratus in the line, "With Jove let us begin,"[1] and in beginning with Homer. He is like his own conception of Ocean,[2] which he describes as the source of every stream and river; for he has given us a model and an inspiration for every department of eloquence. It will be generally admitted that no one has ever surpassed him in the sublimity with which he invests great themes or the propriety with which he handles small. He is at once luxuriant and concise, sprightly and serious, remarkable at once for his fullness and his brevity, and supreme not merely for poetic, but for oratorical power as well. (47.) For, to say nothing of his eloquence, which he shows in praise, exhortation, and consolation, do not the ninth book containing the embassy to Achilles, the first describing the quarrel between the chiefs, or the speeches delivered by the counsellors in the second, display all the rules of art to be followed in forensic or deliberative oratory? (48.) As regards the emotions, there can be no one so ill-educated as to deny that the poet was the master of all, tender and vehement alike. Again, in the few lines with which he introduces both of his epics, has he not, I will not say observed, but actually established the law which should govern the composition of the exordium?[3] For, by his invocation of the goodnesses believed to preside over poetry he wins the goodwill of his audience, by his statement of the greatness of his themes he excites their attention and renders them receptive by the briefness of his summary. (49.) Who can narrate more briefly than the hero[4] who brings the news of Patroclus' death, or more vividly than he[5] who describes the battle between the Curetes and the Aetolians? Then consider his similes, his amplifications, his illustrations, digressions, indications of fact, inferences, and all the other methods of proof and refutation which he employs. They are so numerous that the majority of writers on the principles of rhetoric have gone to his works for examples of all these things. (50.) And as for perorations, what can ever be equal to the prayers which Priam addresses to Achilles[6] when he comes to beg for the body of his son? Again, does he not transcend the limits of human genius in his choice of words, his reflections, figures, and the arrangement of his whole work, with the result that it requires a powerful mind, I will not say to imitate, for that is impossible, but even to appreciate his excellences? (51.) But he has in truth outdistanced all that have come after him in every department of eloquence, above all, he has outstripped all other writers of epic, the contrast in their case being especially striking owing to the similarity of the material with which they deal.

(II.1) It is from these and other authors worthy of our study that we must draw our stock of words, the variety of our figures and our methods of composition, while we must form our minds on the model of every excellence. For there can be no doubt that in art no small portion of our task lies in imitation, since, although invention came first and is all-important, it is expedient to imitate whatever has been invented with success. (2.) And it is a universal rule of life that we should wish to copy what we approve in others. It is for this reason that boys copy the shapes of letters that they may learn to write, and that musicians take the voices of their teachers, painters the works of their predecessors, and peasants the principles of agriculture which have been proved in practice, as models for their imitation. In fact, we may note that the elementary study of every branch of learning is directed by reference to some definite standard that is placed before the learner. (3.) We must, in fact, either be like or unlike those who have proved their excellence. It is rare for nature to produce such resemblance, which is more often the result of imitation. But the very fact that in every subject the procedure to be followed is so much more easy for us than it was for those who had no model to guide them, is a positive drawback, unless we use this dubious advantage with caution and judgment.

(4.) The first point, then, that we must realise is that imitation alone is not sufficient, if only for the reason that a sluggish nature is only too ready to rest content with the inventions of others. For what would have happened in the days when models were not, if men had decided to do and think of nothing that they did not know already? The answer is obvious: nothing would ever have been discovered. (5.) Why, then, is it a crime for us to discover something new? Were primitive men led to make so many discoveries simply by the natural force of their imagination, and shall we not then be spurred on to search for novelty by the very knowledge that those who sought of old were rewarded by success? (6.) And seeing that they, who had none to teach them anything, have handed down such store of knowledge to posterity, shall we refuse to employ the experience which we possess of some things, to discover yet other things, and possess nought that is not owed to the beneficent activity of others? Shall we follow the example of those painters whose sole aim is to be able to copy pictures by using the ruler and the measuring rod?[7] (7.) It is a positive disgrace to be content to owe all our achievement to imitation. For what, I ask again, would have been the result if no one had done more than his predecessors? Livius Andronicus would mark our supreme achievement in poetry and the annals of the *Pontifices*[8] would be our *ne plus ultra* in history. We should still be sailing on rafts, and the art of painting would be restricted to tracing a line round a shadow thrown in the sunlight. (8.) Cast your eyes over the whole of history; you will find that no art has remained just as it was when it was discovered, nor come to a standstill at its very birth, unless indeed we are ready to pass special condemnation on our own generation on the ground that it is so barren of invention that no further development is possible; and it is undoubtedly true that no development is possible for those who restrict themselves to imitation. (9.) But if we are forbidden to add anything to the existing stock of knowledge, how can we ever hope for the birth of our ideal orator? For of all the greatest orators with whom we are as yet acquainted, there is not one who has not some deficiency or blemish. And even those who do not aim at supreme excellence, ought to press toward the mark rather than be content to follow in the tracks of others. (10.) For the man whose aim is to prove himself better than another, even if he does not surpass him, may hope to equal him. But he can never hope to equal him, if he thinks it his duty merely to tread in his footsteps: for the mere follower must always lag behind. Further, it is generally easier to make some advance than to repeat what has been done by others, since there is nothing harder than to produce an exact likeness, and nature herself has so far failed in this endeavor that there is always some difference which enables us to distinguish even the things which seem most like and most equal to one another. (11.) Again, whatever is like another object, must necessarily be inferior to the object of its imitation, just as the shadow is inferior to the substance, the portrait to the features which it portrays, and the acting of the player to the feelings which he endeavors to reproduce. The same is true of oratory. For the models which we select for imitation have a genuine and natural force, whereas all imitation is artificial and molded to a purpose which was not that of the original orator. (12.) This is the reason why declamations have less life and vigor than actual speeches, since the subject is fictitious in the one and real in the other. Again, the greatest qualities of the orator are beyond all imitation, by which I mean, talent, invention, force, facility and all the qualities which are independent of art. (13.) Consequently, there are many who, after excerpting certain words from published speeches or borrowing certain particular rhythms, think that they have produced a perfect copy of the works which they have read, despite the fact that words become obsolete or current with the lapse of years, the one sure standard being contemporary usage; and they are not good or bad in virtue of their inherent nature (for in themselves they are no more than mere sounds), but solely in virtue of the aptitude and propriety (or the reverse) with which they are arranged, while rhythmical composition must be adapted to the theme in hand and will derive its main charm from its variety.

(14.) Consequently the nicest judgment is required in the examination of everything connected with this department of study. First we must consider whom to imitate. For there are many who have shown a passionate desire to imitate the worst and most decadent authors. Secondly, we must consider what it is that we should set ourselves to imitate in the authors thus chosen. (15.) For even great authors have their blemishes, for which they have been censured by competent critics and have even reproached each other. I only wish that imitators were more likely to improve on the good things than to exaggerate the blemishes of the authors whom they seek to copy. And even those who have sufficient critical acumen to avoid the faults of their models will not find it sufficient to produce a copy of their merits, amounting to no more than a superficial resemblance, or rather recalling those sloughs which, according to Epicurus, are continually given off by material things. (16.) But this is just what happens to those who mold themselves on the first impressions derived from the style of their model, without devoting themselves to a thorough investigation of its good qualities, and, despite the brilliance of their imitation and the close resemblance of their language and rhythm, not only fail absolutely to attain the force of style and invention possessed by the original, but as a rule degenerate into something worse, and achieve merely those faults which are hardest to distinguish from virtues: they are turgid instead of grand, bald instead of concise, and rash instead of courageous, while extravagance takes the place of wealth, over-emphasis the place of harmony and negligence of simplicity. (17.) As a result, those who flaunt tasteless and insipid thoughts, couched in an uncouth and inharmonious form, think that they are the equals of the ancients; those who lack ornament and epigram, pose as Attic; those who darken their meaning by the abruptness with which they close their periods, count themselves the superiors of Sallust and Thucydides; those who are dreary and jejune, think that they are serious rivals to Pollio, while those who are tame and listless, if only they can produce long enough periods, swear that this is just the manner in which Cicero would have spoken. (18.) I have known some who thought that they had produced a brilliant imitation of the style of that divine orator, by ending their periods with the phrase *esse videatur*.[9] Consequently it is of the first importance that every student should realize what it is that he is to imitate, and should know why it is good.

(19.) The next step is for each student to consult his own powers when he shoulders his burden. For there are some things which, though capable of imitation, may be beyond the capacity of any given individual, either because his natural gifts are insufficient or of a different character. The man whose talent is for the plain style should not seek only what is bold and rugged, nor yet should he who has vigor without control suffer himself through love of subtlety at once to waste his natural energy and fail to attain the elegance at which he aims: for there is nothing so unbecoming as delicacy wedded to ruggedness. (20.) True, I did express the opinion that the instructor whose portrait I painted in my second book, should not confine himself to teaching those things for which he perceived his individual pupils to have most aptitude. For it is his further duty to foster whatever good qualities he may perceive in his pupils, to make good their deficiencies as far as may be, to correct their faults and turn them to better things. For he is the guide and director of the minds of others. It is a harder task to mold one's own nature. (21.) But not even our ideal teacher, however much he may desire that everything that is correct should prevail in his school to the fullest extent, will waste his labor in attempting to develop qualities to the attainment of which he perceives nature's gifts to be opposed.

It is also necessary to avoid the fault to which the majority of students are so prone, namely, the idea that in composing speeches we should imitate the poets and historians, and in writing history or poetry should copy orators and declaimers. (22.) Each branch of literature has its own laws and its own appropriate character. Comedy does not seek to increase its height by the buskin and tragedy does not wear the slipper of comedy. But all forms of eloquence have something in common, and it is to the imitation of this common element that our efforts should be confined.

(23.) There is a further fault to which those persons are liable who devote themselves entirely to the imitation of one particular style: if the rude vigor of some particular author takes their fancy, they cling to it even when the case on which they are engaged calls for an easy and flowing style; if, on the other hand, it is a simple or agreeable style that claims their devotion, they fail to meet the heavy demands of severe and weighty cases. For not only do cases differ in their general aspect, but one part of a case may differ from another, and some things require a gentle and others a violent style, some require an impetuous and others a calm diction, while in some cases it is necessary to instruct and in others to move the audience, in all these instances dissimilar and different methods being necessary. (24.) Consequently I should be reluctant even to advise a student to select one particular author to follow through thick and thin. Demosthenes is by far the most perfect of Greek orators, yet there are some things which others have said better in some contexts as against the many things which he has said better than others. But it does not follow that because we should select one author for special imitation, he should be our only model. (25.) What then? Is it not sufficient to model our every utterance on Cicero? For my own part, I should consider it sufficient, if I could always imitate him successfully. But what harm is there in occasionally borrowing the vigor of Caesar, the vehemence of Caelius, the precision of Pollio or the sound judgment of Calvus? (26.) For quite apart from the fact that a wise man should always, if possible, make whatever is best in each individual author his own, we shall find that, in view of the extreme difficulty of our subject, those who fix their eyes on one model only will always find some one quality which it is almost impossible to acquire therefrom. Consequently, since it is practically impossible for mortal powers to produce a perfect and complete copy of any one chosen author, we shall do well to keep a number of different excellences before our eyes, so that different qualities from different authors may impress themselves on our minds, to be adopted for use in the place that becomes them best.

(27.) But imitation (for I must repeat this point again and again) should not be confined merely to words. We must consider the appropriateness with which those orators handle the circumstances and persons involved in the various cases in which they were engaged, and observe the judgment and powers of arrangement which they reveal, and the manner in which everything they say, not excepting those portions of their speeches which seem designed merely to delight their audience, is concentrated on securing the victory over their opponents. We must note their procedure in the exordium, the method and variety of their statement of facts, the power displayed in proof and refutation, the skill revealed in their appeal to every kind of emotion, and the manner in which they make use of popular applause to serve their case, applause which is most honorable when it is spontaneous and not deliberately courted. If we have thoroughly appreciated all these points, we shall be able to imitate our models with accuracy. (28.) But the man who to these good qualities adds his own, that is to say, who makes good deficiencies and cuts down whatever is redundant, will be the perfect orator of our search; and it is now above all times that such perfection should be attained when there are before us so many more models of oratorical excellence than were available for those who have thus far achieved the highest success. For this glory also shall be theirs, that men shall say of them that while they surpassed their predecessors, they also taught those who came after.

"LONGINUS"

(1st century A.D.?)

INTRODUCTION

The actual authorship and date of *On Sublimity* are in doubt. Because the name "Longinus" appears in the manuscript attributions of authorship, scholars originally accorded the work to Cassius Longinus, a writer of the third century A.D. More careful scrutiny of the manuscripts later showed, however, that the name is actually given at one point as "Dionysius Longinus" and at another point as "Dionysius" *or* "Longinus." No such critic as Dionysius Longinus is known to us, and it seems probable that the original attribution to "Dionysius" or "Longinus" was a guess by Byzantine scholars, who, uncertain of the author's identity, thought it likely that he was either Dionysius of Halicarnassus, the famous critic of the first century A.D., or the third-century Cassius Longinus.

Modern scholars have adduced two major arguments against third-century authorship. First, there are no references in the treatise to literature written after the first century A.D.—and the absence of such references in a well informed third-century critical work would be quite surprising. Second, *On Sublimity* explores themes commonly discussed in the first century, and it involves an explicit refutation of the work of a first-century critic, Caecilius. Contemporary scholars thus ascribe the work to a perceptive first-century critic whom they continue to call "Longinus," although for all practical purposes he is anonymous. Some scholars conclude from the reference to Genesis (Chapter 9) that "Longinus" was a Greek with both Roman and Jewish contacts, but no certain biographical knowledge is possible.

The work as we have it is fragmentary, with perhaps one-third missing from various parts of the treatise. One principal manuscript exists, the tenth-century Paris 2036; a number of other manuscripts, deriving from this source, come from the fifteenth and sixteenth centuries. In addition to its lacunae, the Greek text offers certain difficulties of interpretation for editors and translators, but the general line of argument is quite clear.

On Sublimity is a kind of textbook for prospective orators; its title, *Peri Hypsous,* can also be rendered as "On the High Style," referring primarily to the art of rhetoric. Nevertheless, the treatise has a valid claim to honor as a document in literary criticism: "Longinus" is concerned with a profundity of thought and an excellence of high technique which overlap the area of literary art. Moreover, he does not hesitate to recommend passages of poetry as examples of the sublimity that the orator should strive for.

To assist in introducing his topic and to conclude his general argument, "Longinus" relies on a method of negative development. Chapters 3–5 treat stylistic vices (e. g., bombast) which constitute a *false* sublime. Chapters 41–43 return to this issue in more detail, and the treatise then closes with an analysis of what "Longinus" perceives as a decline of sublimity in his own day. The sublimity that "Longinus" discusses in this final chapter is emphatically moral, not merely a rhetorical quality. The force of his concluding remarks serves in fact to characterize his general critical approach: a consideration of *style* as a bridge between the aesthetic and the ethical modes of criticism.

This general intent seems to be confirmed in "Longinus' " positive development of his topic: his description of the effects of the sublime, and his investigation of the sources of the sublime. The main effect of the sublime, according to "Longinus," is neither persuasion nor pleasure, but an intense experience of "transport" (*ecstasis*). The audience is carried out of itself, entranced by a stylistic power which reveals itself like a flash of lightning (Chapter 1). But "Longinus" insists that the sublime is no mere wave of sentimentality. It produces a controlled kind of ecstasy, depending largely on diction and imagery that are precise, not vague. "Transport" is no momentary emotional thrill, but a significant psychological experience that is capable of being sustained. And perhaps most importantly, it has serious ethical implications—e.g., the disposing of the mind to "lofty ideas" (Chapter 7).

"Longinus" now passes to the central section of his treatise (Chapters 8–40), an exploration of five major sources of the sublime. Two of these (*noesis* and *pathos*) are qualities which the orator or poet must possess "by nature," and three are technical skills (competence in rhetorical figures, diction, and arrangement of words) which can be studied and developed.

Noesis, the first innate quality, is a power of "great intellectual conception," by which the artist is able to frame thoughts that are awe-inspiring in themselves (as exemplified in many passages from Homer, or in the opening of Genesis). But "Longinus" also elucidates *noesis* in a much broader sense. First, he stresses its ethical implications: sublime thoughts are possible only to an artist whose nature is itself sublime, who possesses true "nobility of soul." Thus *noesis* connotes not only a powerful intellect, but an essential high-mindedness. Second, "Longinus" seems to subsume under *noesis* various elements of rhetorical and poetic craft that unify the finished work and imbue it with telling detail and appropriateness of tone (Chapters 10–15): the artist's inherent skill at selection and organization, amplification, emulation of great works, and vivid representation.

To illustrate how selection and organization of material contribute to the achievement of the sublime, "Longinus" comments perceptively on the famous ode of Sappho which deals with the tormenting emotions of love. He shows how Sappho skillfully selected the essential details and unified them to create an intense effect. He concludes that in this poem, and in all other works of similar excellence, nothing irrelevant or inappropriate weakens or clashes with the poet's intention.

This discussion of selection and arrangement leads "Longinus" to a consideration of the proper amplification of material. The term "amplification" (*auxesis*) pertains to the theory of rhetoric, and it was used by earlier writers to refer to quantitative elaboration, the "piling up" of details to support an argumentative point. "Longinus" explicitly rejects this definition. Although his discussion is interrupted by a lacuna in the text, he seems to be aiming at a definition predicated on quality rather than quantity, a concept of amplification as relevant to poetry as to rhetoric. The sublime can be achieved through the artist's inherent skill at using small details, but the avoidance of redundancy is essential. In an eloquent passage "Longinus" compares the widely divergent but equally effective skills of Demosthenes and Cicero, both successful at "elevated" amplification.

Still another aspect of *noesis* is the artist's talent for "imitation" (*mimesis*) of other great writers. The sublime can often be attained if the artist judiciously attempts to emulate the way that Homer, Plato, or Demosthenes would have expressed a thought. Using such spiritual models, the artist tends to rise to their level—and perhaps even to participate in their visions, much as the priestess at Delphi became the inspired and possessed instrument of the will of Apollo himself. Clearly no mere "copying" is involved; instead, the process encourages the raising of oneself to the level of the sublime thought and expression that characterizes great human beings.

The artist's inherent talent for vivid representation (*phantasia*) is one of the most important aspects of *noesis*. Indeed, a major difference between sublimity and mere bombast is the presence in a poem or speech of precise, evocative images. To startle, move, and uplift his audience, the artist must be able to utilize imagery as a medium. (In one sense, "Longinus' " argument anticipates modern notions of an "objective correlative.")

The text of *On Sublimity* includes only a brief treatment (in Chapter 8) of *pathos,* the second innate quality of the successful artist. Yet several of "Longinus' " other discussions—e.g., his analysis of Sappho's ode—have significant implications for this topic. By *pathos* "Longinus" means the artist's capacity for strong and inspired emotion. He asserts that an emotional "gust" in a speech or poem can be an invaluable aid in the quest for sublimity, but he also implies that this power is to be tempered by *noesis,* that the ideal artist maintains the two faculties in delicate conjunction. In fact, one classical scholar has recently suggested that this aspect of "Longinus'" theory approximates T. S. Eliot's concept of the ideal artist's "unified sensibility."[1]

The concepts of *noesis* and *pathos* continue to underlie "Longinus'" thinking even after he turns (in Chapter 16) to a lengthy discussion of stylistic skills that the prospective artist can consciously study and practice. In analyzing the contribution to sublimity made by various devices of style, "Longinus" usually speaks in terms of their emotional appeal, but he often warns against excess and asserts the need for intellectual control. He proceeds to elucidate the use of such devices as oaths, rhetorical questions, asyndeton (lack of connectives between words and phrases), anaphora (repetition), hyperbaton (abnormal sequence of words and thoughts), the imaginary second person, and periphrasis. In these chapters "Longinus'" technical explanations are fairly traditional, but his true quality as a critic shows forth in his brilliant analyses of the excellence of the passages he chooses for illustration. His discussion of the intellectual and emotional connotations of the oath in Demosthenes' *On the Crown* (Chapter 16) is representative of his best critical technique.

"Longinus'" technical analysis is interrupted in Chapters 33–37. Here he poses a question of great importance in criticism, and his answer extends and clarifies his own philosophy of the sublime. "Longinus" asks whether a poet who has no great virtues but makes no technical errors is superior to one who displays genius but commits errors as well. Would one rather be Homer who occasionally nods amidst much overwhelming greatness, or Apollonius of Rhodes who makes no technical mistakes but never sounds the note of genius? For "Longinus" sublimity is manifestly a product of genius: it cannot be subverted by any quantity of minor errors, and it cannot be achieved by any quantity of mere technical skills. In a passage of surpassing eloquence "Longinus" envisions mankind as having been created by nature to be spectators of the awesome magnificence of the universe. Whenever the grandeur and transcendent beauty of this universe is expressed successfully in art, the sublime is achieved. Such an artistic symbolization of cosmic magnificence is grandly unaffected by the existence of minor technical errors.

"Longinus'" treatise has enjoyed a wide influence in post-Renaissance literary criticism. Popularized by Boileau's translation in 1674, *On the Sublime* became a key document in the critical syntheses of the neoclassical age. It served partly as a necessary supplement to Horace's *Ars Poetica*, "Longinus'" stirring affirmation of "sublimity" balancing Horace's more conservative insistence on "decorum." Alexander Pope in his *Essay on Criticism* (1709) asserted that the great poets were able to "snatch a grace beyond the reach of art," and he praised "Longinus" as a critic "Whose own example strengthens all his laws,/ And is himself the great Sublime he draws." Joseph Addison's *Spectator* essays on *Paradise Lost* (1711–12) relied explicitly on "Longinus" for a critical rationale: according to Addison, the grandeur and sweep of Milton's epic, its essential "sublimity," rendered irrelevant any violation of traditional rules.

The increased influence of *On Sublimity* in eighteenth-century criticism was in part a prefiguration of romantic poetics.[2] In the philosophical treatises on sublimity presented by Edmund Burke and Immanuel Kant, "Longinus' " remarks became the starting point for new idealist philosophies. More significantly, "Longinus' " emphasis on the personality of the artist, especially in regard to inspiration and "genius," helped to prepare for the critical orientation of the major German and British romantics. Ironically, however, most nineteenth-century romantics tended to neglect "Longinus," apparently with the feeling that his outlook was too elementary.[3]

In the modern era, however, the influence of *On Sublimity* has been diverse. Matthew Arnold used "Longinus' " method in "The Study of Poetry" (1880), attempting to define a quality of greatness in literature by isolating eleven short passages as "touchstones," their beauty to be recognized by a flash of insight rather than by rigorous analysis. Carl Jung used the notion of *ecstasis* in 1925 to describe man's aesthetic encounter with the world of archetypal images: "No wonder, then, that at the moment when a typical situation occurs, we feel suddenly aware of an extraordinary release, as though transported, or caught up by an overwhelming power. At such moments we are no longer individuals, but the race: the voice of all mankind resounds in us."[4] Northrop Frye has used *ecstasis* as a companion concept to Aristole's *katharsis*: works of literature may be tentatively categorized according to which of the two responses they encourage.[5]

"Longinus' " greatest influence in modern criticism has been in the area of stylistics. The American "new critics," in particular, have returned to Longinian co-ordinates of criticism; according to Allen Tate, "Longinus' " great relevance derives from the fact that he "implicitly claims for Thought and Diction, two of the nonstructural elements in Aristotle's analysis of tragedy, a degree of objectivity that Aristotle's rhetorical view of poetic language could not include."[6] Significantly, the neo-Aristotelian "Chicago critics" have found "Longinus" to be one of the very few thinkers other than Aristotle himself whose outlook is compatible with theirs, and they have occasionally attempted to balance a sense of Aristotelian "structure" with a sense of Longinian "style," especially in trying to come to terms with lyric poetry.[7]

In both the range and depth of his influence, then, the anonymous rhetorician who wrote *Peri Hypsous* continues as a major force in Western criticism.

The text which follows (and most of the notes) are from D. A. Russell, tr. "Longinus," *On Sublimity* (Oxford: Clarendon Press, 1965) and reprinted by permission of the publisher.

ON SUBLIMITY

PREFACE

(I.1.) You will recall, my dear Postumius Terentianus, that when we were reading together Caecilius' monograph *On Sublimity*, we felt that it was inadequate to its high subject, and failed to touch the essential points. Nor indeed did it appear to offer the reader much practical help, and this ought to be a writer's principal object. Two things are required of any text-book: first, that it should explain what its subject is; second, and more important, that it should explain how and by what methods we can achieve it. Caecilius tries at immense length to explain to us what sort of thing "the sublime" is, as though we did not know; but he has somehow passed over as unnecessary the question how we can develop our nature to some degree of greatness. (2.) However, we ought perhaps not so much to blame our author for what he has left out as to commend him for his originality and enthusiasm. You have urged me to set down a few notes on sublimity for your own use. Let us then consider whether there is anything in my observations which may be thought useful to public men. You must help me, my friend, by giving your honest opinion in detail, as both your natural candor and your friendship with me require. It was well said that what man has in common with the gods is "doing good and telling the truth." (3.) Your own wide culture dispenses me from any long preliminary definition. Sublimity is a kind of eminence or excellence of discourse. It is the source of the distinction of the very greatest poets and prose writers and the means by which they have given eternal life to their own fame. (4.) For grandeur produces ecstacy rather than persuasion in the hearer; and the combination of wonder and astonishment always proves superior to the merely persuasive and pleasant. This is because persuasion is on the whole something we can control, whereas amazement and wonder exert invincible power and force and get the better of every hearer. Experience in invention and ability to order and arrange material cannot be detected in single passages; we begin to appreciate them only when we see the whole context. Sublimity, on the other hand, produced at the right moment, tears everything up like a whirlwind, and exhibits the orator's whole power at a single blow.

(II.1.) Your own experience will lead you to these and similar considerations. The question from which I must begin is whether there is in fact an art of sublimity or profundity.[1] Some people think it is a complete mistake to reduce things like this to technical rules. Greatness, the argument runs, is a natural product, and does not come by teaching. The only art is to be born like that. They believe moreover that natural products are very much weakened by being reduced to the bare bones of a textbook. (2.) In my view, these arguments can be refuted by considering three points: (i) Though nature is on the whole a law unto herself in matters of emotion and elevation, she is not a random force and does not work altogether without method. (ii) She is herself in every instance a first and primary element of creation, but it is method that is competent to provide and contribute quantities and appropriate occasions for everything, as well as perfect correctness in training and application. (iii) Grandeur is particularly dangerous when left on its own, unaccompanied by knowledge, unsteadied, unballasted, abandoned to mere impulse and ignorant temerity. It often needs the curb as well as the spur.

(3.) What Demosthenes[2] said of life in general is true also of literature: good fortune is the greatest of blessings, but good counsel comes next, and the lack of it destroys the other also. In literature, nature occupies the place of good fortune, art that of good counsel. Most important of all, the very fact that some things in literature depend on nature alone can itself be learned only from art. If the critic of students of this subject will bear these points in mind, he will, I believe, come to realize that the examination of the question before us is by no means useless or superfluous. [Lacuna equivalent to about three printed pages]

FAULTS INCIDENT TO THE EFFORT TO ACHIEVE SUBLIMITY: TURGIDITY, PUERILITY, FALSE EMOTION, FRIGIDITY

(III.1.) . . . restrain the oven's mighty glow.
For if I see but one beside his hearth,
I'll thrust in just one tentacle of storm,
And fire his roof and turn it all to cinders.
I've not yet sung my proper song.[3]

This is not tragedy; it is a parody of the tragic manner—tentacles, vomiting to heaven, making Boreas a flute-player, and so on. The result is not impressiveness but turbid diction and confused imagery. If you examine the details closely, they gradually sink from the terrifying to the contemptible.

Now if untimely turgidity is unpardonable in tragedy, a genre which is naturally magniloquent and tolerant of bombast, it will scarcely be appropriate in writing which has to do with real life. (2.) Hence the ridicule attaching to Gorgias of Leontini's "Xerxes, the Persians' Zeus" and "their living tombs, the vultures," or to various things in Callisthenes, where he has not so much risen to heights as been carried off his feet. Clitarchus is an even more striking example; he is an inflated writer, and, as Sophocles has it, "Blows at his tiny flute, the mouth-band off."[4] Amphicrates, Hegesias, Matris—they are all the same. They often fancy themselves possessed when they are merely playing the fool. (3.) Turgidity is a particularly hard fault to avoid, for it is one to which all who aim at greatness naturally incline, because they seek to escape the charge of weakness and aridity. They act on the principle that "to slip from a great prize is yet a noble fault." (4.) In literature as in the body, puffy and false tumors are bad, and may well bring us to the opposite result from that which we expected. As the saying goes, there is nothing so dry as a man with dropsy. While turgidity is an endeavor to go above the sublime, puerility is the sheer opposite of greatness; it is a thoroughly low, mean and ignoble vice. What do I mean by "puerility"? A pedantic thought, so over-worked that it ends in frigidity. Writers slip into it through aiming at originality, artifice, and (above all) charm, and then coming to grief on the rocks of tawdriness and affection.

(5.) A third kind of fault—what Theodorus called "the pseudo-bacchanalian" —corresponds to these in the field of emotion. It consists of untimely or mean-ingless emotion where none is in place, or immoderate emotion where moderate is in place. Some people often get carried away, like drunkards, into emotions unconnected with the subject, which are simply their own pedantic inven-tion. The audience feels nothing, so that they inevitably make an exhibition of themselves, parading their ecstasies before an audience which does not share them.

(IV.1.) But I reserve the subject of emotion for another place,[5] returning meanwhile to the second fault of those I mentioned: frigidity. This is a constant feature in Timaeus, who is in many ways a competent writer, not without the capacity for greatness on occasion, learned and original, but as unconscious of his own faults as he is censorious of others', and often falling into the grossest child-ishness through his passion for always starting exotic ideas. (2.) I will give one or two examples; Caecilius has already cited most of those available. (i) In praise of Alexander the Great, Timaeus writes: "He conquered all Asia in fewer years than it took Isocrates to write the *Panegyricus* to advocate the Persian war." What a splendid comparison this is—the Macedonian king and the sophist! On the same principle, the Lacedaemonians were very much less brave than Isocrates: it took them thirty years to capture Messene,[6] whereas he took only ten to write the *Panegyricus*! (3.) (ii) Listen also to Timaeus' comment on the Athenians captured in Sicily. "They were punished for their impiety to Hermes and mutila-tion of his statues, and the main agent of their punishment was one who had a family connection with their victim, Hermocrates the son of Hermon." I cannot help wondering, my dear Terentianus, why he does not also write about the tyrant Dionysius, "Because he was impious towards Zeus and Heracles, Dion and Heraclides robbed him of his throne."[7] (4.) But why speak of Timaeus, when those heroes of letters, Xenophon and Plato, for all that they were trained in Socrates' school, forget themselves sometimes for the sake of similar petty pleasures? Thus Xenophon writes in *The Constitution of the Lacedaemonians:* "You could hear their voice less than the voice of stone statues, you could distract their eyes less than the eyes of bronze images; you would think them more bashful than the very maidens in the eyes."[8] It would have been more in keeping with Amphicrates' manner than Xenophon's to speak of the pupils of our eyes as bashful maidens. And what an absurd misconception to think of everybody's pupils as bashful! The shamelessness of a person, we are told, appears nowhere so plainly as in the eyes. Remember the words Achilles used to revile Agamemnon's violent temper: "Drunken sot, with a dog's *eyes!*"[9] (5.) Timaeus, unable to keep his hands off stolen property, as it were, has not left the monopoly of this frigid conceit to Xenophon. He uses it in connection with Agathocles, who eloped with his cousin from the unveiling ceremony of her marriage to another: "Who would have done this, if he had not had harlots in his eyes for pupils (*koras*)?"[10]

(6.) Now here is Plato, the otherwise divine Plato. He wants to express the idea of writing-tablets. "They shall write," he says, "and deposit in the temples memorials of cypress."[11] Again: "As for walls, Megillus, I should concur with Sparta in letting walls sleep in the earth and not get up."[12] (7.) Herodotus' description[13] of beautiful women as "pains on the eyes" is the same sort of thing, though it is to some extent excused by the fact that the speakers are barbarians and drunk—not that it is a good thing to make an exhibition of the triviality of one's mind to posterity, even through the mouths of characters like these.

(V.) All such lapses from dignity arise in literature through a single cause: that desire for novelty of thought which is all the rage today. Evils often come from the same source as blessings; and so, since beauty of style, sublimity, and charm all conduce to successful writing, they are also causes and principles not only of success but of failure. Variation, hyperbole, and the use of plural for singular are like this too; I shall explain below the dangers which they involve.[14]

SOME MARKS OF TRUE SUBLIMITY

At this stage, the question we must put to ourselves for discussion is how to avoid the faults which are so much tied up with sublimity. (VI.) The answer, my friend, is: by first of all achieving a genuine understanding and appreciation of true sublimity. This is difficult; literary judgment comes only as the final product of long experience. However, for the purposes of instruction, I think we can say that an understanding of all this can be acquired. I approach the problem in this way:

(VII.1.) In ordinary life, nothing is truly great which it is great to despise; wealth, honor, reputation, absolute power—anything in short which has a lot of external trappings—can never seem supremely good to the wise man; because it is no small good to despise them. People who could have these advantages if they chose but disdain them out of magnanimity are admired much more than those who actually possess them. It is much the same with elevation in poetry and literature generally. We have to ask ourselves whether any particular example does not give a show of grandeur which, for all its accidental trappings, will, when dissected, prove vain and hollow, the kind of thing which it does a man more honor to despise than to admire. (2.) It is our nature to be elevated and exalted by true sublimity. Filled with joy and pride, we come to believe we have created what we have only heard. (3.) When a man of sense and literary experience hears something many times over, and it fails to dispose his mind to greatness or to leave him with more to reflect upon than was contained in the mere words, but comes instead to seem valueless on repeated inspection, this is not true sublimity: it endures only for the moment of hearing. Real sublimity contains much food for reflection, is difficult or rather impossible to resist, and makes a strong and ineffaceable impression on the memory. (4.) In a word, reckon those things which please everybody all the time as genuinely and finely sublime. When people of different training, way of life, tastes, age, and manners all agree about something, the judgment and assent, as it were, of so many distinct voices lends strength and irrefutability to the conviction that their admiration is rightly directed.

THE FIVE SOURCES OF SUBLIMITY; THE PLAN OF THE BOOK

(VIII.1.) There are, one may say, five most productive sources of sublimity. (Competence in speaking is assumed as a common foundation for all five; nothing is possible without it.) (i) The first and most important is the power to conceive great thoughts; I defined this in my work on Xenophon. (ii) The second is strong and inspired emotion. (These two sources are for the most part natural; the remaining three involve art.) (iii) Certain kinds of figures. (These may be divided into figures of thought and figures of speech.) (iv) Noble diction. This has as subdivisions choice of words and the use of metaphorical and artificial language.[15] (v) Finally, to round off the whole list, dignified and elevated word-arrangement.[16] Let us now examine the points which come under each of these heads. I must first observe, however, that Caecilius has omitted some of the five—emotion, for example. (2.) Now if he thought that sublimity and emotion were one and the same thing and always existed and developed together, he was wrong. Some emotions, such as pity, grief, and fear, are found divorced from sublimity and with a low effect. Conversely, sublimity often occurs apart from emotion. Of the innumerable examples of this I select Homer's bold account of the Aloadae: "Ossa upon Olympus they sought to heap; and on Ossa/Pelion with its shaking forest, to make a path to heaven—" and the even more impressive sequel—"And they would have finished their work. . . ."[17] (3.) In orators, encomia and ceremonial or exhibition pieces always involve grandeur and sub-limity, though they are generally devoid of emotion. Hence those orators who are best at conveying emotion are least good at encomia, and conversely the experts at encomia are not conveyors of emotion. (4.) On the other hand, if Caecilius thought that emotion had no contribution to make to sublimity and therefore thought it not worth mentioning, he was again completely wrong. I should myself have no hesitation in saying that there is nothing so productive of grandeur as noble emotion in the right place. It inspires and possesses our words with a kind of madness and divine spirit.

GREATNESS OF THOUGHT

(IX.1.) The first source, natural greatness, is the most important. Even if it is a matter of endowment rather than acquisition, we must, so far as possible, develop our minds in the direction of greatness and make them always pregnant with noble thoughts. (2.) You ask how this can be done. I wrote elsewhere something like this: "sublimity is the echo of a noble mind." This is why a mere idea, with-out verbal expression, is sometimes admired for its nobility—just as Ajax's silence in the Vision of the Dead is grand and indeed more sublime than any words could have been.[18] (3.) First then we must state what sublimity comes from: the orator must not have low or ignoble thoughts. Those whose thoughts and habits all their lives are trivial and servile cannot possibly produce anything ad-mirable or worthy of eternity. Words will be great if thoughts are weighty. (4.) This is why splendid remarks come naturally to the proud; the man who, when Parmenio said, "I should have been content". . . .[19] [Lacuna equivalent to about nine pages]

SUCCESSFUL AND UNSUCCESSFUL WAYS OF REPRESENTING SUPERNATURAL BEINGS AND OF EXCITING AWE

. . . the interval between earth and heaven. (5.) One might say that this is the measure not so much of strife as of Homer.[20] Contrast the line about Darkness in Hesiod—if the *Shield* is by Hesiod: "Mucus dripped from her nostrils."[21] This gives a repulsive picture, not one to excite awe. But how does Homer magnify the divine power? "As far as a man can peer through the mist,/Sitting on watch, look-ing over the wine-dark sea,/So long is the stride of the gods' thundering horses."[22] He uses a cosmic distance to measure this speed. This enormously im-pressive image would make anybody say, and with reason that, if the horses of the gods took two strides like that, they would find there was not enough room

in the world. (6.) The imaginative pictures in the Battle of the Gods are also
very remarkable:

> And the great heavens and Olympus trumpeted
>   around them.
> Aïdoneus, lord of the dead, was frightened in his
>   depths;
> And in fright he jumped from his throne, and shouted,
> For fear the earth-shaker Poseidon might break
>   through the ground,
> And gods and men might see
> The foul and terrible halls, which even the gods
>   detest.[32]

Do you see how the earth is torn from its foundations, Tartarus laid bare, and
the whole universe overthrown and broken up, so that all things—Heaven and
Hell, things mortal and things immortal—war together and are at risk together
in that ancient battle? (7.) But, terrifying as all this is, it is blasphemous and
indecent unless it is interpreted allegorically; in relating the gods' wounds, quarrels, revenges, tears, imprisonments, and manifold misfortunes, Homer, as it
seems to me, has done his best to make the men of the Trojan war gods, and the
gods men. If men are unhappy, there is always death as a harbor in trouble; what
he has done for his gods is to make them immortal indeed, but immortally miserable.

(8.) Much better than the Battle of the Gods are the passages which represent
divinity as genuinely unsoiled and great and pure. The lines about Poseidon,
much discussed by my predecessors, exemplify this:

> The high hills and the forest trembled,
> And the peaks and the city of Troy and the Achaean
>   ships
> Under the immortal feet of Poseidon as he went his
>   way.
> He drove over the waves, and the sea-monsters gam-
>   bolled around him,
> Coming up everywhere out of the deep; they recog-
>   nized their king.
> The sea parted in joy; and the horses flew onward.[24]

(9.) Similarly, the lawgiver of the Jews, no ordinary man—for he understood
and expressed God's power in accordance with its worth—writes at the beginning
of his *Laws*: "God said"—now what?—" 'Let there be light,' and there was light;
'Let there be earth,' and there was earth."[25]

(10.) Perhaps it will not be out of place, my friend, if I add a further Homeric
example—from the human sphere this time—so that we can see how the poet

is accustomed to enter into the greatness of his heroes. Darkness falls suddenly. Thickest night blinds the Greek army. Ajax is bewildered. "O Father Zeus," he cries, "Deliver the sons of the Achaeans out of the mist,/Make the sky clear, and let us see;/In the light—kill us."[26] The feeling here is genuinely Ajax's. He does not pray for life—that would be a request unworthy of a hero—but having no good use for his courage in the paralyzing darkness, and so angered at his inactivity in the battle, he asks for light, and quickly: he will at all costs find a shroud worthy of his valor, though Zeus be arrayed against him.

COMPARISON BETWEEN THE ILIAD AND THE ODYSSEY

(11.) In this passage, it is the real Homer, the gale of whose genius fans the excitement of battle; the poet "Rages like Ares, spear-brandishing, or the deadly fire/Raging in the mountains, in the thickets of the deep wood./Foam shows at his mouth."[27] In the *Odyssey*, on the other hand—and there are many reasons for adding this to our inquiry—he demonstrates that when a great mind begins to decline, a love of story-telling characterizes its old age. (12.) We can tell that the *Odyssey* was his second work from various considerations, in particular from his insertion of the residue of the Trojan troubles in the poem in the form of episodes, and the way in which he pays tribute of lamentation and pity to the heroes, treating them as persons long known. The *Odyssey* is simply an epilogue to the *Iliad*: "There lies warlike Ajax, there Achilles,/There Patroclus, the gods' peer as a counsellor,/And there my own dear son."[28] (13.) For the same reason, I maintain, he made the whole body of the *Iliad*, which was written at the height of his powers, dramatic and exciting, whereas most of the *Odyssey* consists of narrative, which is a characteristic of old age. Homer in the *Odyssey* may be compared to the setting sun: the size remains without the force. He no longer sustains the tension as it was in the tale of Troy, nor the consistent level of elevation which never admitted any falling off. The outpouring of passions crowding one or another has gone; so has the versatility, the realism, the abundance of imagery taken from the life. We see greatness on the ebb. It is as though the Ocean were withdrawing into itself and flowing quietly in its own bed. Homer is lost in the realm of the fabulous and incredible. (14.) In saying this, I have not forgotten the storms in the *Odyssey*, the story of Cyclops, and a few other episodes; I am speaking of old age—but it is the old age of a Homer. The point about all these stories is that the mythical element in them predominates over the realistic.

I digressed into this topic, as I said, to illustrate how easy it is for great genius to be perverted in decline into nonsense. I mean things like the story of the wineskin, the tale of the men kept as pigs in Circe's palace ("howling piglets," Zoilus called them), the feeding of Zeus by the doves (as though he were a chick in the nest), the ten days on the raft without food, and the improbabilities of the murder of the suitors.[29] What can we say of all this but that it really is "the dreaming of a Zeus"? (15.) There is also a second reason for discussing the *Odyssey*. I want you to understand that the decline of emotional power in great writers and poets turns to a capacity for depicting manners. The realistic description of Odysseus' household forms a kind of comedy of manners.

SELECTION AND ORGANIZATION OF MATERIAL

(X.1.) Now have we any other means of making our writing sublime? Every topic naturally includes certain elements which are inherent in its raw material. It follows that sublimity will be achieved if we consistently select the most important of these inherent features and learn to organize them as a unity by combining one with another. The first of these procedures attracts the reader by the selection of details, the second by the compression of those selected.

Consider Sappho's treatment of the feelings involved in the madness of being in love. She uses the attendant circumstances and draws on real life at every point. And in what does she show her quality? In her skill in selecting the outstanding details and making a unity of them:

> (2.) To me he seems a peer of the gods, the man who sits facing
>   you and hears your sweet voice
> And lovely laughter; it flutters my heart in my breast.
> When I see you only for a moment, I cannot speak;
>   My tongue is broken, a subtle fire runs under my skin; my
> eyes cannot see, my ears hum;
>   Cold sweat pours off me; shivering grips me all over; I am
> paler than grass; I seem near to dying;
>   But all must be endured. . . .[30]

(3.) Do you not admire the way in which she brings everything together—mind and body, hearing and tongue, eyes and skin? She seems to have lost them all, and to be looking for them as though they were external to her. She is cold and hot, mad and sane, frightened and near death, all by turns. The result is that we see in her not a single emotion, but a complex of emotions. Lovers experience all this; Sappho's excellence, as I have said, lies in her adoption and combination of the most striking details.

A similar point can be made about the descriptions of storms in Homer who always picks out the most terrifying aspects. (4.) The author of the *Arimaspea* on the other hand expects these lines to excite terror:

> This too is a great wonder to us in our hearts:
> There are men living on water, far from land, on the deep sea:
> Miserable they are, for hard is their lot;

They give their eyes to the stars, their lives to the sea;
Often they raise their hands in prayer to the gods,
As their bowels heave in pain.[31]

Anyone can see that this is more polished than awe-inspiring. (5.) Now compare it with Homer (I select one example out of many):

He fell upon them as upon a swift ship falls a wave,
Huge, wind-reared by the clouds. The ship
Is curtained in foam, a hideous blast of wind
Roars in the sail. The sailors shudder in terror:
They being carried away from under death, but only just.[32]

(6.) Aratus rtied to transfer the same thought: "A little plank wards off Hades."[33] But this is smooth and unimpressive, not frightening. Moreover, by saying "a plank wards off Hades," he has got rid of the danger. The plank *does* keep death away. Homer, on the other hand, does not banish the cause of fear at a stroke; he gives a vivid picture of men, one might almost say, facing death many times for every wave that comes. Notice also the forced combination of naturally uncompoundable prepositions: *hupek*, "away from under." Homer has tortured the words to correspond with the emotion of the moment, and expressed the emotion magnificently by thus crushing words together. He has in effect stamped the special character of the danger on the diction: "they are being carried away from under death."

(7.) Compare Archilochus on the shipwreck, and Demosthenes on the arrival of the news ("It was evening . . .").[34] In short, one might say that these writers have taken only the very best pieces, polished them up and fitted them together. They have inserted nothing inflated, undignified, or pedantic. Such things ruin the whole effect, because they produce, as it were, gaps or crevices, and so spoil the impressive thoughts which have been built into a structure whose cohesion depends upon their mutual relations.

AMPLIFICATION

(XI.1.) The quality called "amplification" is connected with those we have been considering. It is found when the facts or the issues at stake allow many starts and pauses in each section. You wheel up one impressive unit after another to give a series of increasing importance. (2.) There are innumerable varieties of amplification: it may be produced by commonplaces, by exaggeration or intensification of facts or arguments, or by a build-up of action or emotion. The orator should realize, however, that none of these will have its full effect without sublimity. Passages expressing pity or disparagement are no doubt an exception; but in any other instance of amplification, if you take away the sublime element, you take the soul away from the body. Without the strengthening influence of the sublimity, the effective element in the whole loses all its vigor and solidity. (3.) What is the difference between this precept and the point made above about the inclusion of vital details and their combination in a unity? What in general is the difference between amplification and sublimity? I must define my position briefly on these points, in order to make myself clear.

(XII.1.) I do not feel satisfied with the definition given by the rhetoricians: "amplification is expression which adds grandeur to its subject." This might just as well be a definition of sublimity or emotion or tropes. All these add grandeur of some kind. The difference lies, in my opinion, in the fact that sublimity depends on elevation, whereas amplification involves extension; sublimity exists often in a single thought, amplification cannot exist without a certain quantity and superfluity. (2.) To give a general definition, amplification is an aggregation of all the details and topics which constitute a situation, strengthening the argument by dwelling on it; it differs from proof in that the latter demonstrates the point made. . . . [Lacuna equivalent to about three pages]

SAME GENERAL SUBJECT CONTINUED: A COMPARISON BETWEEN PLATO AND DEMOSTHENES, WITH A WORD ON CICERO

(3.) . . . spreads out richly in many directions into an open sea of grandeur. Accordingly, Demosthenes, the more emotional of the two, displays in abundance the fire and heat of passion, while Plato, consistently magnificent, solemn and grand, is much less intense—without of course being in the least frigid. (4.) These seem to me, my dear Terentianus—if a Greek is allowed an opinion—to be also the differences between the grandeur of Cicero and the grandeur of Demosthenes. Demosthenes has an abrupt sublimity; Cicero spreads himself. Demosthenes burns and ravages; he has violence, rapidity, strength and force, and shows them in everything; he can be compared to a thunderbolt or a flash of lightning. Cicero, on the other hand, is like a spreading conflagration. He ranges everywhere and rolls majestically on. His huge fires endure; they are renewed in various forms from time to time and repeatedly fed with fresh fuel.—(5.) But this is a comparison which your countrymen can make better than I. Anyway, the place for the intense, Demosthenic kind of sublimity is in indignant exaggeration, the violent emotion, and in general wherever the hearer has to be struck with amazement. The place for expansiveness is where he has to be deluged with words. This treatment is appropriate in *loci communes,* epilogues, digressions, all descriptive and exhibition pieces, historical or scientific topics, and many other departments.

(XIII.1.) To return to Plato, and the way in which he combines the "soundless flow"[35] of his smooth style with grandeur. A passage you have read in the

Republic[36] makes the point: "Men without experience of wisdom and virtue and always occupied with feasting and that kind of thing naturally go downhill and wander through life on a low plane of existence. They never look upwards to the truth and never rise, they never taste certain or pure pleasure. Like cattle, they always look down, bowed earthwards and tablewards; they feed and they breed, and their greediness in these directions makes them kick and butt till they kill one another with iron horns and hooves, because they can never be satisfied."

IMITATION OF EARLIER WRITERS AS A MEANS TO SUBLIMITY

(2.) Plato, if we will read him with attention, illustrates yet another road to sublimity, besides those we have discussed. This is the way of imitation and emulation of great writers of the past. Here too, my friend, is an aim to which we must hold fast. Many are possessed by a spirit not their own. It is like what we are told of the Pythia at Delphi: she is in contact with the tripod near the cleft in the ground which (so they say) exhales a divine vapor, and she is thereupon made pregnant by the supernatural power and prophesies as one inspired. Similarly, the genius of the ancients acts as a kind of oracular cavern, and effluences flow from it into the minds of their imitators. Even those previously not much inclined to prophesy become inspired and share the enthusiasm which comes from the greatness of others. (3.) Was Herodotus the only "most Homeric" writer? Surely Stesichorus and Archilochus earned the name before him. So, more than any, did Plato, who diverted to himself countless rills from the Homeric spring. (If Ammonius had not selected and written up detailed examples of this, I might have had to prove the point myself.) (4.) In all this process there is no plagiarism. It resembles rather the reproduction of good character in statues and works of art.[37] Plato could not have put such a brilliant finish on his philosophical doctrines or so often risen to poetical subjects and poetical language, if he had not tried, and tried wholeheartedly, to compete for the prize against Homer, like a young aspirant challenging an admired master. To break a lance in this way may well have been a brash and contentious thing to do, but the competition proved anything but valueless. As Hesiod says, "this strife is good for men."[38] Truly it is a noble contest and prize of honor, and one well worth winning, in which to be defeated by one's elders is itself no disgrace.

(XIV.1.) We can apply this to ourselves. When we are working on something which needs loftiness of expression and greatness of thought, it is good to imagine how Homer would have said the same thing, or how Plato or Demosthenes or (in history) Thucydides would have invested it with sublimity. These great figures, presented to us as objects of emulation and, as it were, shining before our gaze, will somehow elevate our minds to the greatness of which we form a mental image. (2.) They will be even more effective if we ask ourselves "How would Homer or Demosthenes have reacted to what I am saying, if he had been here? What would his feelings have been?" It makes it a great occasion, if you imagine such a jury or audience for your own speech, and pretend that you are answering for what you write before judges and witnesses of such heroic stature. (3.) Even more stimulating is the further thought: "How will posterity take what I am writing?" If a man is afraid of saying anything which will outlast his own life and age, the conceptions of his mind are bound to be incomplete and abortive; they will miscarry and never be brought to birth whole and perfect for the day of posthumous fame.

VISUALIZATION (PHANTASIA)

(XV.1.) Another thing which is very productive of grandeur, magnificence, and urgency, my young friend, is visualization (*phantasia*). I use this word for what some people call image-production. The term *phantasia* is used generally for anything which in any way suggests a thought productive of speech;[39] but the word has also come into fashion for the situation in which enthusiasm and emotion make the speaker *see* what he is saying and bring it *visually* before his audience. (2.) It will not escape you that rhetorical visualization has a different intention from that of the poets: in poetry the aim is astonishment, in oratory it is clarity. Both, however, seek emotion and excitement: "Mother, I beg you, do not drive them at me, / The women with the blood in their eyes and the snakes—They are here, they are here, jumping right up to me."[40] Or again: "O, O! She'll kill me. Where shall I escape?"[41] The poet himself saw the Erinyes, and has as good as made his audience see what he imagined. (3.) Now Euripides devotes most pains to producing a tragic effect with two emotions, madness and love. In these he is supremely successful. At the same time, he does not lack the courage to attempt other types of visualization. Though not formed by nature for grandeur, he often forces himself to be tragic. When the moment for greatness comes, he (in Homer's words) "Whips flank and buttocks with his tail / And drives himself to fight."[42] (4.) For example, here is Helios handing the reins to Phaethon:

> "Drive on, but do not enter Libyan air—
> It has no moisture in it, and will let
> Your wheel fall through—"

and again:

> "Steer towards the seven Pleiads."
> The boy listened so far, then seized the reins,
> Whipped up the winged team, and let them go.
> To heaven's expanse they flew.
> His father rode behind on Sirius,
> Giving the boy advice: "That's your way, there:
> Turn here, turn there."[43]

May one not say that the writer's soul has mounted the chariot, has taken wing with the horses and shares the danger? Had it not been up among those heavenly bodies and moved in their courses, he could never have visualized such things. Compare, too, his Cassandra: "Ye Trojans, lovers of horses . . ."[44] (5.) Aeschylus, of course, ventures on the most heroic visualizations; he is like his own Seven against Thebes—

> Seven men of war, commanders of companies,
> Killing a bull into a black-bound shield,
> Dipping their hands in the bull's blood,
> Took oath by Ares, by Enyo, by bloodthirsty Terror—

in a joint pledge of death in which they showed themselves no mercy. At the same time, he does sometimes leave his thoughts unworked, tangled, and hard. The ambitious Euripides does not shirk even these risks. (6.) For example, there is in Aeschylus a remarkable description of the palace of Lycurgus in its divine seizure at the moment of Dionysus' epiphany: "The palace was possessed, the house went bacchanal." Euripides expresses the same thought less harshly: "The whole mountain went bacchanal with them."[45] (7.) There is another magnificent visualization in Sophocles' account of Oedipus dying and giving himself burial to the accompaniment of a sign from heaven,[46] and in the appearance of Achilles to the departing fleet over his tomb.[47] Simonides has perhaps described this scene more vividly than anyone else; but it is impossible to quote everything. (8.) The poetical examples, as I said, have a quality of exaggeration which belongs to fable and goes far beyond credibility. In an orator's visualizations, on the other hand, it is the element of fact and truth which makes for success; when the content of the passage is poetical and fabulous and does not shrink from any impossibility, the result is a shocking and outrageous abnormality. This is what happens with the shock orators of our own day; like tragic actors, these fine fellows *see* the Erinyes, and are incapable of understanding that when Orestes says "Let me go; you are one of my Erinyes, / You are hugging me tight, to throw me into Hell."[48] he visualizes all this because he is mad.

(9.) What then is the effect of rhetorical visualization? There is much it can do to bring urgency and passion into our words; but it is when it is closely involved with factual arguments that it enslaves the hearer as well as persuading him. "Suppose you heard a shout this very moment outside the court, and someone said that the prison had been broken open and the prisoners had escaped—no one, young or old, would be so casual as not to give what help he could. And if someone then came forward and said 'This is the man who let them out,' our friend would never get a hearing; it would be the end of him."[49] (10.) There is a similar instance in Hyperides' defense of himself when he was on trial for the proposal to liberate the slaves which he put forward after the defeat.[50] "It was not the proposer," he said, "who drew up this decree: it was the battle of Chaeronea." Here the orator uses a visualization actually in the moment of making his factual argument, with the result that his thought has taken him beyond the limits of mere persuasiveness. (11.) Now our natural instinct is, in all such cases, to attend to the stronger influence, so that we are diverted from the demonstration to the astonishment caused by the visualization, which by its very brilliance conceals the factual aspect. This is a natural reaction: when two things are joined together, the stronger attracts to itself the force of the weaker. (12.) This will suffice for an account of sublimity of thought produced by greatness of mind, imitation, or visualization.

FIGURES
An Example to Illustrate the Right Use of Figures: The "Oath"
in "On the Crown"

(XVI.1.) The next topic is that of figures. Properly handled, figures constitute, as I said, no small part of sublimity. It would be a vast, or rather infinite, labor to enumerate them all; what I shall do is to expound a few of those which generate sublimity, simply in order to confirm my point.

(2.) Here is Demosthenes putting forward a demonstrative argument on behalf of his policy.[51] What would have been the natural way to put it? "You have not done wrong, you who fought for the liberty of Greece; you have examples to prove this close at home: the men of Marathon, of Salamis, of Plataea did not do wrong." But instead of this he was suddenly inspired to give voice to the oath by the heroes of Greece: "By those who risked their lives at Marathon, you have not done wrong!" Observe what he effects by this single figure of conjuration, or "apostrophe" as I call it here. He deifies his audience's ancestors, suggesting that it is right to take an oath by men who fell so bravely, as though they were gods. He inspires the judges with the temper of those who risked their lives. He transforms his demonstration into an extraordinary piece of sublimity and passion, and into the convincingness of this unusual and amazing oath. At the same time he injects into his hearers' minds a healing specific, so as to lighten their hearts by these paeans of praise and make them as proud of the battle with Philip as of the triumphs of Marathon and Salamis. In short, the figure enables him to run away with his audience. (3.) Now the origin of this oath is said to be in the lines of Eupolis: "By Marathon, by *my* battle, / No one shall grieve me and escape rejoicing."[52] The greatness therefore depends not on the mere form of the oath, but on place, manner, occasion, and purpose. In Eupolis, there is nothing but the oath; he is speaking to the Athenians while their fortunes are still high and they need no comfort; and instead of immortalizing the men in order to engender in the audience a proper estimation of their valor, he wanders away from the actual people who risked their lives to an inanimate object, namely the battle. In Demosthenes, on the other hand, the oath is addressed to a defeated nation, to make them no longer think of Chaeronea as a disaster. It embraces, as I said, a demonstration that they "did no wrong," an illustrative example, a confirmation, an encomium, and an exhortation. (4.) Moreover, because he was faced with the possible objection "your policies brought us to defeat—and yet you swear by victories!" he brings his thought back under control and makes it safe and unanswerable, showing that sobriety is needed even under the influence of inspiration: "By those who *risked their lives* at Marathon, and *fought in the ships* at Salamis and Artemisium, and *formed the line* at Plataea!" He never says *conquered;* throughout he withholds the word for the final issue, because it was a happy issue, and the opposite to that of Chaeronea. From the same motives he forestalls his audience by adding immediately: "all of whom were buried at the city's expense, Aeschines—all, not only the successful."

THE RELATION BETWEEN FIGURES AND SUBLIMITY

(XVII.1.) At this point, my friend, I feel I ought not to pass over an observation of my own. It shall be very brief: figures are natural allies of sublimity and themselves profit wonderfully from the alliance. I will explain how this happens. Playing tricks by means of figures is a peculiarly suspect procedure. It raises the suspicion of a trap, a deep design, a fallacy. It is to be avoided in addressing a judge who has power to decide, and especially in addressing tyrants, kings, governors, or anybody in a high place. Such a person immediately becomes angry if he is led astray like a foolish child by some skillful orator's figures. He takes the fallacy as indicating contempt for himself. He becomes like a wild animal. Even if he controls his temper, he is now completely conditioned against being convinced by what is said. A figure is therefore generally thought to be best when the fact that it is a figure is concealed. (2.) This sublimity and emotion are a defense and a wonderful aid against the suspicion which the use of figures engenders. The artifice of the trick is lost to sight in the surrounding brillance of beauty and grandeur, and it escapes all suspicion. "By the men of Marathon . . ." is proof enough. For how did Demosthenes conceal the figure in that passage? By sheer brilliance of course. As fainter lights disappear when the sunshine surrounds them, so the sophisms of rhetoric are dimmed when they are enveloped in encircling grandeur. Something like this happens in painting: when light and shadow are juxtaposed in colors on the same plane, the light seems more prominent to the eye, and both stands out and actually appears much nearer. Similarly, in literature, emotional and sublime features seem closer to the mind's eye, both because of a certain natural kinship[53] and because of their brilliance. Consequently, they always show up above the figures, and overshadow and eclipse their artifice.

RHETORICAL QUESTIONS

(XVIII.1.) What are we to say of inquiries and questions? Should we not say that they increase the realism and vigor of the writing by the actual form of the figure?[54] "Or—tell me—do you want to go round asking one another 'Is there any news?' ? What could be hotter news than that a Macedonian is conquering Greece? 'Is Philip dead?' 'No, but he's ill.' What difference does it make to you? If anything happens to him, you will soon create another Philip."[55] Again: "Let us sail to Macedonia. 'Where shall we anchor?' says someone. The war itself will find out Philip's weak spots."[56] Put in the straightforward form, this would have been quite insignificant; as it is, the impassioned rapidity of question and answer and the device of making an objection to oneself have made the remark, in virtue of its figurative form, not only more sublime but more credible. (2.) For emotion carries us away more easily when it seems to be generated by the occasion rather than deliberately assumed by the speaker, and the self-directed question and its answer represent precisely this momentary quality of emotion. Just as people who are unexpectedly plied with questions become annoyed and reply to the point with vigor and exact truth, so the figure of question and answer arrests the hearer and cheats him into believing that all the points made were raised and are being put into words on the spur of the moment. Again—this sentence in Herodotus is believed to be a particularly fine example of sublimity— . . . [Lacuna equivalent to about three pages]

ASYNDETON

(XX.1.) The conjunction of several figures in one phrase also has a very stirring almost getting ahead of the speaker: "Engaging their shields, they pushed, fought, slew, died" (Xenophon.)[57] (2.) "We went as you told us, noble Odysseus, up the woods,/ We saw a beautiful palace built in the glades," says Homer's Eurylochus.[58] Disconnected and yet hurried phrases convey the impression of an agitation which both obstructs the reader and drives him on. Such is the effect of Homer's asyndeta.

ASYNDETON COMBINED WITH ANAPHORA

(XX.1.) The conjunction of several figures in one phrase also has a very stirring effect. Two or three may be joined together in a kind of team, jointly contributing strength, persuasiveness, charm. An example is the passage in *Against Midias*,[59] where asyndeton is combined with anaphora and vivid description. "The aggressor would do many things—some of which his victim would not even be able to tell anyone else—with gesture, with look, with voice." (2.) Then, to save the sentence from monotony and a stationary effect—for this goes with inertia, whereas disorder goes with emotion, which is a disturbance and movement of the mind—he leaps immediately to fresh instances of asyndeton and epanaphora: "With gesture, with look, with voice, when he insults, when he acts as an enemy, when he slaps the fellow, when he slaps him on the ears. . . ." The orator is doing here exactly what the bully does—hitting the jury in the mind with blow after blow. (3.) Then he comes down with a fresh onslaught, like a sudden squall: ". . . when he slaps the fellow, when he slaps him on the ears. That rouses people, that makes them lose control, when they are not used to being insulted. No one could bring out the horror of such a moment by a mere report." Here Demosthenes keeps up the natural effect of epanaphora and asyndeton by frequent variation. His order becomes disorderly, and his disorder in turn acquires a certain order.

POLYSYNDETON

(XXI.1.) Now add the conjunctions, as Isocrates' pupils do. "Again, one must not omit this point that the aggressor would do many things, first with gesture, then with look, and finally with voice." As you proceed with these insertions, it will become clear that the urgent and harsh character of the emotion loses its sting and becomes a spent fire as soon as you level it down to smoothness by the conjunctions. (2.) If you tie a runner's arms to his side, you take away his speed; likewise, emotion frets at being impeded by conjunctions and other additions, because it loses the free abandon of its movement, and the sense of being, as it were, catapulted out.

HYPERBATON

(XXII.1.) Hyperbaton belongs to the same general class. It is an arrangement of words or thoughts which differs from the normal sequence. . . .[60] It is a very real mark of urgent emotion. People who in real life feel anger, fear, or indignation, or are distracted by jealousy or some other emotion (it is impossible to say how many emotions there are; they are without number), often put one thing forward and then rush off to another, irrationally inserting some remark, and then hark back again to their first point. They seem to be blown this way and that by their excitement, as if by a veering wind. They inflict innumerable variations on the expression, the thought, and the natural sequence. Thus hyperbaton is a means by which, in the best authors, imitation approaches the effect of nature. Art is perfect when it looks like nature, nature is felicitous when it embraces concealed art. Consider the words of Dionysius of Phocaea in Herodotus: "Now, for our affairs are on the razor's edge, men of Ionia, whether we are to be free or slaves—and worse than slaves, runaways—so if you will bear hardships now, you will suffer temporarily but be able to overcome your enemies."[61] (2.) The natural order of thought would have been: "Men of Ionia, now is the time for you to bear hardships, for our affairs are on the razor's edge." The speaker has displaced "men of Ionia"; he begins with the cause of fear, as though the alarm was so pressing that he did not even have time to address the audience by name. He has also diverted the order of thought. Before saying that they must suffer hardship themselves (that is the gist of his exhortation), he first gives the reason why it is necessary, by saying "our affairs are on the razor's edge." The result is that he seems to be giving not a premeditated speech but one forced on him by the circumstances. (3.) It is even more characteristic of Thucydides to show ingenuity in separating by transpositions even things which are by nature completely unified and indivisible. Demosthenes is less wilful in this than Thucydides, but no one uses this kind of effect more lavishly. His transpositions produce not only a great sense of urgency but the appearance of extemporization, as he drags his hearers with him into the hazards of his long hyperbata. (4.) He often holds in suspense the meaning which he set out to convey and, introducing one extraneous item after another in an alien and unusual place before getting to the main point, throws the hearer into a panic lest the sentence collapse altogether, and forces him in his excitement to share the speaker's peril, before, at long last and beyond all expectation, appositely paying off at the end the long due conclusion; the very audacity and hazardousness of the hyperbata add to the astounding effect. There are so many examples that I forbear to give any.

CHANGES OF CASE, TENSE, PERSON, NUMBER, GENDER; PLURAL FOR SINGULAR AND SINGULAR FOR PLURAL

(XXIII.1.) What is called polyptoton, like accumulation, variation, and climax, is, as you know, extremely effective and contributes both to ornament and to sublimity and emotion of every kind.[62] How do variations in case, tense, person, number, and gender diversify and stimulate the style? (2.) My answer to this is that, as regards variations of number, the lesser effect (though a real one) is produced by instances in which singular forms are seen on reflection to be plural in sense: "The innumerable host/Were scattered over the sandy beach, and shouted." More worthy of note are the examples in which plurals give a more grandiose effect, and court success by the sense of multitude expressed by the grammatical number. (3.) An example comes in Sophocles, where Oedipus says:

> Weddings, weddings,
> You bred me and again released my seed,

> Made fathers, brothers, children, blood of the kin,
> Brides, wives, mothers—all
> The deeds most horrid ever seen in men.[63]

All this is about Oedipus on the one hand and Jocasta on the other, but the expansion of the number to the plural forms pluralizes the misfortunes also. Another example is: "Hectors and Sarpedons came forth."[64] Another is the Platonic passage about the Athenians, which I have quoted elsewhere:[65] (4.) "No Pelopses or Cadmuses or Aegyptuses or Danauses or other barbarians by birth have settled among us; we are pure Greeks, with no barbarian blood," and so on. Such an agglomeration of names in crowds naturally makes the facts sound more impressive. But the practice is only to be followed when the subject admits amplification, abundance, hyperbole, or emotion—one or more of these. Only a sophist has bells on his harness wherever he goes.

(XXIV.1.) The contrary device—the contraction of plurals into singulars—also sometimes produces a sublime effect. "The whole Peloponnese was divided."[66] "When Phrynichus produced *The Capture of Miletus* the theater burst into tears" ("theater" for "spectators.").[67] To compress the separate individuals into the corresponding unity produces a more solid effect. (2.) The cause of the effect is the same in both cases. Where the nouns are singular, it is a mark of unexpected emotion to pluralize them.[68] Where they are plural, to unite the plurality under one well-sounding word is again surprising because of the opposite transformation of the facts.

VIVID PRESENT TENSE

(XXV.) To represent past events as present is to turn a narrative into a thing of immediate urgency. "A man who has fallen under Cyrus' horse and is being trampled strikes the horse in the belly with his sword. The horse, convulsed, shakes Cyrus off. He falls." (Xenophon[69]). This is common in Thucydides.

IMAGINARY SECOND PERSON

(XXVI.1.) Urgency may also be conveyed by the replacement of one grammatical person by another. It often gives the hearer the sense of being in the midst of the danger himself. "You would say they were tireless, never wearied in war,/So eagerly they fought" (Homer[70]). "May you never be drenched in the sea in that month!" (Aratus[71]). (2.) "You will sail upstream from Elephantine, and then you will come to a smooth plain. After crossing this, you will embark on another boat and sail for two days. Then you will come to a great city called Meroe" (Herodotus[72]). Do you see, my friend, how he grips your mind and takes it on tour through all these places, making hearing as good as seeing? All such forms of expression, being directed to an actual person, bring the hearer into the presence of real events. (3.) Moreover, if you speak as though to an individual and not to a large company, you will affect him more and make him more attentive and excited, because the personal address stimulates: "You could not tell with whom Tydides stood."[73]

LAPSES INTO DIRECT SPEECH

(XXVII.1.) Sometimes a writer, in the course of a narrative in the third person, makes a sudden change and speaks in the person of his character. This kind of thing is an outburst of emotion.

> Hector shouted aloud to the Trojans
> To rush for the ships, and leave the spoils of the dead.
> "If I see anyone away from the ships of his own accord,
> I will have him killed on the spot." [74]

Here the poet has given the narrative to himself, as appropriate to him, and then suddenly and without warning has put the abrupt threat in the mouth of the angry prince. It would have been flat if he had added "Hector said." As it is, the change of construction is so sudden that it has outstripped its creator. (2.) Hence the use of this figure is appropriate when the urgency of the moment gives the writer no chance to delay, but forces on him an immediate change from one person to another. "Ceyx was distressed at this, and ordered the children to depart. 'For I am unable to help you. Go therefore to some other country, so as to save yourselves without harming me'" (Hecataeus[75]). (3.) Somewhat different is the method by which Demosthenes in *Against Aristogiton*[76] makes variation of person produce the effect of strong emotion and rapid change of tone: "Will none of you be found to feel bile or anger at the violence of this shameless monster, who—you vile wretch, your right of free speech is barred not by gates and doors which can be opened, but . . . !" He makes the change before the sense is complete, and in effect divides a single thought between two persons in his passion ("who—you vile wretch . . . !"), as well as turning to Aristogiton and giving the impression of abandoning the course of his argument—with the sole result, so strong is the emotion, of giving it added intensity. (4.) So also Penelope:

> Herald, why have the proud suitors sent you here?
> Is it to tell Odysseus' maidservants
> To stop their work and get dinner for them?
> After their wooing, may they never meet again!

May this be their last dinner here—
You who gather together so often and waste wealth,
Who never listened to your fathers when you were children
And they told you what kind of man Odysseus was![77]

PERIPHRASIS

(XXVIII.1.) No one, I fancy, would question the fact that periphrasis is a means to sublimity. As in music the melody is made sweeter by what is called the accompaniment, so periphrasis is often heard in concert with the plain words and enhances them with a new resonance. This is especially true if it contains nothing bombastic or tasteless but only what is pleasantly blended. (2.) There is a sufficient example in Plato, at the beginning of the Funeral Speech: "These men have received their due, and having received it they go on their fated journey, escorted publicly by their country and privately each by his own kindred."[78] Plato here calls death a "fated journey" and the bestowal of regular funeral rites a public escort by the country. This surely adds no inconsiderable impressiveness to the thought. He has lyricized the bare prose, enveloping it in the harmony of the beautiful periphrasis. (3.) "You believe labor to be the guide to a pleasant life; you have gathered into your souls the noblest and most heroic of possessions: you enjoy being praised more than anything else in the world" (Xenophon[79]). In this passage "you make labor the guide to a pleasant life" is put for "you are willing to labor." This and the other expansions invest the praise with a certain grandeur of conception. (4.) Another example is the inimitable sentence of Herodotus: "The goddess struck the Scythians who plundered the temple with a feminine disease."[80]

(XXIX.1.) Periphrasis, however, is a particularly dangerous device if it is not used with moderation. It soon comes to be heavy and dull, smelling of empty phrases and coarseness of fiber. This is why Plato—who is fond of the figure and sometimes uses it unseasonably—is ridiculed for the sentence in the Laws[81] which runs: "Neither silvern wealth nor golden should be permitted to establish itself in the city." If he had wanted to prohibit cattle, says the critic, he would have talked of "ovine and bovine" wealth.

CONCLUSION OF THE SECTION ON FIGURES

(2.) So much, my dear Terentianus, by way of digression on the theory of the use of those figures which conduce to sublimity. They all make style more emotional and excited, and emotion is as essential a part of sublimity as characterization is of charm.[82] [Lacuna of about three pages]

DICTION
General Remarks

(**XXX.**1.) Thought and expression are of course very much involved with each other. We have therefore next to consider whether any topics still remain in the field of diction. The choice of correct and magnificent words is a source of immense power to entice and charm the hearer. This is something which all orators and other writers cultivate intensely. It makes grandeur, beauty, old-world charm, weight, force, strength, and a kind of luster bloom upon our words as upon beautiful statues; it gives things life and makes them speak. But I suspect there is no need for me to make this point; you know it well. (2.) It is indeed true that beautiful words are the light that illuminates thought. Magniloquence, however, is not always serviceable: to dress up trivial material in grand and solemn language is like putting a huge tragic mask on a little child. In poetry and history, however. . . . [Lacuna equivalent to about three pages]

USE OF EVERYDAY WORDS

(**XXXI.**1.) . . . and productive, as is Anacreon's "I no longer turn my mind to the Thracian filly."[83] Similarly, Theopompus' much admired phrase seems to me to be particularly expressive because of the aptness of the analogy, though Caecilius manages to find fault with it: "Philip was excellent at stomaching facts." An idiomatic phrase is sometimes much more vivid than an ornament of speech, for it is immediately recognized from everyday experience, and the familiar is inevitably easier to credit. "To stomach facts" is thus used vividly of a man who endures unpleasantness and squalor patiently, and indeed with pleasure, for the sake of gain. (2.) There are similar things in Herodotus: "Cleomenes in his madness cut his own flesh into little pieces with a knife till he had sliced himself to death," "Pythes continued fighting on the ship until he was cut into joints."[84] These phrases come within an inch of being vulgar, but they are so expressive that they avoid vulgarity.

METAPHORS

(**XXXII.**1) As regards number of metaphors, Caecilius seems to agree with the propounders of the rule that not more than two or at most three may be used of the same subject. Here too Demosthenes is our canon. The right occasions are when emotions come flooding in and bring the multiplication of metaphors with them as a necessary accompaniment. (2.) "Vile flatterers, mutilators of their countries, who have given away liberty as a drinking present, first to Philip and now to Alexander, measuring happiness by the belly and the basest impulses overthrowing liberty and freedom from despotism, which Greeks of old regarded as the canons and standards of the good."[85] In this passage the orator's anger against traitors obscures the multiplicity of his metaphors. (3.) This is why Aristotle and Theophrastus say that there are ways of softening bold metaphors —namely by saying "as if," "as it were," "if I may put it so," or "if we may venture on a bold expression." Apology, they say, is a remedy for audacity. (4.) I accept this doctrine, but I would add—and I said the same about figures—that strong and appropriate emotions and genuine sublimity are a specific palliative for multiplied or daring metaphors, because their nature is to sweep and drive all these other things along with the surging tide of their movement. Indeed it might be truer to say that they *demand* the hazardous. They never allow the hearer leisure to count the metaphors, because he too shares the speaker's enthusiasm.

(5.) At the same time, nothing gives distinction to commonplaces and descriptions so well as a continuous series of tropes. This is the medium in which the description of man's bodily tabernacle is worked out so elaborately in Xenophon and yet more superlatively by Plato.[86] Thus Plato calls the head the "citadel" of the body; the neck is an "isthmus" constructed between the head and the chest; the vertebrae, he says, are fixed underneath "like pivots." Pleasure is a "lure of evil" for mankind: the tongue is a "taste-meter." The heart is a "knot of veins" and "fountain of the blood that moves impetuously round," allocated to the "guard-room." The word he uses for the various passages of the canals is "alleys." "Against the throbbing of the heart," he continues, "in the expectation of danger and in the excitation of anger, when it gets hot, they contrived a means of succor, implanting in us the lungs, soft, bloodless and with cavities, a sort of cushion, so that when anger boils up in the heart, the latter's throbbing is against a yielding obstacle, so that it comes to no harm." Again: he calls the seat of the desires "the women's quarters," and the seat of anger "the men's quarters." The spleen is for him "a napkin for the inner parts, which therefore grows big and festering through being filled with secretions." "And thereafter," he says again, "they buried the whole under a canopy of flesh," putting the flesh on "as a protection against dangers from without, like felting." Blood he called "fodder of the flesh." For the purpose of nutrition, he says also, "they irrigated the body, cutting channels as in gardens, so that the streams of the veins might flow as it were from an incoming stream, making the body an aqueduct." Finally: when the end is at hand, the soul's "ship's cables" are "loosed," and she herself "set free." (6.) The passage contains countless similar examples; but these are enough to make my point, namely that tropes are naturally grand, that metaphors conduce to sublimity, and that passages involving emotion and description are the most suitable field for them. (7.) At the same time, it is plain without my saying it that the use of tropes, like all other good things in literature, always tempts one to go too far. This is what people ridicule most in Plato, who is often carried away by a sort of literary madness into crude, harsh metaphors or allegorical fustian. "It is not easy to understand that a city ought to be mixed like a bowl of wine, wherein the wine seethes with madness, but when chastened by another, sober god, and achieving a proper communion with him, produces a good and moderate drink."[87] To call water "a sober god," says the critic, and mixture "chastening," is the language of a poet who is far from sober himself.

DIGRESSION: GENIUS *VERSUS* MEDIOCRITY

(8.) Faults of this kind formed the subject of Caecilius' attack in his book on Lysias, in which he had the audacity to declare Lysias in all respects superior to Plato. He has in fact given way without discrimination to two emotions: loving Lysias more deeply than he loves himself, he yet hates Plato with an even greater intensity. His motive, however, is desire to score a point, and his assumptions are not, as he believed, generally accepted. In preferring Lysias to Plato he thinks he is preferring a faultless and pure writer to one who makes many mistakes. But the facts are far from supporting his view.

(XXIII.1.) Let us consider a really pure and correct writer. We have then to ask ourselves in general terms whether grandeur attended by some faults of execution is to be preferred, in prose or poetry, to a modest success of impeccable soundness. We must also ask whether the greater *number* of good qualities or the greater good qualities ought properly to win the literary prizes. These questions are relevant to a discussion of sublimity, and urgently require an answer. (2.) I am certain in the first place that great geniuses are least "pure." Exactness in every detail involves a risk of meanness; with grandeur, as with great wealth, there ought to be something overlooked. It may also be inevitable that low or mediocre abilities should maintain themselves generally at a correct and safe level, simply because they take no risks and do not aim at the heights, whereas greatness, just because it is greatness, incurs danger. (3.) I am aware also of a second point. All human affairs are, in the nature of things, better known on their worse side; the memory of mistakes is ineffaceable, that of goodness is soon gone. (4.) I have myself cited not a few mistakes in Homer and other great writers, not because I take pleasure in their slips, but because I consider them not so much voluntary mistakes as oversights let fall at random through inattention and with the negligence of genius. I do, however, think that the greater good qualities, even if not consistently maintained, are always more likely to win the prize—if for no other reason, because of the greatness of spirit they reveal. Apollonius makes no mistakes in the *Argonautica*; Theocritus is very felicitous in the *Pastorals,* apart from a few passages not connected with the theme; but would you rather be Homer or Apollonius? (5.) Is the Eratosthenes of that flawless little poem *Erigone* a greater poet than Archilochus, with his abundant, uncontrolled flood, that bursting forth of the divine spirit which is so hard to bring under the rule of law? Take lyric poetry: would you rather be Bacchylides or Pindar? Take tragedy: would you rather be Ion of Chios or Sophocles? Ion and Bacchylides are impeccable, uniformly beautiful writers in the polished manner; but it is Pindar and Sophocles who sometimes set the world on fire with their vehemence, for all that their flame often goes out without reason and they collapse dismally. Indeed, no one in his senses would reckon all Ion's works put together as the equivalent of the one play *Oedipus.*

(XXXIV.1.) If good points were totted up, not judged by their real value, Hyperides would in every way surpass Demosthenes. He is more versatile,[88] and has more good qualities. He is second-best at everything, like a pentathlon competitor; always beaten by the others for first place, he remains the best of the non-specialists. (2.) In fact, he reproduces all the good features of Demosthenes, except his word-arrangement, and also has for good measure the excellences and graces of Lysias. He knows how to talk simply where appropriate; he does not deliver himself of everything in the same tone, like Demosthenes. His expression of character has sweetness and delicacy. Urbanity, sophisticated sarcasm, good breeding, skill in handling irony, humor neither rude nor tasteless but flavored with true Attic salt, an ingenuity in attack with a strong comic element and a sharp sting to its apt fun—all this produces inimitable charm. He has moreover great talents for exciting pity, and a remarkable facility for narrating myths with copiousness and developing general topics with fluency. For example, while his account of Leto is in his more poetic manner, his Funeral Speech is an unrivalled example of the epideictic style.[89] (3.) Demosthenes, by contrast, has no sense of character. He lacks fluency, smoothness, and capacity for the epideictic manner; in fact he is practically without all the qualities I have been describing. When he forces himself to be funny or witty, he makes people laugh at him rather than with him. When he wants to come near to being charming, he is furthest removed from it. If he had tried to write the little speech on Phryne or that on Athenogenes,[90] he would have been an even better advertisement for Hyperides. (4.) Yet Hyperides' beauties, though numerous, are without grandeur: "inert in the heart of a sober man," they leave the hearer at peace. Nobody feels frightened reading Hyperides. But when Demosthenes begins to speak, he concentrates in himself excellences finished to the highest perfection of his sublime genius—the intensity of lofty speech, living emotions, abundance, acuteness, speed where speed is vital, all his unapproachable vehemence and power. He concentrates it all in himself—they are divine gifts, it is almost blasphemous to call them human—and so outpoints all his rivals, compensating with the beauties he has even for those which he lacks. The crash of his thunder, the brilliance of his lightning make all other orators, of all ages, insignificant. It would be easier to open your eyes to an approaching thunderbolt than to face up to his unremitting emotional blows.

(XXXV.1.) To return to Plato and Lysias, there is, as I said, a further difference between them. Lysias is much inferior not only in the importance of the good qualities concerned but in their number; and at the same time he exceeds Plato in the number of his failings even more than he falls short in his good qualities.

(2.) What then was the vision which inspired those divine writers who disdained exactness of detail and aimed at the greatest prizes in literature? They saw many things. One was the fact that nature made man to be no humble or lowly creature, but brought him into life and into the universe as into a great festival, to be both a spectator and an enthusiastic contestant in its competitions. She implanted in our minds from the start an irresistible desire for anything which is great and, in relation to ourselves, supernatural. (3.) The universe therefore is not wide enough for the range of human speculation and intellect. Our thoughts often travel beyond the boundaries of our surroundings. If anyone wants to know what we were born for, let him look round at life and contemplate the splendor, grandeur, and beauty in which it everywhere abounds. (4.) It is a natural inclination that leads us to admire not the little streams, however pellucid and however useful, but the Nile, the Danube, the Rhine, and above all the Ocean. Nor do we feel so much awe before the little flame we kindle, because it keeps its light clear and pure, as before the fires of heaven, though they are often obscured. We do not think our flame more worthy of admiration than the craters of Etna, whose eruptions bring up rocks and whole hills out of the depths, and sometimes pour forth rivers of the earth-born, spontaneous fire. (5.) A single comment fits all these examples: the useful and necessary are readily available to man, it is the unusual which always excites our wonder.

(XXXVI.1.) So when we come to great geniuses in literature—where, by contrast, grandeur is not divorced from service and utility—we have to conclude that such men, for all their faults, tower far above mortal stature. Other literary qualities prove their users to be human; sublimity raises us towards the spiritual greatness of god. Freedom from error does indeed save us from blame, but it is only greatness that wins admiration. (2.) Need I add that every one of those great men redeems all his mistakes many times over by a single sublime stroke? Finally, if you picked out all the mistakes in Homer, Demosthenes, Plato, and all the other really great men, and put them together, the total would be found to be a minute fraction of the successes which those heroic figures have to their credit. Posterity and human experience—judges whose sanity envy cannot question—place the crown of victory on their heads. They keep their prize irrevocably, and will do so, "So long as waters flow and tall trees flourish."[91]

(3.) It has been remarked that "the failed Colossus is no better than the

Doryphorus of Polyclitus."[92] There are many ways of answering this. We may say that accuracy is admired in art and grandeur in nature, and it is *by nature* that man is endowed with the power of speech; or again that statues are expected to represent the human form, whereas, as I said, something higher than human is sought in literature. (4.) At this point I have a suggestion to make which takes us back to the beginning of the book. Impeccability is generally a product of art; erratic excellence comes from natural greatness; therefore, art must always come to the aid of nature, and the combination of the two may well be perfection. It seemed necessary to settle this point for the sake of our inquiry; but everyone is at liberty to enjoy what he takes pleasure in.

SIMILES

(XXXVII.) We must now return to the main argument. Next to metaphors come comparisons and similes. The only difference is. . . . [Lacuna equivalent to about three pages]

HYPERBOLE

(XXXVIII.1.) . . . such expressions as: "Unless you've got your brains in your heels and are walking on them."[93] The important thing to know is how far to push a given hyperbole; it sometimes destroys it to go too far; too much tension results in relaxation, and may indeed end in the contrary of the intended effect. (2.) Thus Isocrates' zeal for amplifying everything made him do a childish thing. The argument of his *Panegyricus* is that Athens surpasses Sparta in services to the Greek race. Right at the beginning we find the following: "Secondly, the power of speech is such that it can make great things lowly, give grandeur to the trivial, say what is old in a new fashion, and lend an appearance of antiquity to recent events."[94] Is Isocrates then about to reverse the positions of Athens and Sparta? The encomium on the power of speech is equivalent to an introduction recommending the reader not to believe what he is told. (3.) I suspect that what we said of the best figures is true of the best hyperboles: they are those which avoid being seen for what they are. The desired effect is achieved when they are connected with some impressive circumstance and in moments of high emotion. Thucydides' account of those killed in Sicily is an example: "The Syracusans came down and massacred them, especially those in the river. The water was stained; but despite the blood and the dirt, men continued to drink it, and many still fought for it."[95] It is the intense emotion of the moment which makes it credible that dirt and blood should still be fought for as drink. (4.) Herodotus has something similar about Thermopylae: "Meanwhile though they defended themselves with swords (those who still had them), and with hands and mouths, the barbarians buried them with their missiles."[96] What is meant by fighting armed men with mouths or being buried with missiles? Still, it is credible; for we form the impression that the hyperbole is a reasonable product of the situation, not that the situation has been chosen for the sake of the hyperbole. (5.) As I keep saying, acts and emotions which approach ecstasy provide a justification for, and an antidote to, any linguistic audacity. This is why comic hyperboles, for all their incredibility, are convincing because we laugh at them so much: "He had a farm, but it didn't stretch as far as a Laconic letter." Laughter is emotion in pleasure. (6.) There are hyperboles which belittle as well those which exaggerate. Intensification is the factor common to the two species, vilification being in a sense an amplification of lowness.

WORD-ARRANGEMENT OR COMPOSITION

(XXXIX.1) There remains the fifth of the factors contributing to sublimity which we originally enumerated. This was a certain kind of composition or word-arrangement. Having set out my conclusions on this subject fully in two books, I shall here add only so much as is essential for our present subject.

EFFECT OF RHYTHM

Harmony is a natural instrument not only of conviction and pleasure in mankind, but also to a remarkable degree of grandeur and emotion. (2.) The flute fills the audience with certain emotions and makes them in a manner of speaking beside themselves and possessed. It sets a rhythm, it makes the hearer move to the rhythm and assimilate himself to the tune, "untouched by the Muses though he be."[97] The notes of the lyre, though they have no meaning, also, as you know, often cast a wonderful spell of harmony with their varied sounds and blended and mingled notes. (3.) Yet all these are but spurious images and imitations of persuasion, not the genuine activities proper to human nature of which I spoke.[98] Composition, on the other hand, is a harmony of words, man's natural instrument, penetrating not only the ears but the very soul. It arouses all kinds of conceptions of words and thoughts and objects, beauty and melody—all things native and natural to mankind. The combination and variety of its sounds convey the speaker's emotions to the minds of those around him and make the hearers share them. It fits his great thoughts into a coherent structure by the way in which it builds up patterns of words. Shall we not then believe that by all these methods it bewitches us and elevates to grandeur, dignity, and sublimity both every thought which comes within its compass and ourselves as well, holding as it does complete domination over our minds? It is absurd to question facts so generally agreed. Experience is proof enough.

(4.) The idea which Demosthenes uses in speaking of the decree[99] is reputed very sublime, and is indeed splendid. "This decree made the danger which then surrounded the city pass away like a cloud (*touto to psēphisma ton tote tē polei peristanta kindunon parelthein epoiēsen hōsper nephos*)." But the effect depends as much on the harmony as on the thought. The whole passage is based on dactylic rhythms, and these are very noble and grand. (This is why they form the heroic, the noblest meter we know.) . . . [A short phrase missing] . . . but make any change you like in the order: "*touto to psēphisma hōsper nephos epoiēse ton tote kindūnon parelthein,*" or cut off a syllable: "*epoiēse parelthein hōs nephos.*" You will immediately see how the harmony echoes the sublimity. The phrase *hōspēr nephos* rests on its long first unit (− −) which measures four shorts; the removal of a syllable (*hōs nephos*) at once curtails and mutilates the grand effect. Now lengthen the phrase: "*parelthein epoiēsen hōsperei nephos.*" It still means the same, but the effect is different, because the sheer sublimity is broken up and undone by the breaking up of the run of long syllables at the end.

EFFECT OF PERIOD STRUCTURE

(XL.1.) I come now to a principle of particular importance for lending grandeur to our words. The beauty of the body depends on the way in which the limbs are joined together, each one when severed from the others having nothing remarkable about it, but the whole together forming a perfect unity. Similarly great thoughts which lack connection are themselves wasted and waste the total sublime effect, whereas if they co-operate to form a unity and are linked by the bonds of harmony, they come to life and speak just by virtue of the periodic structure. It is indeed generally true that, in periods, grandeur results from the total contribution of many elements. (2.) I have shown elsewhere[100] that many poets and other writers who are not naturally sublime, and may indeed be quite unqualified for grandeur, and who use in general common and everyday words which carry with them no special effect, nevertheless acquire magnificence and splendor, and avoid being thought low or mean, solely by the way in which they arrange and fit together their words. Philistus, Aristophanes sometimes, Euripides generally, are among the many examples. (3.) Thus Heracles says after the killing of the children: "I'm full of troubles, there's no room for more."[101] This is a very ordinary remark, but it has become sublime, as the situation demands.[102] If you re-arrange it, it will become apparent that it is in the composition, not in the sense, that Euripides' greatness appears. (4.) Dirce is being pulled about by the bull: "And where it could, it writhed and twisted round, / Dragging at everything, rock, woman, oak, / Juggling with them all."[103] The conception is fine in itself, but it has been improved by the fact that the word-harmony is not hurried and does not run smoothly; the words are propped up by one another and rest on the intervals between them; set wide apart like that, they give the impression of solid strength.

FEATURES DESTRUCTIVE OF SUBLIMITY
(1) Bad and Affected Rhythm

(XLI.1.) Nothing is so damaging to a sublime effect as effeminate and agitated rhythm, pyrrhics ($\cup\cup$), trochees ($-\cup$ or $\cup\cup\cup$) and dichorei ($-\cup-\cup$); they turn into a regular jig. All the rhythmical elements immediately appear artificial and cheap, being constantly repeated in a monotonous fashion without the slightest emotional effect. (2.) Worst of all, just as songs distract an audience from the action[104] and compel attention for themselves, so the rhythmical parts of speech produce on the hearer the effect not of speech but of rhythm, so that they foresee the coming endings and sometimes themselves beat time for the speaker and anticipate him in giving the step, just as in a dance.

(2) The "Chopped Up" Style

(3.) Phrases too closely knit[105] are also devoid of grandeur, as are those which are chopped up into short elements consisting of short syllables, bolted together, as it were, and rough at the joints.

(3) Excessive Brevity

(XLII.) Excessively cramped expression also does damage to sublimity. It cripples grandeur to compress it into too short a space. I do not mean proper compression, but cutting up into tiny pieces. Cramping mutilates sense; brevity gives directness. Conversely with fully extended expressions: anything developed at unseasonable length falls dead.[106]

(4) Undignified Vocabulary

(XLIII.1.) Lowness of diction also destroys grandeur.
     The description of the storm in Herodotus is magnificent in conception, but includes expressions which are below the dignity of the subject.[107] "The sea seethed" is one instance: the cacophony does much to dissipate the sublime effect. "The wind slacked" is another example; yet another is the "unpleasant end" which awaited those who were thrown against the wreckage. "Slack" is

an undignified, colloquial word; "unpleasant" is inappropriate to such an experience. (2.) Similarly, Theopompus first gives a magnificent setting to the descent of the Persian king on Egypt, and then ruins it all with a few words:

"What city or nation in Asia did not send its embassy to the King? What thing of beauty or value, product of the earth or work of art, was not brought him as a gift? There were many precious coverlets and cloaks, purple, embroidered, and white; there were many gold tents fitted out with all necessities; there were many robes and beds of great price. There were silver vessels and worked gold, drinking cups and bowls, some studded with jewels, some elaborately and preciously wrought. Countless myriads of arms were there, Greek and barbarian. There were multitudes of pack animals and victims fattened for slaughter, many bushels of condiments, many bags and sacks and pots of onions and every other necessity. There was so much salt meat of every kind that travellers approaching from a distance mistook the huge heaps for cliffs or hills thrusting up from the plain."

(3.) He passes from the sublime to the mean; the development of the scene should have been the other way round. By mixing up the bags and the condiments and the sacks in the splendid account of the whole expedition, he conjures up the vision of a kitchen. Suppose one actually had these beautiful objects before one's eyes, and then dumped some bags and sacks in the middle of the gold and jewelled bowls, the silver vessels, the gold tents, and the drinking-cups —the effect would be disgusting. It is the same with style: if you insert words like this when they are not wanted, they make a blot on the context. (4.) It was open to Theopompus to give a general description of the "hills" which he says were raised, and, having made this change,[108] to proceed to the rest of the preparations, mentioning camels and multitudes of beasts of burden carrying everything needed for luxury and pleasure of the table, or speaking of "heaps of all kinds of seeds and everything that makes for fine cuisine and dainty living." If he had wanted at all costs to make the king self-supporting, he could have talked of "all the refinements of maîtres-d'hôtel and chefs." (5.) It is wrong to descend, in a sublime passage, to the filthy and contemptible, unless we are absolutely compelled to do so. We ought to use words worthy of things. We ought to imitate nature, who, in creating man, did not set our private parts or the excretions of our body in the face, but concealed them as well as she could, and, as Xenophon says,[109] made the channels of these organs as remote as possible, so as not to spoil the beauty of the creature as a whole.

CONCLUSION OF CHAPS. 39–43

(6.) There is no urgent need to enumerate in detail features which produce a low effect. We have explained what makes style noble and sublime; the opposite qualities will obviously make it low and undignified.

APPENDIX: CAUSES OF THE DECLINE OF LITERATURE

(XLIV.1.) I shall not hesitate to add for your instruction, my dear Terentianus, one further topic, so as to clear up a question put to me the other day by one of the philosophers.

"I wonder," he said, "and so no doubt do many others, why it is that in our age there are minds which are strikingly persuasive and practical, shrewd, versatile, and well endowed with the ability to write agreeably, but no sublime or really great minds, except perhaps here and there. There is a universal dearth of literature." (2.) "Are we to believe," he went on, "the common explanation that democracy nurtures greatness, and great writers flourished with democracy and died with it? Freedom, the argument goes, nourishes and encourages the thoughts of the great, as well as exciting their enthusiasm for rivalry with one another and their ambition for the prize. (3.) In addition the availability of political reward sharpens and polishes up orators' talents by giving them exercise; they shine forth, free in a free world. We of the present day, on the other hand," he continued, "seem to have learned in infancy to live under justified slavery, swathed round from our first tender thoughts in the same habits and customs, never allowed to taste that fair and fecund spring of literature, freedom. We end up as flatterers in the grand manner." (4.) He went on to say how the same argument explained why, unlike other capacities, that of the orator could never belong to a slave. "The inability to speak freely and the consciousness of being a prisoner at once assert themselves, battered into him as they have been by the blows of habit. (5.) As Homer says,[110] 'The day of slavery takes half one's manhood away.' I don't know if it's true, but I understand that the cages in which dwarfs or Pygmies are kept not only prevent the growth of the prisoners but cripple them because of the fastening which constricts the body. One might describe all slavery, even the most justified,[111] as a cage for the soul, a universal prison."

(6.) "My good friend," I replied, "it is easy to find fault with the present situation; indeed it is a human characteristic to do so. But I wonder whether what destroys great minds is not the peace of the world, but the unlimited war which lays hold on our desires, and all the passions which beset and ravage our modern life. Avarice, the insatiable disease from which we all suffer, and love of pleasure are our two slavemasters; or perhaps one should say that they sink our ship of life with all hands. Avarice is a mean disease; love of pleasure is base through and through. (7.) I cannot see how we can honor, or rather deify, unlimited wealth as we do without admitting into our souls the evils which attach to it. When wealth is measureless and uncontrolled, extravagance comes with it, sticking close beside it, and, as they say, keeping step. The moment wealth opens the way into cities and houses, extravagance also enters and dwells therein. These evils then become chronic in people's lives, and, as the philoso-phers say, nest and breed. They are soon busy producing offspring: greed, pride, and luxury are their all too legitimate children. If these offspring of wealth are allowed to mature, they breed in turn those inexorable tyrants of the soul, insolence, lawlessness, and shamelessness. (8.) It is an inevitable process. Men will no longer open their eyes or give thought to their reputation with posterity. The ruin of their lives is gradually consummated in a cycle of such vices. Greatness of mind wanes, fades, and loses its attraction when men spend their admiration on their mortal parts and neglect to develop the immortal. (9.) One who has been bribed to give a judgment will no longer be a free and sound judge of rightness and nobility. The corrupt man inevitably thinks his own side's claim just and fair. Yet nowadays bribery is the arbiter of the life and fortunes of every one of us—not to mention chasing after other people's deaths and conspiring about wills. We are all so enslaved by avarice that we buy the power of making profit out of everything at the price of our souls. Amid such pestilen-tial corruption of human life, how can we expect any free, uncorrupt judge of great things of permanent value to be left to us? How can we hope not to lose our case to the corrupt practices of the love of gain? (10.) Perhaps people like us are better as subjects than given our freedom. Greed would flood the world in woe, if it were really released and let out of the cage, to prey on its neighbors. (11.) "Idleness," I went on to say, "was the bane of present-day minds. We all live with it. Our whole régime of effort and relaxation[112] is devoted to praise and pleasure, not to the useful results that deserve emulation and honor. (12.) 'Best to let these things be,'[113] and proceed to our next subject. This was emotion, to which we promised to devote a separate treatise. It occupies as I said, a very important place among the constituents of literature in general, and sublimity in particular. . . ." [A few words missing at the end]

PLOTINUS

(205–269/270 A.D.)

INTRODUCTION

The principal source of biographical information about Plotinus is the Life of
Plotinus written by his most eminent student, Porphyry. From this and other
sources we learn that the eminent Neoplatonist philosopher was born in Egypt
and lived the early part of his life there. He attended the lectures of various
philosophers at Alexandria but without enthusiasm until he came under the
influence of Ammonius Saccas, with whom he studied until 242 A.D. At that
time he joined the Persian expedition of Emperor Gordian in the expectation
of becoming more closely acquainted with Persian philosophy, but when Gordian
died the expedition failed and Plotinus went to Rome where he founded his
own school. He conceived of a plan to establish a city, Platonopolis, which was
to be the realization of Plato's *Republic*; but, although his friend, Emperor
Gallienus, showed interest in the project, the plan was never realized. With
regard to Plotinus' personality we know that he had a great reputation for
kindness and was named the guardian of the children of a number of his
friends. He lived an intensely spiritual life and, according to Porphyry, he
achieved ecstatic union with God four times in the six years during which
Porphyry was his disciple. It was Porphyry who divided his writings into six
books of nine chapters each and it is from the chapter divisions that the title
Enneads (units of nine) was derived for the work as a whole.

As in the case of his predecessor, Plato, Plotinus' aesthetic theory is
intimately connected with metaphysical considerations. Characteristically, Plotinus
rejects the commonly held position (propounded by the Stoics) that beauty
results from the existence of symmetry in all the parts of an object. He cites
entities such as the virtues and the soul to which symmetry in the ordinary
sense does not apply and yet which must be considered supremely beautiful.
Plotinus solves this difficulty by adopting the Platonic position that beauty
results from a communion of all things that are called beautiful and the always
existing ideal form of beauty. The beautiful object achieves essential unity
through its participation in the absolute principle of beauty. The task of judging

beauty is attributed to a faculty of the soul which is capable of perceiving the presence of the ideal unifying principle of beauty in material things whether they be letters and words, colors and lines, or sounds and harmonies.

Plotinus' comments on art do not derive from an inquiry into "aesthetics"; instead, his position is essentially *theological,* proceeding directly from a concept of God. What Plato called "the One" is now emphasized as a totally active force, radiating outwards as the source and sustaining principle of all being. This premise allows for an elevation of the status of art. According to Plotinus, the artistic imitation is not merely a static copy of the objects it represents: it is also a manifestation of the *divine idea* which the object itself imitates. Plotinus supports this thesis by declaring that art can imitate objects which have never yet existed or which are incapable of sensuous apprehension; as an example he cites the representation of Zeus by Phidias, who had to envision the form that the great Olympian god might take if he were to manifest himself to our senses.

Plotinus is important, of course, for carrying Platonic themes into Hellenistic criticism. But his work also has great significance for the whole subsequent history of Western poetics: he is the first real "Neoplatonic" critic. Plotinus developed a strategy by means of which later critics, from Augustine to Shelley, could reconcile Platonic "imitation" with reverence for art. In short, the aesthetic experience could be interpreted as an encounter with a higher spiritual reality.

The translation of the selections used here is by Stephen MacKenna in Plotinus, *The Enneads,* 4th ed. rev. by B. S. Page (London: Faber and Faber; New York: Pantheon Books of Random House, 1969) and has been reprinted by permission of the publishers.

from THE ENNEADS

BEAUTY

(1.) Beauty addresses itself chiefly to sight; but there is a beauty for the hearing too, as in certain combinations of words and in all kinds of music, for melodies and cadences are beautiful; and minds that lift themselves above the realm of sense to a higher order are aware of beauty in the conduct of life, in actions, in character, in the pursuits of the intellect; and there is the beauty of the virtues. What loftier beauty there may be, yet, our argument will bring to light.

What, then, is it that gives comeliness to material forms and draws the ear to the sweetness perceived in sounds, and what is the secret of the beauty there is in all that derives from soul?

Is there some one principle from which all take their grace, or is there a beauty peculiar to the embodied and another for the bodiless? Finally, one or many, what would such a principle be?

Consider that some things, material shapes for instance, are gracious not by anything inherent but by something communicated, while others are lovely of themselves, as, for example, virtue.

The same bodies appear sometimes beautiful, sometimes not; so that there is a good deal between being body and being beautiful.

What, then, is this something that shows itself in certain material forms? This is the natural beginning of our inquiry.

What is it that attracts the eyes of those to whom a beautiful object is presented, and calls them, lures them, towards it, and fills them with joy at the sight? If we possess ourselves of this, we have at once a standpoint for the wider survey.

Almost everyone declares that the symmetry of parts towards each other and towards a whole, with, besides, a certain charm of color, constitutes the beauty recognized by the eye, that in visible things, as indeed in all else, universally, the beautiful thing is essentially symmetrical, patterned.

But think what this means.

Only a compound can be beautiful, never anything devoid of parts; and only a whole; the several parts will have beauty, not in themselves, but only as working together to give a comely total. Yet beauty in an aggregate demands beauty in details: it cannot be constructed out of ugliness; its law must run throughout.

All the loveliness of color and even the light of the sun, being devoid of parts and so not beautiful by symmetry, must be ruled out of the realm of beauty. And how comes gold to be a beautiful thing? And lightning by night, and the stars, why are these so fair?

In sounds also the simple must be proscribed, though often in a whole noble composition each several tone is delicious in itself.

Again since the one face, constant in symmetry, appears sometimes fair and sometimes not, can we doubt that beauty is something more than symmetry, that symmetry itself owes its beauty to a remoter principle?

Turn to what is attractive in methods of life or in the expression of thought; are we to call in symmetry here? What symmetry is to be found in noble conduct, or excellent laws, in any form of mental pursuit?

What symmetry can there be in points of abstract thought?

The symmetry of being accordant with each other? But there may be accordance or entire identity where there is nothing but ugliness: the proposition that honesty is merely a generous artlessness chimes in the most perfect harmony with the proposition that morality means weakness of will; the accordance is complete.

Then again, all the virtues are a beauty of the soul, a beauty authentic beyond any of these others; but how does symmetry enter here? The soul, it is true, is not a simple unity, but still its virtue cannot have the symmetry of size or of number: what standard of measurement could preside over the compromise or the coalescence of the soul's faculties or purposes?

Finally, how by this theory would there be beauty in the intellectual-principle, essentially the solitary?

(2.) Let us, then, go back to the source, and indicate at once the principle that bestows beauty on material things.

Undoubtedly this principle exists; it is something that is perceived at the first glance, something which the soul names as from an ancient knowledge and, recognizing, welcomes it, enters into unison with it.

But let the soul fall in with the ugly and at once it shrinks within itself, denies the thing, turns away from it, not accordant, resenting it.

Our interpretation is that the soul—by the very truth of its nature, by its affiliation to the noblest existents in the hierarchy of being—when it sees anything of that kin, or any trace of that kinship, thrills with an immediate delight, takes its own to itself, and thus stirs anew to the sense of its nature and of all its affinity.

But, is there any such likeness between the loveliness of this world and the splendors in the supreme? Such a likeness in the particulars would make the two orders alike: but what is there in common between beauty here and beauty there?

We hold that all the loveliness of this world comes by communion in ideal-form.

All shapelessness whose kind admits of pattern and form, as long as it remains outside of reason and idea, is ugly by that very isolation from the divine reason-principle. And this is the absolute ugly: an ugly thing is something that has not been entirely mastered by pattern, that is by reason, the matter not yielding at all points and in all respects to ideal-form.

But where the ideal-form has entered, it has grouped and coordinated what from a diversity of parts was to become a unity: it has rallied confusion into co-operation: it has made the sum one harmonious coherence: for the idea is a unity and what it molds must come to unity as far as multiplicity may.

And on what has thus been compacted to unity, beauty enthrones itself, giving itself to the parts as to the sum: when it lights on some natural unity, a thing of like parts, then it gives itself to that whole. Thus, for an illustration, there is the beauty, conferred by craftsmanship, of all a house with all its parts, and the beauty which some natural quality may give to a single stone.

This, then, is how the material thing becomes beautiful—by communicating in the reason-principle that flows from the divine.

(3.) And the soul includes a faculty peculiarly addressed to beauty—one incomparably sure in the appreciation of its own, when soul entire is enlisted to support its judgment.

Or perhaps the faculty acts immediately, affirming the beautiful where it finds something accordant with the ideal-form within itself, using this idea as a canon of accuracy in its decision.

But what accordance is there between the material and that which antedates all matter?

On what principle does the architect, when he finds the house standing before him correspondent with his inner ideal of a house, pronounce it beautiful? Is it not that the house before him, the stones apart, is the inner idea stamped upon the mass of exterior matter, the indivisible exhibited in diversity?

So with the perceptive faculty: discerning in certain objects the ideal-form which has bound and controlled shapeless matter, opposed in nature to idea, seeing further stamped upon the common shapes some shape excellent above the common, it gathers into unity what still remains fragmentary, catches it up and carries it within, no longer a thing of parts, and presents it to the inner ideal-principle as something concordant and congenial, a natural friend: the joy here is like that of a good man who discerns in a youth the early signs of a virtue consonant with the achieved perfection within his own soul.

The beauty of color is also the outcome of a unification: it derives from shape, from the conquest of the darkness inherent in matter by the pouring-in of light, the unembodied, which is a rational-principle and an ideal-form.

Hence it is that fire itself is splendid beyond all material bodies, holding the rank of ideal-principle to the other elements, making ever upwards, the subtlest and sprightliest of all bodies, as very near to the unembodied; itself alone admitting no other, all the others penetrated by it: for they take warmth but this is never cold; it has color primally; they receive the form of color from it: hence the splendor of its light, the splendor that belongs to the idea. And all that has resisted and is but uncertainly held by its light remains outside of beauty, as not having absorbed the plenitude of the form of color.

And harmonies unheard in sound create the harmonies we hear and wake the soul to the consciousness of beauty, showing it the one essence in another kind: for the measures of our sensible music are not arbitrary but are determined by the principle whose labor is to dominate matter and bring pattern into being.

Thus far of the beauties of the realm of sense, images and shadow-pictures, fugitives that have entered into matter—to adorn, and to ravish, where they are seen.

(4.) But there are earlier and loftier beauties than these. In the sense-bound life we are no longer granted to know them, but the soul, taking no help from the organs, sees and proclaims them. To the vision of these we must mount, leaving sense to its own low place.

As it is not for those to speak of the graceful forms of the material world who have never seen them or known their grace—men born blind, let us suppose —in the same way those must be silent upon the beauty of noble conduct and of learning and all that order who have never cared for such things, nor may those tell of the splendor of virtue who have never known the face of justice and of moral-wisdom beautiful beyond the beauty of evening and of dawn.

Such vision is for those only who see with the soul's sight—and at the vision, they will rejoice, and awe will fall upon them and a trouble deeper than all the rest could ever stir, for now they are moving in the realm of truth.

This is the spirit that beauty must ever induce, wonderment and a delicious trouble, longing and love and a trembling that is all delight. For the unseen all this may be felt as for the seen; and this the souls feel for it, every soul in some degree, but those the more deeply that are the more truly apt to this higher love—just as all take delight in the beauty of the body but all are not stung as sharply, and those only that feel the keener wound are known as lovers.

(5.) These lovers, then, lovers of the beauty outside of sense, must be made to declare themselves.

What do you feel in presence of the grace you discern in actions, in manners, in sound morality, in all the works and fruits of virtue, in the beauty of souls? When you see that you yourselves are beautiful within, what do you feel? What is this Dionysiac exultation that thrills through your being, this straining upwards of all your soul, this longing to break away from the body and live sunken within the veritable self?

These are no other than the emotions of souls under the spell of love.

ON THE INTELLECTUAL BEAUTY

(1.) It is a principle with us that one who has attained to the vision of the intellectual cosmos and grasped the beauty of the authentic intellect will be able also to come to understand the father and transcendent of that divine being. It concerns us, then, to try to see and say, for ourselves and as far as such matters may be told, how the beauty of the divine intellect and of the intellectual cosmos may be revealed to contemplation.

Let us go to the realm of magnitudes:—suppose two blocks of stone lying side by side: one is unpatterned, quite untouched by art; the other has been minutely wrought by the craftsman's hands into some statue of god or man, a Grace or a Muse, or if a human being, not a portrait but a creation in which the sculptor's art has concentrated all loveliness.

Now it must be seen that the stone thus brought under the artist's hand to the beauty of form is beautiful not as stone—for so the crude block would be as pleasant—but in virtue of the form or idea introduced by the art. This form is not in the material; it is in the designer before ever it enters the stone; and the artificer holds it not by his equipment of eyes and hands but by his participation in his art. The beauty, therefore, exists in a far higher state in the art; for it does not come over integrally into the work; that original beauty is not transferred; what comes over is a derivative and a minor: and even that shows itself upon the statue not integrally and with entire realization of intention but only in so far as it has subdued the resistance of the material.

Art, then, creating in the image of its own nature and content, and working by the idea or reason-principle of the beautiful object it is to produce, must itself be beautiful in a far higher and purer degree since it is the seat and source of that beauty, indwelling in the art, which must naturally be more complete than any comeliness of the external. In the degree in which the beauty is diffused by entering into matter, it is so much the weaker than that concentrated in unity; everything that reaches outwards is the less for it, strength less strong, heat less hot, every power less potent, and so beauty less beautiful.

Then again every prime cause must be, within itself, more powerful than its effect can be: the musical does not derive from an unmusical source but from music; and so the art exhibited in the material work derives from an art yet higher.

Still the arts are not to be slighted on the ground that they create by imitation of natural objects; for, to begin with, these natural objects are themselves imitations; then, we must recognize that they give no bare reproduction of the thing seen but go back to the reason-principles from which nature itself derives, and, furthermore, that much of their work is all their own; they are holders of beauty and add where nature is lacking. Thus Pheidias wrought the Zeus upon no model among things of sense but by apprehending what form Zeus must take if he chose to become manifest to sight.

(2.) But let us leave the arts and consider those works produced by nature and admitted to be naturally beautiful which the creations of art are charged with imitating, all reasoning life and unreasoning things alike, but especially the consummate among them, where the molder and maker has subdued the material and given the form he desired. Now what is the beauty here? It has nothing to do with the blood or the menstrual process: either there is also a color and form apart from all this or there is nothing unless sheer ugliness or (at best) a bare recipient as it were the mere matter of beauty.

Whence shone forth the beauty of Helen, battle-sought; or of all those women like in loveliness to Aphrodite; or of Aphrodite herself; or of any human being that has been perfect in beauty; or of any of these gods manifest to sight, or unseen but carrying what would be beauty if we saw?

In all these is it not the form-idea, something of that realm but communicated to the produced from within the producer, just as in works of art, we held, it is communicated from the arts to their creations? Now we can surely not believe that, while the made thing and the reason-principle thus impressed upon matter are beautiful, yet the principle not so alloyed but resting still with the creator—the idea primal and immaterial—is not beauty.

If material extension were in itself the ground of beauty, then the creating principle, being without extension, could not be beautiful: but beauty cannot be made to depend upon magnitude since, whether in a large object or a small, the one idea equally moves and forms the mind by its inherent power. A further indication is that as long as the object remains outside us we know nothing of it; it affects us by entry; but only as an ideal-form can it enter through the eyes which are not of scope to take an extended mass: we are, no doubt, simultaneouly possessed of the magnitude which, however, we take in not as mass but an elaboration upon the presented form.

Then again the principle producing the beauty must be, itself, ugly, neutral, or beautiful: ugly, it could not produce the opposite; neutral, why should its product be the one rather than the other? The nature, then, which creates things so lovely must be itself of a far earlier beauty; we, undisciplined in discernment of the inward, knowing nothing of it, run after the outer, never understanding that it is the inner which stirs us; we are in the case of one who sees his own reflection but not realizing whence it comes goes in pursuit of it.

NOTES

ARISTOPHANES: THE FROGS

1. Armor for the leg below the knee.
2. This seems to be a slip of memory on the part of Aristophanes. *The Persians* is reliably dated 472 B.C., *The Seven Against Thebes* 467 B.C.—R.L.
3. The heroine of a lost play named after her. Her story is similar to that of Phaidra, insofar as she made advances to Bellerophon, her husband's guest, was refused, and told her husband that Bellerophon had tried to seduce her.—R.L.
4. No one is willing to be *trierarch*. The *trierarchy,* a special duty or liturgy imposed on rich citizens, involved the outfitting and upkeep of a trireme (war galley), as well as the nominal command of the vessel on active service.—R.L.
5. *His nurses . . . life?* The nurse-procuress could be Phaidra's nurse in *Hippolytus.* In *Auge,* the heroine gave birth in the temple of Athene. In *Aeolus,* Makareus and Kanake, brother and sister, are involved in a love affair. For musings on life, see the fragment from Euripides' lost *Polyeidus:* "Who knows if life be not thought death, or death be life in the world below?" There is a similar thought in the lost *Phrixus.*—R.L.

PLATO: INTRODUCTION

1. See Richard P. McKeon, "The Concept of Imitation in Antiquity," in *Critics and Criticism: Ancient and Modern,* ed. by R. S. Crane (Chicago, Ill., 1952), pp. 147–75, and W. J. Verdenius, *Mimesis: Plato's Doctrine of Artistic Imitation and Its Meaning to Us* (Leyden, 1962).
2. Allen H. Gilbert, "Plato's *Ion,* Comic and Serious," in *Studies in Honor of De W. T. Starnes* (Austin, Texas, 1967), pp. 259–69.

PHAEDRUS

1. A sanctuary and oracular shrine of Zeus, located in the mountains of Epirus.

GORGIAS

1. Originally, choral hymns that were sung to Dionysus. Developed into a formal art form by Arion of Corinth (ca. 600 B.C.) and introduced into Athens by Lasus

of Hermione, dithyrambic poetry became one of the competitive subjects at the Greek festivals. In Plato's time it was the most important type of lyric poetry.

ION

1. Professional reciters of poetry.
2. Greek festival celebrated annually at Athens.
3. Or, "I think I have well deserved the golden crown given me by the Homeridae."—JOWETT'S EDITORS. The latter were reciters of Homer's poetry and claimed to be his descendants.
4. Mythical attendants of the nature goddess Cybele, who engaged in orgiastic ritual dances.
5. See Note 1 to *Phaedrus*.
6. Originally, a choral song in honor of Apollo or his sister Artemis.
7. *Iliad* XXIII.335.
8. *Iliad* XI.639–40.
9. *Iliad* XXIV.80
10. *Odyssey* XX.351.
11. *Iliad* XII.200.

THE REPUBLIC
Book III

1. Spoken by the ghost of Achilles, *Odyssey* XI.489.
2. *Iliad* XX.64.
3. Said by Achilles when he tries, in vain, to embrace the ghost of Patroclus, *Iliad* XXIII.103.
4. *Odyssey* X.495.
5. *Iliad* XVI.856.
6. *Iliad* XXIII.100.
7. *Odyssey* XXIV.6 (refers to the souls of the slain suitors of Penelope).
8. Appropriate.
9. Mourning his friend Patroclus, *Iliad* XXIV.10.
10. Perhaps in a metaphorical sense, "reeling." Plato has slightly altered the text of Homer.—JOWETT'S EDITORS.
11. *Iliad* XVIII.23.
12. When he saw Achilles mistreating the body of his son Hector, *Iliad* XXII.414.
13. The speaker is Thetis, the mother of Achilles, *Iliad* XVIII.54.
14. Zeus when he saw Hector pursued by Achilles, *Iliad* XXII.168.
15. *Iliad* XVI.433.
16. *Iliad* I.599.
17. *Odyssey* XVII.383ff.
18. Or, "if his words are accompanied by actions."—B.J.
19. *Iliad* IV.412.

20. *Iliad* III.3.
21. *Iliad* IV.431.
22. Spoken by Achilles to his king Agamemnon, *Iliad* I.225.
23. Odysseus is the speaker, *Odyssey* IX.8.
24. *Odyssey* XII.342.
25. *Iliad* XIV.294ff.
26. *Odyssey* VIII.266.
27. Odysseus is speaking, *Odyssey* XX.17.
28. Quoted by Suidas (a historical and literary encyclopedia compiled about 1,000 A.D.) as ascribed to Hesiod.
29. *Iliad* IX.515.
30. *Iliad* XXIV.175.
31. Cf. *Republic* X.595.
32. *Iliad* XXII.15ff.
33. *Iliad* XXI.130, 223ff.
34. *Iliad* XXIII.151.
35. *Iliad* XXII.395.
36. *Iliad* XXIII.175.
37. From the *Niobe* of Aeschylus.
38. Agamemnon and Menelaus, *Iliad* I.15.
39. A wreath or garland worn on the head.
40. Juror.
41. I.e. the four notes of the tetrachord.—B.J.
42. Socrates expresses himself carelessly in accordance with his assumed ignorance of the details of the subject. In the first part of the sentence he appears to be speaking of paeonic rhythms which are in the ratio of $3/2$; in the second part, of dactylic and anapaestic rhythms, which are in the ratio of $1/1$; in the last clause, of iambic and trochaic rhythms, which are in the ratio of $1/2$ or $2/1$.—B.J. In classical prosody, a long syllable is the equivalent of two short ones. The dactylic (—$\cup\cup$) and anapaestic ($\cup\cup$—) feet, each consisting of one long and two shorts, thus have a 1:1 ratio; the iambic ($\cup$—) and trochaic (—$\cup$) a 1:2 or 2:1 ratio; and the paean (first p., —$\cup\cup\cup$; second p., $\cup$—$\cup\cup$; third $\cup\cup$—$\cup$; fourth, $\cup\cup\cup$—) a 3:2 ratio.

THE REPUBLIC
Book X

1. Stories taken from epic poetry often served as the plots of Greek tragedies. Thus Homer was considered the first tragic poet.
2. Or (probably better), "we have been accustomed to assume that there is one single idea corresponding to each group of particulars; and to these we give the same name (as we give the idea)."—JOWETT'S EDITORS, note abridged.
3. Or, "with his nouns and verbs."—B.J.
4. Dactylic hexameter.
5. Or, "law and the principle which the community in every case has pronounced to be the best."—JOWETT'S EDITORS.

6. Reading and sense uncertain. The origin of all these quotations is unknown.—JOWETT'S EDITORS.

7. I.e. imitative poetry. The word imitation, in the recent argument, had not the same sense as in Book III; but it has always been implied that there might be poetry which is not imitative.—JOWETT'S EDITORS.

8. Text doubtful. Perhaps "you demanded . . . this admission should be made."—JOWETT'S EDITORS.

9. *Odyssey* XI–XII.

10. I.e. those who were not incurable, but had further punishment to endure.—JOWETT'S EDITORS.

11. War galley; the earliest kind of a Greek warship.

L A W S

1. *Laws* V.741E.
2. *Laws* VI.764C.
3. *Laws* VI.765D.
4. Cf. *Republic* X.607A.
5. Or, . . . "even though the pleasure of music is not counted."—JOWETT'S EDITORS.
6. *Laws* I.644D.E.
7. *Laws* I.628.
8. *Odyssey* III.26ff.
9. The shortest metrical foot in classical verse, consisting of two short syllables (∪∪).
10. The solemn dance of the chorus in Greek tragedy.
11. Cf. *Republic* III.398A and X.607A.
12. Public square in which the popular political assembly met.

A R I S T O T L E :   I N T R O D U C T I O N

1. For a full discussion of this problem see O. B. Hardison's commentary in L. Golden and O. B. Hardison, Jr., *Aristotle's Poetics: A Translation and Commentary for Students of Literature* (Englewood Cliffs, N.J., 1968), pp. 230–37.

2. On the basis of the evidence from Book 10 of the *Republic,* the "copying" theory of imitation which is mentioned in the text has generally been attributed to Plato. Some scholars, however, having surveyed the entire corpus of Plato's work, have also attributed to him a more sophisticated view of imitation. See Richard McKeon, "Literary Criticism and the Concept of Imitation in Antiquity," in *Critics and Criticism: Ancient and Modern,* ed. R. S. Crane (Chicago, 1952), pp. 160–68; W. J. Verdenius, *Mimesis: Plato's Doctrine of Artistic Imitation and Its Meaning to Us* (Leyden, 1962); and L. Golden, "*Mimesis* and *Katharsis*," *Classical Philology,* LXIV (1969), 143–53.

3. See, for example, Suzanne Langer, *Feeling and Form* (New York, 1953), p. 352: "'Imitation' is used by Aristotle in much the same sense in which I use 'semblance'"; Roman Ingarden, "A Marginal Commentary on Aristotle's *Poetics* —Part II," tr. Helen Michejda, *Journal of Aesthetics and Art Criticism,* XX (1961–62), 282: "It

seems probable that Aristotle had in mind the same thing that in my book, *Das literarische Kunstwerk*, I called 'objective consistency' . . . within the framework of the world presented in the work"; and Northrop Frye, *Anatomy of Criticism* (Princeton, N.J., 1957), p. 113: the fictive imagination involves the "transmutation of experience into mimesis, of life into art, of routine into play."

4. *Aristotle's Theory of Poetry and Fine Art*, 4th ed. (New York, 1951), pp. 121–62.
5. "The Mimetic Principle" in *The World's Body*, 2nd ed. (Baton Rouge, La., 1968), pp. 196–97.
6. *Aristotle's Poetics* (Note 1), pp. 281–96.
7. An excellent warning against the confusion of the aesthetic principles of the *Poetics* with the non-aesthetic principles of the *Politics* has been given by Richard McKeon (Note 2), pp. 165–66.
8. For a discussion of Lessing's view see Ingram Bywater, ed., *Aristotle on the Art of Poetry* (London and New York, 1909), pp. 160–61.
9. Gerald F. Else, *Aristotle's Poetics: The Argument* (Cambridge, Mass., 1957), pp. 224–32, 423–47.
10. S. O. Haupt, *Wirkt die Tragödie auf das Gemüt oder den Verstand oder die Moralität der Zuschauer?* (Berlin, 1915) and *Die Lösung der Katharsis Theorie des Aristoteles* (Znaim, 1911).
11. Leon Golden, "Catharsis," *Transactions of the American Philological Association*, XCIII (1962), 51–60. See also his *"Mimesis* and *Katharsis," Classical Philology*, LXIV (1969), 145–53.
12. H. D. F. Kitto, "Catharsis," in *The Classical Tradition: Literary and Historical Studies in Honor of Harry Caplan* (Ithaca, N.Y., 1966), pp. 133–47.
13. See J. M. Bremer, *Hamartia: Tragic Error in the Poetics of Aristotle and in Greek Tragedy* (Amsterdam, 1969); R. D. Dawe, "Some Reflections on *Ate* and *Hamartia," Harvard Studies in Classical Philology*, LXXII (1968), 81–123; Martin Ostwald, "Aristotle on *Hamartia* and Sophocles' *Oedipus Tyrannos*," in *Festschrift Ernst Kapp* (Hamburg, 1958), pp. 93–108.
14. "Tragedy and the Common Man," in Sylvan Barnet *et al*, eds., *Aspects of the Drama* (Boston, 1962), p. 64.

THE POETICS

1. See Plato, Note 1 to *Phaedrus*.
2. Dramatic representations of short scenes from daily life, involving dancing, music, and dialogue.
3. Poetry originally concerned with texts taken from the epic and presented with a flute or lyre accompaniment.
4. There is a lacuna in the text at this point where the name of another writer of nomic poetry was probably mentioned.
5. This poem is no longer attributed to Homer.
6. A form of drama in which the chorus was dressed as satyrs. In historical times a satyr play was presented as the fourth play in a tetralogy produced at Athenian dramatic festivals. The theme of the satyr play was mocking or "satirical" in tone,

contrasting with the seriousness of the other three dramas associated with it. Aristotle viewed the satyr play as a stage in the development of mature tragedy.

7. Athenian magistrates.

8. There is no word in the Greek text for "proper," but I have followed the practice of several other translators who add a modifier to the term "magnitude" where it is logically warranted. The term "representation" has also been added to the final clause of this sentence because of Aristotle's insistence that the pleasure of tragedy is achieved *through imitation* (Chapter XIV, lines 15–16).

9. Text is corrupt here.

10. A lost play by the 4th century tragic poet Theodectes.

11. Unknown. Possibly, a variant title for a tragedy by Sophocles.

12. The *Cresphontes* and the *Iphigenia,* the former no longer extant, are plays by Euripides. We have no further information concerning the *Helle.*

13. According to some scholars, a play by Euripides; others believe it to be a work of the dithyrambic poet Timotheus.

14. Euripides' play about the Amazon queen.

15. Medea escaped in a magic chariot in Euripides' tragedy.

16. A birthmark on the descendants of the armed men who, as legend has it, sprang up when Cadmus sowed the dragon's teeth at Thebes.

17. A lost drama by Sophocles.

18. Having had her tongue cut out by Tereus, Philomela disclosed the story of her rape through the web she wove.

19. The second play of the Aeschylean trilogy known as the *Oresteia.* The play describes Orestes' murder of his mother Clytemnestra, in vengeance for her killing of his father Agamemnon, and the subsequent madness visited upon him by the Erinyes in punishment for his crime.

20. Nothing more is known of these two plays, the *Tydeus* and the *Phinidae.*

21. Text is in dispute here.

22. The *Phthiotian Women* and *Peleus,* neither now extant, were probably written by Sophocles.

23. The *Daughters of Phorcis* and *Prometheus* are both by Aeschylus.

24. Opening line of the *Iliad.*

25. The passage that begins here is corrupt and difficult to interpret.

26. There is a lacuna in the text here. Massilia (Marseilles) was founded by Greeks from Phorcis.

27. "At her right breast" (*Iliad* V.393). Two words meaning "right" are quoted to illustrate Aristotle's point here.

28. This passage offers a number of difficulties in text and interpretation. The essential point is that the prose lines quoted can be technically turned into verse if enough licenses are allowed. The first phrase may be translated "I saw Epichares going to Marathon." The text of the second phrase is corrupt and does not have a clear meaning as it stands.

29. A lost play.

30. "Someone small, worthless, and unseemly" (*Odyssey* IX.515).

31. "Having set down [for him] an unseemly chair and a small table" (*Odyssey* XX.259).

32. "The shores cry out" (*Iliad* XVII.265).

33. One of the poems of the Trojan cycle once attributed to Homer. It described Paris' abduction of Helen and is no longer extant.

34. Part of the ancient epic cycle of poems composed after the Homeric epics by poets who are now unknown. The work has not survived.

35. The *Award of the Arms* may refer to the existing play *Ajax* of Sophocles or to a lost tragedy by Aeschylus. A play entitled *Neoptolemus* is attributed by Suidas (a literary and historical encyclopedia compiled around the year 1,000) to a tragic poet named Nicomachus. We have no further record of *Eurypylus*, the *Beggar*, and the *Return Voyage* as titles of tragedies.

36. Sophocles' *Laconian Woman* is lost. A play entitled the *Sack of Troy* is attributed to Iophon, who was the son of Sophocles and a tragic poet in his own right. Sophocles' *Sinon* has not survived. The *Women of Troy* is an extant play by Euripides.

37. Dactylic hexameter.

38. Musical competitions and athletic contests held, in honor of Apollo, every four years in Delphi.

39. Probably a lost play by Aeschylus.

40. There is a lacuna in the text here that I have filled by translating Bywater's suggested reading, *hēmarte de di'*.

41. "First of all, the mules" (*Iliad* I.50).

42. *Iliad* X.316.

43. *Iliad* IX.202.

44. *Iliad* XVIII.489.

45. The problem here is that words that are spelled the same way change their meaning when given different accents. In the first phrase quoted, *didomen* can be either a present indicative or an infinitive used as an imperative, depending on the way it is accented; in the second phrase, *ou* can be either a relative pronoun or a negative adverb, depending on the way it is accented.

46. The problem treated here is the effect that punctuation has on the meaning of a sentence. Thus, by means of different punctuations the word "before" in Empedocles' statement could be referred either to the phrase that precedes it, "things unmixed," or to the word that follows it, "mixed."

47. The word "more" has a form in Greek that can also be translated as "full."

48. In Homer, Icarius is Penelope's father.

49. Translating *kai ei adunaton,* suggested by Vahlen to fill a lacuna in the text at this point.

DEMETRIUS: ON STYLE

1. An apparent reference to *Rhetoric* III.viii.4–6, but Aristotle's discussion of rhythm does not deal with any theory of styles, nor does he use the adjective "impressive." —from G.M.A.G.

2. *History of the Peloponnesian War* II.48.

3. Here Demetrius makes an important advance when he speaks of the *general*

rhythmic character of a clause without trying to analyze it into exact feet. The sentence quoted is *tōn men peri ta mēdenos axia philosophountōn* ("they were philosophizing about matters of no importance," the rhythm of which is ——ᴜᴜᴜ—ᴜᴜ—ᴜᴜᴜᴜ——). Thus it neither begins nor ends with a paeon; yet it is termed generally paeonic.—G.M.A.G.

4. Demetrius' example here is an unidentified clause: *hēkōn hēmōn eis tēn chōrān* in which all the syllables are long. The term "heroic meter" usually refers to the dactylic hexameter. His example has no dactyl and only four feet. Thus it can be said to be heroic only in the same general sense as the clause from Theophrastus was called paeonic.—G.M.A.G., note abridged.

5. The opening words of Thucydides' *History of the Peloponnesian War* and Herodotus' *Histories*.

6. *History of the Peloponnesian War* II.102.

7. *Aias d' ho megas aien ep' Hektori chalkokorustē* (*Iliad* XVI.358).

8. *History of the Peloponnesian War* II.49.

9. *Republic* III.411A–B.

10. *Odyssey* IX.190.

11. *Men* and *de* ["on the one hand" and "but on the other"] is the simplest way to express an antithesis in Greek. . . . We do not possess the context of the sentence here quoted: *hē men gar nēsos hēn echomen dēlē men kai porrōthen estin, hupsēlē kai tracheia, kai ta men chrēsima kai ergasima mikra autēs esti, ta de arga polla, smikras autēs ousēs.* (The island we occupy is visible from afar, high and rough, and the parts of it that are workable and cultivated are small, but the uncultivated parts are large, considering its size.) Actually, the *de* answers the last *men* only. *Men* was used alone when the second member of an antithesis remained unexpressed.—G.M.A.G.

12. *Iliad* II.497.

13. *Phaedrus* 246E.

14. *Iliad* XIV.433 or XXI.I.

15. *Odyssey* V. 203.

16. Demetrius quotes the first four words only of the Homeric line *kai nu k'oduromenoisin edu phaos ēelioio* (the light of the sun set upon their lamentations) from the scene of Patroclus' burial, *Iliad* XXIII.154.—G.M.A.G.

17. *Odyssey* XII.73. Substitution of the nominative for the genitive.

18. *Iliad* II.671. Epanaphora is the repetition of the same word at the beginning of succeeding clauses, here also succeeding lines. Dialysis (disconnection) is the name here given to lack of connectives, elsewhere also called asyndeton.—G.M.A.G.

19. The source of the quotation is unknown. The term synapheia is here used of the repetition of the *same* connective (*kai*). This figure is called *polysyndeton* by Quintilian (IX.iii.51).—G.M.A.G.

20. Demetrius expects his readers to remember Homer's description of the waves breaking on the shore in *Iliad* XIII.798–800: "Many a clashing wave of the loud-roaring sea, high-arched, white-crested; first one comes, then another. . . ."—G.M.A.G.

21. A brief and inexact quotation from *History of the Peloponnesian War* IV.12.—G.M.A.G., note abridged.

22. Anadiplōsis is the immediate repetition of a word. This sentence is not found in

Herodotus' description of the Caucasus, but a near-anadiplōsis does occur in his *Histories* I.203, where he says of the Caucasus: "Of mountains in number the greatest, and in greatness the highest."—G.M.A.G.

23. Isocrates was notorious for his avoidance of hiatus, that is, the clash of vowels which comes from a word that ends in a vowel being followed by one that begins with a vowel.—G.M.A.G.

24. All Demetrius' examples are proper names, except *chiōn.*—G.M.A.G.

25. The example (omitted in translation) of sounds that lose by being elided is an unidentified sentence: *panta ta nea kai kala estin* (all that is young is also beautiful) where the last two words would normally be elided into *kal' estin* or, and this is the form he gives, *kala 'stin* to avoid hiatus.—G.M.A.G.

26. The seven vowels in Greek are: a, e, ē, i, o, u, ō; ē and ō were always long; a, i, and u could be long or short.—G.M.A.G.

27. *Odyssey* XI.595–98. The Sisyphus passage was a favorite with critics. . . . Here, however, Demetrius quotes only three words and is concerned with the hiatus between the last two.—G.M.A.G.

28. *History of the Peloponnesian War* VI.1. Here again Demetrius quotes only three words with a hiatus between the first two.—G.M.A.G., note abridged.

29. *History of the Peloponnesian War* I.24. This example (omitted in translation) has many long syllables:

> *taūtēn kátōkēsān mēn Kērkўrāioi ōikistēs dē ĕgĕnĕtó*
> (the Corcyraeans colonized it. The founder was),

but our immediate concern is the hiatus in *oi* and *e* in the last four words.—G.M.A.G., note abridged.

30. This is a sound point that Aristotle does not make in his discussion of metaphors, and Demetrius may well be deliberately improving on him. The reference is to *Iliad* XX.218.—G.M.A.G.

31. *On the Crown* 136.

32. The reference is to *Rhetoric* III.xi.3–4, where Aristotle says that such metaphors put the action vividly before our eyes. He gives the same examples as Demetrius, namely, *Iliad* IV.126 and XIII.799.—G.M.A.G., note abridged.

33. *Iliad* XIII.339.

34. *Iliad* XXI.388.

35. *Anabasis* I.viii.18.

36. The quotation may be from the didactic poet, Theognis of Megara (6th century B.C.) or from the tragic poet of the last 5th century B.C.—G.M.A.G.

37. The "eyes of the vine" means the buds, and *ophthalmos* (eye) was used in many other common metaphors. A modern equivalent would be "the eye of a needle." —G.M.A.G.

38. The instances given in this section are *sphondulos* which means both vertebra and the whorl of a spindle; *kleis*, key and also collar-bone; and *ktenes*, ribs, incisor teeth, and also the comb of a loom.—G.M.A.G.

39. *Cyropaideia* I.iv.21. The distinction here is between the prose simile and the Homeric kind here called *parabolē poiĕtikē* (poetic comparison). It is a distinction that needed making and is not made by Aristotle.—G.M.A.G.

40. The Greek examples in the last sentence are *nomothetēs*, lawgiver, and *architektōn,*

but architect is not an English compound, nor is master-builder a single word.—
G.M.A.G.

41. Demetrius' example, *sitopompia* for *hē pompē tou sitou* is not particularly impressive either in Greek or in English. Eyelid or flagstaff might be more impressive.—
G.M.A.G., note abridged.

42. *Anabasis* I.v.2. The word translated "relays" is *diadechomenoi,* which is a compound word, so that this is not a digression.—G.M.A.G.

43. *Odyssey* IX.394. "Sizzled" is used of the Cyclops' eye when the burning stake is driven into it. "Lapping" is used of wolves and dogs in *Iliad* XVI.161.—G.M.A.G., note abridged.

44. *Historia Animalium* II.497 and 610.

45. *Allēgoria* seems to be used here in the general sense of meaning something else than one says rather than in our more restricted sense of allegory. The meaning of the example is that the whole city and country will be devastated.—G.M.A.G., note abridged.

46. The line (about the cupping-glass) is used by Aristotle both in *Rhetoric* III.ii.12 and *Poetics* 1458A.—G.M.A.G.

47. I.e., Dionysius was once a great ruler like you, but he is now living in Corinth as a private citizen.—from G.M.A.G.

48. The Greek for "to pass over in silence," that is, not to express what is implied, is *aposiōpēsis*. Repetition here is *dilogia*, that is, repeating words from one clause to another—G.M.A.G., note abridged.

49. *Anabasis* I.viii.20.

50. Ibid I.viii.10.

51. Demetrius here quotes only in part *Iliad* XVI.358, which he quoted in full, as an example of dysphony, in section 48 (see Note 7). Here our attention is drawn to the repetition of the long *a* and *ai* sounds in *Aias d'ho megas aien . . .* but we are meant to remember the line as a whole which contains both repetition of sound and lack of euphony.—G.M.A.G., note abridged.

52. *Odyssey* XIX.7–13.

53. Probably awnings or drapes.—from G.M.A.G.

54. *Iliad* XII.113.

55. *History of the Peloponnesian War* IV.64 and *Odyssey* XIX.172.

56. The lacuna indicated in the text must have contained not only some such expression as is added here, but also a reference to the fourth kind. It can be supplied from Aristotle's account in *Rhetoric* III.iii.1–4 which Demetrius is obviously following.
—G.M.A.G.

57. Demetrius gives one example:

hēkōn hēmōn eis tēn chōrān, pāsēs hēmōn orthēs ousēs,

of which he gave the first five words as an example of "heroic" meter in section 42 (see Note 4). All the syllables are long.—G.M.A.G., note abridged.

58. Some name has obviously dropped out. It may have been any lowly or weak character. The suggestion of Thersites, the ugly and obstreperous rank-and-filer in *Iliad* II will do as well as any other.—G.M.A.G.

59. *Anabasis* IV.iv.3.

60. Source unknown.
61. Magistrate.
62. Hesiod, *Work and Days* 40.
63. The first two examples are used by Dolon of the horses of Rhesus: "they are whiter than snow, and run like the wind" in *Iliad* X.437. This certainly does not seem frigid. The third is from *Iliad* IV.443 and describes Eris or Strife. Here Demetrius' criticism is more justified.—G.M.A.G.
64. Demetrius is still dealing with the impressive style.—G.M.A.G.
65. Source of the quotations is unknown.—G.M.A.G.

HORACE: INTRODUCTION

1. See Richard McKeon's "Literary Criticism and the Concept of Imitation in Antiquity," in *Critics and Criticism: Ancient and Modern,* ed. R. S. Crane (Chicago, 1952), especially pp. 168–72.
2. *Works,* ed. Albert Feuillerat (Cambridge, Mass., 1922–23), III, 9.
3. See Marvin T. Herrick's *The Fusion of Horatian and Aristotelian Literary Criticism, 1550–1580* (University of Illinois Studies in Language and Literature, XXXII, no. 1; Urbana, Ill., 1946).

ARS POETICA

1. The *Ars Poetica* is a letter of advice addressed to a father and his two sons bearing the family name of Piso.
2. People saved from a shipwreck placed a picture on the scene as a votive offering in the temple.
3. Horace refers to the days of old when such men as M. Cornelius Cethegus wore a loincloth (*cinctus*) under the toga instead of the tunic of later times.
4. Perhaps a reference to the Portus Julius, an artificial harbor formed by constructing a channel to connect Lake Lucrinus with Lake Avernus.
5. Probably the draining of the Pontine Marshes.
6. Horace may be referring to the straightening of the course of the Tiber to prevent flooding of farm land.
7. Dactylic hexameter.
8. The elegiac couplet, consisting of a hexameter and a pentameter.
9. The iambic trimeter was the measure used in dialogue both in comedy and tragedy.
10. A lightweight shoe worn by ancient Greek and Roman comic actors.
11. The high, thick-soled shoe worn by ancient Greek and Roman tragic actors.
12. Chremes is a name used by the Roman poet Terence in his comedies. Peleus and Telephus are mythical figures (the father of Achilles and the son-in-law of Priam, respectively) and Euripidian characters.
13. Epic poets, probably later than Homer, whose subjects were the legends revolving around the Trojan and Theban wars.
14. A paraphrase of the opening lines of the *Odyssey*.

15. The mythical warrior Meleager, uncle of Diomedes, a hero in the Trojan war, dies before the latter is born.—The "twin eggs" refer to the birth of Helen of Troy. Zeus had visited her mother Leda in the form of a swan, and she produced two eggs. From one Helen emerged and from the other Castor and Pollux.
16. Campus Martius in Rome.
17. Tragedy or "goat song" was supposed to take its name from the prize in a competition: a he-goat. This derivation, however, is no longer accepted.
18. See Note 6 to Aristotle's *Poetics*.
19. Typical characters (slave, maid, old man) in the New Comedy.
20. Epithet given by the poet's admirers.
21. They produced hellbore, medicine made from a herb supposedly effective in the treatment of madness.
22. A female monster; a bugbear.
23. An ancient classification of Roman citizens into *seniores* and *iuniores*.
24. Booksellers in ancient Rome.
25. Region in ancient Macedonia. The Pierian Spring was sacred to the Muses, and its water was said to be a source of inspiration.
26. A festival at Delphi, including musical and athletic contests—next in importance to the Olympic games.

QUINTILIAN: INSTITUTIO ORATORIA

1. *Phaenomena* 1.
2. *Iliad* XXI.196.
3. Beginning; introduction.
4. Antilochus in the *Iliad* XVIII.18.
5. Phoenix, *Iliad* IX.529.
6. *Iliad* XXIV.486ff.
7. Refers to copying by dividing the surface of the picture to be copied, and of the material on which the copy is to be made, into a number of equal squares.—H.E.B.
8. The Annales Maximi kept by the Pontifex Maximus, containing the list of the consuls and giving a curt summary of the events of each consulate.—H.E.B.
9. Would seem to be.

"LONGINUS": INTRODUCTION

1. Roy Arthur Swanson, "'Longinus': Noesis and Pathos," *Classical Bulletin*, XLVI (November, 1969), 1–5.
2. See Samuel Holt Monk, *The Sublime: A Study of Critical Theories in Eighteenth-Century England* (New York, 1934).
3. See the "Introduction" to *"Longinus" on the Sublime*, ed. D. A. Russell (Oxford, 1964), pp. xlvii-xlviii.
4. "On the Relation of Analytical Psychology to Poetic Art," tr. H. G. and Cary F. Baynes, in *Modern Continental Literary Criticism*, ed. O. B. Hardison (New York, 1962), p. 286.

5. *Anatomy of Criticism* (Princeton, 1957), p. 65.
6. "Longinus and the 'New Criticism,'" in *Collected Essays* (Denver, 1959), p. 511.
7. See especially Elder Olson, "The Argument of Longinus' *On the Sublime*," in *Critics and Criticism: Ancient and Modern,* ed. R. S. Crane (Chicago, 1952); and Hoyt Trowbridge, "'Leda and the Swan': A Longinian Analysis," *Modern Philology,* LI (November, 1953).

ON SUBLIMITY

1. This is to translate *bathous*. The simple, 18th-century emendation *pathous* means "emotion." The English word "bathos" seems to have acquired its meaning from a misunderstanding of the passage.—D.A.R. See Pope's *Peri Bathous; or, Martinus Scriblerus, His Treatise of the Art of Sinking in Poetry* (1727/28).
2. *Orations* XXIII.113.
3. Aeschylus, fragment 281 in Nauck's *Tragicorum Graecorum Fragmenta* (ed. 2). But it is not certain that the passage is not rather by Sophocles. The speaker is Boreas, the North Wind, who is enraged with King Erechtheus of Athens because he will not give him his daughter Orithyia. As the passage is incomplete, the point of some of the critical comment is lost.—D.A.R.
4. Fragment 701, Nauck, op. cit.—D.A.R.
5. Presumably in the lost passage.—D.A.R.
6. In the 8th century B.C. According to other sources this war lasted 20 years.—D.A.R., note abridged.
7. Dionysius II, expelled in 356.—D.A.R.
8. The word *korē* means both "girl" and "pupil"; Xenophon replaces it by *parthenos,* which means unambiguously "maiden."—D.A.R.
9. *Iliad* I.225.
10. . . . The "unveiling ceremony" was normally held on the third day after the marriage.—D.A.R.
11. *Laws* 741C.
12. *Laws* 778D.
13. *Histories* V.18.
14. See chapters 23 and 38.—D.A.R.
15. Or "and coined words."—D.A.R.
16. *Sunthesis;* Latin "compositio," but narrower in sense than "composition" in non-technical English. See chaps. 39–42.—D.A.R.
17. *Odyssey* XI.315–17.
18. *Odyssey* XI.563. Note that this is not an example, but a simile illustrating the point that ideas in themselves can be grand.—D.A.R.
19. Parmenio said to Alexander that if he were Alexander he would be content, and would not go on fighting. "So would I, if I were Parmenio," replied Alexander.—D.A.R.
20. *Iliad* IV.440ff., where Strife is described as having her head in the sky and walking on the earth. "Longinus" means that Homer too is a colossus of cosmic dimensions.—D.A.R.
21. *Shield of Heracles* 267.

22. *Iliad* V.770–2.
23. See *Iliad* XXI.388 and XX.61ff.
24. See *Iliad* XIII.18ff. and XX.60.
25. Controversy about the genuineness of this reference to Genesis i has raged since the 18th century.—D.A.R., note abridged.
26. *Iliad* XVII.645ff.
27. *Iliad* XV.605ff.
28. Spoken by Nestor, *Odyssey* III.109ff.
29. For these various stories, see *Odyssey* X.17ff., X.237ff., XII.447ff., XXII.79ff.—D.A.R.
30. Sappho, fragment 31. See D. L. Page, *Sappho and Alcaeus,* chap. 2.—D.A.R., note abridged.
31. From a lost poem attributed to Aristeas of Proconnesus, a prophet of Apollo said to have travelled in Siberia in the 7th century B.C.—D.A.R., note abridged.
32. *Iliad* XV.624ff.
33. *Phaenomena* 299.
34. The example from Archilochus cannot be certainly identified. That from Demosthenes (*On the Crown* 169) describes the alarm at Athens when news arrived of Philip's occupation of Elatea (339 B.C.).—D.A.R., note abridged.
35. *Theaetetus* 144B.
36. *Republic* IX.586A (slightly abridged).
37. Text uncertain: perhaps "the reproduction of beauty of form. . . ."—D.A.R.
38. *Work and Days* 24: healthy rivalry contrasted with the strife that produces war. —D.A.R.
39. A Stoic definition.—D.A.R.
40. Euripides, *Orestes* 255–57. Orestes sees the Furies.—D.A.R.
41. Euripides, *Iphigenia in Tauris* 291. Again Orestes and the Furies.—D.A.R.
42. *Iliad* XX.170.
43. Fragment 779, Nauck op. cit. . . . The passages quoted [from Euripides' lost *Phaethon*] seem to be from a messenger's speech recounting Phaethon's fall.— D.A.R.
44. Fragment 935, Nauck op. cit. Perhaps from the *Alexandros.* As the context is lost, we do not know the point.—D.A.R., note abridged.
45. Aeschylus, fragment 58, Nauck, op. cit.; Euripides, *Bacchae* 726.—D.A.R., note abridged.
46. Final scene of *Oedipus Coloneus.*
47. Probably in the lost *Polyxena.*—D.A.R., note abridged.
48. Euripides, *Orestes* 264–65.
49. Demosthenes, *Oration,* XXIV.208.
50. I.e. after Philip's victory at Chaeronea (338 B.C.). The speech is not extant.—D.A.R.
51. *Oration* XVIII.208.
52. From the lost comedy *Demoi.* Eupolis parodies Euripides, *Medea* 395ff.—D.A.R.
53. See below, chap. 35.—D.A.R.
54. Note that these remarks are themselves cast as rhetorical questions.—D.A.R.
55. Demosthenes, *Orations* IV.10.
56. Ibid., 44.
57. *Hellenica* IV.iii.19.
58. *Odyssey* X.251–52.

59. Demosthenes, *Orations* XXI.72.
60. Probably a few words are missing here.—D.A.R.
61. *Histories* VI.11.
62. Polyptoton is the occurrence of the same word in various inflexions. It is not certain whether "Longinus" thinks of accumulation (*athroismos*), variation (*metabole*), and climax as species of it or as distinct.—D.A.R., note abridged.
63. *Oedipus Tyrannus* 1403ff.
64. A line of an unknown tragedy.—D.A.R.
65. *Menexenus* 245D. Not quoted in any other extant part of this book.—D.A.R.
66. Demosthenes, *Orations,* XVIII.18.
67. Herodotus, *Histories* VI.21.
68. Or, "it is a mark of emotion to pluralize them unexpectedly."—D.A.R.
69. *Cyropaedia* VII.i.37.
70. *Iliad* XV.697.
71. *Phaenomena* 287.
72. *Histories* II.29.
73. *Iliad* V.85.
74. *Iliad* XV.346.
75. Fragment 30, Jacoby.—D.A.R.
76. *Oration* XXV (a spurious speech). The passage is from §27.—D.A.R.
77. *Odyssey* IV.681ff.
78. *Menexenus* 236D.
79. *Cyropaedia* I.v.12.
80. *Histories* I.105.
81. 801B.
82. "Pathos" (emotion) characterizes truly "sublime" writing; "ēthos" (realistic depiction of manners or humors) belongs rather to lower, more human and even comic, genres; cf. the *Iliad-Odyssey* contrast, IX.13–15. "Hēdonē" (pleasure, charm) is the typical aim and effect of this second kind of literature.—D.A.R., note abridged.
83. Fragment 96, Bergk, *Poetae Lyrici Graeci.* "Filly" is a probable, but not certain, supplement. "Longinus' " text here is uncertain. Perhaps: ". . . But not Anacreon's I turn my mind. . . ' ."—D.A.R.
84. *Histories* VI.75, VII.181.
85. Demosthenes, *Orations* XVIII.296.
86. Xenophon, *Memorabilia* I.iv.5ff; Plato *Timaeus* 65C–85E ("Longinus" picks various details out of this long passage, and runs them together).—D.A.R., note abridged.
87. *Laws* VI.773C.
88. Or perhaps "fluent."—D.A.R.
89. The speech in which the myth of Leto was told is lost: the Funeral Speech is extant (*Oration* 2). "Epideictic": i.e. written as a demonstration of skill; the term applies to panegyrics, etc. Cf. chap. 8.—D.A.R.
90. The first is lost; the second is *Oration* 3 (5).—D.A.R.
91. "Epigram on the tomb of Midias," ascribed to Homer; see Plato *Phaedrus* 264D. —D.A.R.
92. It is not certain whether "Longinus" means the Colossus of Rhodes or some other large statue.—D.A.R., note abridged.
93. Demosthenes, *Orations* VII.45—a speech generally thought to be spurious.—D.A.R.

94. *Panegyricus* 8.
95. *History of the Peloponnesian War* VII.84.
96. *Histories* VII.225.
97. Euripides, fragment 663, Nauck, op. cit.—D.A.R.
98. Presumably in the work referred to in chap. 39.1.—D.A.R.
99. The decree making provision for war after Philip's occupation of Elatea.—D.A.R., note abridged.
100. Presumably in the two books on "composition."—D.A.R.
101. Euripides, *Hercules Furens* 1245.
102. Or, "in accordance with its structure."—D.A.R.
103. From Euripides' lost *Antiope* (fragment 221, Nauck, op. cit.). The Greek contains the words *perix helixas* and *petran drun,* and these are the effects to which "Longinus' " comment refers.—D.A.R.
104. Of a play, presumably.—D.A.R.
105. Obscure: is this the same as the "chopped up" manner or a separate fault?—D.A.R.
106. Again an obscure section; partly because "Longinus" seems to intend it as an example of "brevity."—D.A.R.
107. *Histories* VII.188, 191; VIII.13.
108. Translation doubtful. Perhaps "and then make a change of arrangement and proceed. . . ."—D.A.R.
109. *Memorabilia* I.iv.6.
110. *Odyssey* XVII.322–33.
111. Translate as though the adjective *dikaios* means the same as it does just above; but perhaps [it should read] "justly exercised," i.e., humane.—D.A.R.
112. Or, "all our effort and all that we undertake."—D.A.R.
113. Euripides, *Electra* 379.

BIBLIOGRAPHY

GENERAL INTRODUCTION

Atkins, J. W. H. *Literary Criticism in Antiquity.* 2 vols. See under Plato bibliography.

D'Alton, J. F. *Roman Literary Theory and Criticism: A Study in Tendencies.* London: Longmans, Green, 1931.

Else, Gerald F. "Classical Poetics." *Encyclopedia of Poetry and Poetics,* ed. by Alex Preminger, Frank J. Warnke and O. B. Hardison, Jr. Princeton: Princeton University Press, 1965.

Gomme, A. W. *The Greek Attitude to Poetry and History.* Berkeley: University of California Press, 1954. An important study by one of the foremost scholars of the 20th century who combines eminence as an historian with literary sensitivity.

Grube, G. M. A. *The Greek and Roman Critics.* See under Plato bibliography.

Harriott, Rosemary. *Poetry and Criticism before Plato.* London: Methuen, 1969. A useful survey of the early history of Greek literary criticism.

Jaeger, Werner. *Paideia,* tr. by Gilbert Highet. 3 vols. Oxford: Oxford University Press, 1939–44. A profound and influential work that treats with great perception the major themes of Greek culture.

Kitto, H. D. F. *Poiesis.* Berkeley and Los Angeles: University of California Press, 1966.

Lanata, Giuliana, ed. and tr. *Poetica pre-Platonica: testimonianze e frammenti.* Florence: "La Nuova Italia," 1963. A useful collection of passages concerned with the nature of poetry from the works of earlier Greek authors.

Parsons, Edward A. *The Alexandrian Library.* New York: Elsevier, 1952.

Pfeiffer, Rudolf. *History of Classical Scholarship, from the Beginnings to the End of the Hellenistic Age.* New York: Oxford University Press, 1968.

Saintsbury, George. *A History of Criticism and Literary Taste in Europe.* 3 vols. Edinburgh and London: Blackwood, 1900–04. This work has been highly influential for decades and, with its limitations, is still useful today.

Sikes, E. E. *The Greek View of Poetry.* London: Methuen, 1931.

Snell, Bruno. *Poetry and Society.* Bloomington: Indiana University Press, 1961. A volume containing many stimulating ideas about Greek poetry by one of the most influential scholars of the 20th century.

Webster, T. B. L. "Greek Theories of Art and Literature down to 400 B.C." *Classical Quarterly,* XXXIII (1939), 166–79.

Wimsatt, W. K. and Cleanth Brooks. *Literary Criticism: A Short History.* Part 1. New York: Knopf, 1967. An important, thought-provoking book.

ARISTOPHANES

Cornford, Francis M. *The Origin of Attic Comedy,* ed. by Theodore H. Gaster. Garden City, N. Y.: Anchor Books, 1961. A recent reprinting of an early important and controversial study of the genesis of comedy in the Greek world.

Dover, K. J. *Aristophanic Comedy.* Berkeley: University of California Press, 1972. Best treatment to date.

———, ed. Aristophanes: *Clouds.* Oxford: Oxford University Press, 1968. This edition with introduction and commentary is now the standard Greek text of this important play.

Ehrenberg, Victor. *The People of Aristophanes.* 3rd rev. ed. New York: Schocken Books, 1962. A major study using the plays of Aristophanes as a source of information about ancient Athenian society.

Gomme, A. W. *More Essays in Greek History and Literature.* Oxford: Blackwell, 1962. This volume contains an essay entitled "Aristophanes and Politics" which is representative of the author's sensitive appreciation of the inter-relationships which exist between art and society.

Grube, G. M. A. *The Greek and Roman Critics.* See under Plato bibliography.

Jaeger, Werner. *Paideia: The Ideals of Greek Culture,* tr. by Gilbert Highet. 3 vols. Oxford: Oxford University Press, 1939–44. One of the most important and perceptive studies of Greek culture that we possess, this work contains a valuable section on "The Comic Poetry of Aristophanes."

Lever, Katherine. *The Art of Greek Comedy.* London: Methuen, 1956. A comparatively recent standard survey of the subject.

Littlefield, David J., comp. *Twentieth Century Interpretations of The Frogs.* Englewood Cliffs, N.J.: Prentice-Hall, 1968. A useful collection of scholarly views concerning this play.

Murray, Gilbert. *Aristophanes: A Study.* New York: Oxford University Press, 1933. A standard work by one of the most influential classicists of this century.

Norwood, Gilbert. *Greek Comedy.* London: Methuen, 1931. A now somewhat outdated but still useful survey of the subject.

Pickard-Cambridge, A. W. *Dithyramb, Tragedy, and Comedy.* 2nd edition, revised by T. B. L. Webster. Oxford: Clarendon Press, 1962. A standard and extremely important reference work.

Stanford, W. B., ed. Aristophanes: *The Frogs.* 2nd ed. London: Macmillan, 1963. This edition with introduction and commentary is now the standard Greek text of this important play.

Strauss, Leo. *Socrates and Aristophanes.* New York: Basic Books, 1966. A recent study by an imaginative and stimulating political philosopher.

Whitman, Cedric H. *Aristophanes and the Comic Hero.* Cambridge, Mass.: Harvard University Press, 1964. A major study of Aristophanes by a scholar widely known for his work on Homer and Sophocles.

P L A T O

Atkins, J. W. H. *Literary Criticism in Antiquity*. Cambridge: Cambridge University Press, 1934, vol. I, pp. 33–70. This standard history of classical literary criticism is still a useful and reliable guide although somewhat dated in its approach to the subject.

Brumbaugh, Robert S. "A New Interpretation of Plato's Republic." *Journal of Philosophy*, LXIV (1967), 661–70.

Carter, Robert E. "Plato and Inspiration," *Journal of the History of Philosophy*, V(1967), 111–21.

Cherniss, Harold. "Plato (1950–1957)." *Lustrum: Internationale Forschungsberichte aus dem Bereich des klassischen Altertums*, IV (1959), 5–316; V (1960), 321–648; see especially 520–54.

Crombie, Ian M. *An Examination of Plato's Doctrine*. 2 vols. London: Routledge and Kegan Paul, 1962.

Gallop, D. "Image and Reality in Plato's *Republic*," *Archiv für Geschichte der Philosophie*, XLVII (1965), 113–31.

Gilbert, Allen H. "Plato's *Ion*, Comic and Serious." *Studies in Honor of De W. T. Starnes*. Austin: University of Texas Press, 1967, pp. 259–84.

Gould, Thomas R. "Plato's Hostility to Art." *Arion*, III (1964), 70–91.

Greene, W. Chase. "Plato's View of Poetry." *Harvard Studies in Classical Philology*, XXIX (1918), 1–76.

Grube, G. M. A. *The Greek and Roman Critics*. Toronto: Toronto University Press, 1965, pp. 46–65. A scholarly history of classical literary criticism by one of the leading authorities in this field which usefully brings up to date our knowledge of the relevant scholarship.

Havelock, Eric A. *Preface to Plato*. Cambridge, Mass.: Harvard University Press, 1963.

Henning, Roslyn B. "A Performing Musician Looks at the *Ion*." *Classical Journal*, LIX (1964), 241–47.

Levinson, Ronald B. "Plato's *Phaedrus* and the New Criticism," *Archiv für die Geschichte der Philosophie*, XLVI (1964), 293–309.

Lodge, Rupert C. *Plato's Theory of Art*. London: Routledge and Kegan Paul, 1953. A scholarly and thorough study of Plato's treatment of art throughout the dialogues.

McKeon, Richard. "Literary Criticism and the Concept of Imitation in Antiquity." *Critics and Criticism: Ancient and Modern*, ed. R. S. Crane. Chicago: University of Chicago Press, 1952, pp. 147–75.

Maguire, Joseph P. "Beauty and the Fine Arts in Plato: Some *Aporiai*." *Harvard Studies in Classical Philology*, LXX (1965), 171–93.

———. "The Differentiation of Art in Plato's Aesthetics." *Harvard Studies in Classical Philology*, LXVIII (1964), 389–410.

Morrow, Gen R. *Plato's Cretan City: A Historical Interpretation of the Laws*. Princeton: Princeton University Press, 1960. This major scholarly work is the definitive study of Plato's *Laws*.

Murphy, Neville R. *The Interpretation of Plato's Republic*. Oxford: Oxford University Press, 1951. A standard, scholarly study of the *Republic*.

Philip, J. A. "*Mimesis* in the *Sophistes* of Plato," *Transactions of the American Philological Association*, XCII (1961), 453–68.

Ringbom, Sixten. "Plato on Images," *Theoria*, XXXI (1965), 86–109.

Steward, Douglas J. "Man and Myth in Plato's Universe." *Bucknell Review*, XIII, (1965), 72–90.

Tate, J. " 'Imitation' in Plato's *Republic*." *Classical Quarterly*, XXII (1928), 16–24.

———. "Plato and 'Imitation.' " *Classical Quarterly*, XXVI (1932), 161–69.

Verdenius, W. J. *Mimesis: Plato's Doctrine of Artistic Imitation and Its Meaning to Us*. Leiden: Brill, 1949. An important and perceptive study which emphasizes the positive values which Plato attributes to artistic *mimesis*.

Warren, John G. *Greek Aesthetic Theory: A Study of Callistic and Aesthetic Concepts in the Works of Plato and Aristotle*. New York: Barnes and Noble, 1962. This study of the important concepts of classical aesthetics is specifically directed at the student of modern literature.

ARISTOTLE

1. *Bibliographies of Studies on Aristotle's* Poetics.

Cooper, Lane, and Alfred Gudeman. *A Bibliography of the Poetics of Aristotle*. New Haven, Conn.: Yale University Press, 1928.

Else, Gerald F. "A Survey of Work on Aristotle's *Poetics*, 1940–1952." *Classical Weekly* (now *Classical World*), XLVIII (1955), 73–82.

Herrick, Marvin T. "A Supplement to Cooper and Gudeman's Bibliography of the *Poetics* of Aristotle." *American Journal of Philology*, LII (1931), 168–74.

2. *Texts, Translations, and Commentaries on the* Poetics.

Butcher, S. H. *Aristotle's Theory of Poetry and Fine Art*. New York: Dover Publications, 1951. Butcher offers a helpful translation and a fine series of essays on selected topics in the *Poetics* that manifest excellent literary judgment and perceptive insight into Aristotle's theory of literature. The Greek text which he prints is now out of date.

Bywater, Ingram. *Aristotle on the Art of Poetry*. London and New York: Oxford University Press, 1909. Bywater's Greek text remains authoritative for the study of the *Poetics* although it has recently been improved upon in some details. His commentary and translation, directed mainly at the illumination of philological rather than literary problems, are a model of their type and offer immense assistance to the student of this work.

Cooper, Lane. *Aristotle on the Art of Poetry*. Ithaca, N.Y.: Cornell University Press, 1947. Cooper extensively amplifies and therefore extensively interprets the actual text of the *Poetics* for his readers.

Else, Gerald F. Aristotle: *Poetics*. Ann Arbor: University of Michigan Press, 1967. A translation revised from the author's 1957 edition of the *Poetics* for greater fluency and easier use by those not in command of the Greek text. The translation still depends in various places on Else's own text and interpretation of the work.

––––––. *Aristotle's Poetics: The Argument.* Cambridge, Mass.: Harvard University Press, 1957. A stimulating and controversial edition which makes many new suggestions about the text and interpretation of the *Poetics.* Even where Else's suggestions are not accepted they offer an excellent point of departure for rethinking important concepts in the *Poetics.*

Fergusson, Francis, ed. *Aristotle's Poetics.* New York: Hill and Wang, 1961. The editor's introduction is perceptive and provides a number of references to classical and modern literature in illustration of Aristotle's meaning. Butcher's translation is presented in this text but without his commentaries.

Gilbert, Allan H., tr. Aristotle's *Poetics,* in *Literary Criticism: Plato to Dryden,* New York: American Book Co., 1940, pp. 63–124. A sound translation making use of a number of important 20th century editions of the *Poetics* and especially those of Gudeman and Rostagni.

Golden, Leon and Hardison, O. B. *Aristotle's Poetics: A Translation and Commentary for Students of Literature.* Englewood Cliffs, N.J.: Prentice-Hall, 1968. The translation aspires to be both literal and idiomatic and the commentary provides a chapter-by-chapter discussion of all of the major concepts in the *Poetics.* New interpretations of important ideas are presented together with a review of standard scholarly opinions.

Grube, G. M. A. *Aristotle on Poetry and Style.* New York: Library of Liberal Arts, 1958. A sound and literal translation together with a good general introduction to the *Poetics.* Relevant sections of Aristotle's *Rhetoric* are included in this edition.

Gudeman, Alfred. *Aristoteles' PERI POIETIKES.* Berlin and Leipzig, 1934. Greek text, notes and extensive commentary making significant use of the Arabic tradition of the *Poetics.*

Hardy, J. Aristote: *Poétique* (Collection des Universités de France publiée sous le patronage de l'Association Guillaume Budé). Paris, 1952. A scholarly Greek text and very useful French translation of facing pages. This edition with its perceptive notes is a major aid to the understanding and interpretation of the *Poetics.*

Kassel, Rudolf. *Aristotelis de Arte Poetica Liber* (Oxford Classical Texts). Oxford: Oxford University Press, 1965. This is an updating of Bywater's original Oxford text which takes into consideration all of the sources for Aristotle's original text. An informative preface describes the state of our knowledge of the text of the *Poetics* at the present time.

Lucas, D. W. Aristotle: *Poetics.* Oxford: Clarendon Press, 1968. Kassel's Oxford text is reproduced with valuable and extensive notes and appendices of varying quality on the major ideas presented in the *Poetics.*

Potts, L. J. *Aristotle on the Art of Fiction.* Cambridge: Cambridge University Press, 1959 (2nd print. rev.). A not always idiomatic translation that is challenging for some of the interpretations it puts upon the Greek. Brief but useful introduction and notes accompany the translation.

Rostagni, Augusto. *Aristotele Poetica.* Turin: Chiantore, 1945. One of the most distinguished of modern editions of the *Poetics.* An extensive and scholarly introduction and detailed commentary accompany the Greek text.

Telford, K. *Aristotle's Poetics: Translation and Analysis.* Chicago: Regnery, 1965. A literal translation together with a chapter-by-chapter commentary that sets the argument of the *Poetics* against the background of Aristotle's general philosophical mood.

Valgimigli, E., ed. Aristotle: *De Arte Poetica. Guillelmo de Moerbeke, Interprete.* Revised with prefaces and indices added by A. Franceschini and L. Minio-Paluello. Bruges: Brouwer, 1953. A major scholarly edition which presents the text of William of Moerbeke's important and extremely literal Latin translation of the *Poetics.*

3. *Interpretative Studies of Major Themes in the* Poetics.

Braam, P. van. "Aristotle's Use of *Hamartia.*" *Classical Quarterly,* VI (1912), 266–72.

Dale, A. M. "Ethos and Dianoia: Character and Thought in Aristotle's *Poetics.*" *AUMLA: Journal of the Australasian Universities Language and Literature Association,* XI (1959), 3–16.

Dawe, R. D. "Some Reflections on *Ate* and *Hamartia.*" *Harvard Studies in Classical Philology,* LXXII (1967), 89–123.

Else, Gerald F. " 'Imitation' in the Fifth Century." *Classical Philology,* LIII (1958), 73–90.

Golden, Leon. "Catharsis." *Transactions of the American Philological Association,* XCIII (1962), 51–60.

———. "Is Tragedy the 'Imitation of a Serious Action'?" *Greek, Roman and Byzantine Studies,* VI (1965), 283–89.

———. "*Mimesis* and *Katharsis.*" *Classical Philology,* LXIV (1969), 145–53.

Goldstein, Harvey D. "Mimesis and Catharsis Reexamined." *Journal of Aesthetics and Art Criticism,* XXIV (1966), 567–77.

Gomperz, Theodor. *Zu Aristoteles' Poetik,* II, III. Vienna, 1896.

———. "Ein Beitrag zur Kritik und Erklärung der Kapitel 1–6." *Sitzungsberichte der Kaiserlichen Akademie der Wissenschaften in Wien.* Philosophisch-Historische Classe, I–VI (1888), 543–82.

Gresseth, Gerald K. "The System of Aristotle's *Poetics.*" *Transactions of the American Philological Association,* LXXXIX (1958), 312–35.

Harsh, Philip, W. "Hamartia Again." *Transactions of the American Philological Association,* LXXVI (1945), 47–58.

House, Humphry. *Aristotle's Poetics: A Course of Eight Lectures,* rev. by C. Hardie. London: R. Hart Davis, 1956.

Jones, John. *On Aristotle and Greek Tragedy.* London: Oxford University Press 1962.

Kerrane, Kevin. "Aristotle's *Poetics* in Modern Literary Criticism" (unpublished doctoral dissertation, University of North Carolina, 1968).

Lucas, D. W. "Pity, Terror, and *Peripeteia.*" *Classical Quarterly,* XII (1962), 52–60.

McKeon, Richard. "Literary Criticism and the Concept of Imitation in Antiquity." *Critics and Criticism: Ancient and Modern,* ed. R. S. Crane. Chicago: University of Chicago Press, 1952, pp. 147–75.

Montmollin, Daniel de. *La Poétique d' Aristote: Texte primitif et additions ultérieures.* Neuchâtel: Messeiller, 1951.

———. "Le Sens du terme *philanthropon* dans *La Poétique* d'Aristote." *Phoenix,* XIX (1965), 15–23.

Murray, Gilbert. "An Essay in the Theory of Poetry." *Yale Review,* X (1921), 482–99.

Olson, Elder, ed. *Aristotle's Poetics and English Literature: A Collection of Critical Essays.* Chicago: University of Chicago Press, 1965.

Ostwald, Martin. "Aristotle on *Hamartia* and Sophocles' *Oedipus Tyrannus.*" *Festschrift Ernst Kapp*. Hamburg, 1958, pp. 93–108.

Solmsen, Friedrich. "The Origins and Methods of Aristotle's *Poetics.*" *Classical Quarterly,* XXIX (1935), 192–201.

Stanford, W. B. "On a Recent Interpretation of the Tragic Catharsis." *Hermathena,* LXXXV (1955), 52–56.

Vahlen, Johannes. *Beiträge zu Aristoteles' Poetik*. Leipzig, Berlin, 1914.

DEMETRIUS

Atkins, J. W. H. *Literary Criticism in Antiquity,* vol. II, pp. 175–209. See under Plato bibliography.

Grube, G. M. A. *A Greek Critic: Demetrius on Style*. Toronto: University of Toronto Press, 1961. An important, recent edition of Demetrius which takes some controversial positions about this critic.

———. "The Date of Demetrius on Style." *Phoenix* (1964), 294–302.

———. *The Greek and Roman Critics,* pp. 110–21. See under Plato bibliography.

Roberts, W. Rhys, ed. *Demetrius on Style*. Cambridge: Cambridge University Press, 1902. A standard, authoritative edition of Demetrius.

Schenkeveld, Dirk M. *Studies in Demetrius On Style*. Amsterdam: Hakkert, 1964.

HORACE

Atkins, J. W. H. *Literary Criticism in Antiquity,* vol. II, pp. 47–103. See under Plato bibliography.

Brink, Charles O. *Horace on Poetry*. Cambridge: Cambridge University Press, 1963 (vol. I, Prolegomena, 1963; vol. II, Commentary, 1971.) A major work of scholarship on Horace's literary theories by one of the leading scholars in this field.

D'Alton, J. F. *Roman Literary Theory and Criticism: A Study in Tendencies*. London: Longmans, Green, 1931.

Dilke, O. A. W. "When Was the *Ars Poetica* Written?" *Bulletin of the Institute of Classical Studies,* University of London, V (1958), 49–57.

Duckworth, George. "Horace's Hexameters and the Date of the *Ars Poetica.*" *Transactions of the American Philological Association,* XCVI (1965), 73–95.

Elmore, Jefferson. "A New Dating of Horace's *De Arte Poetica.*" *Classical Philology,* XXX (1935), 1–9.

Fairclough, H. Rushton. "Horace's View of Relations Between Satire and Comedy." *American Journal of Philology,* XXXIV (1913), 183–93.

Fiske, George C. "Lucilius, the *Ars Poetica* of Horace, and Persius." *Harvard Studies in Classical Philology,* XXIV (1913), 1–36.

———. *Lucilius and Horace, a Study in the Classical Theory of Imitation*. (University of Wisconsin Studies in Language and Literature, VII. Madison, 1920.)

———. and Grant, Mary A. "Cicero's *Orator* and Horace's *Ars Poetica.*" *Harvard Studies in Classical Philology,* XXXV (1924), 1–74.

Fraenkel, Eduard. *Horace.* Oxford: Oxford University Press, 1957. A very important study of the poet's work by one of the most prominent and influential 20th-century scholars.

Frank, Tenney. "Horace on Contemporary Poetry." *Classical Journal,* XIII (1917–18), 550–64.

———. "Horace's Definition of Poetry." *Classical Journal,* XXXI (1935–36), 167–74.

Getty, Robert J. "Recent Work on Horace." *Classical World,* LII (1959), 167–88, 246–47.

Greenberg, Nathan A. "The Use of *Poiema* and *Poiesis.*" *Harvard Studies in Classical Philology,* LXV (1961), 263–89.

Grube, G. M. A. *The Greek and Roman Critics,* pp. 231–55. See under Plato bibliography.

Hack, Roy K. "The Doctrine of Literary Forms." *Harvard Studies in Classical Philology,* XXVII (1916), 1–65.

Haight, Elizabeth H. "Horace on Art: *ut pictura poiesis.*" *Classical Journal,* XLVII (1952), 157–62.

Hendrickson, George L. "Satura—the Genesis of a Literary Form." *Classical Philology,* VI (1911), 129–43.

Herrick, Marvin T. *The Fusion of Horatian and Aristotelian Literary Criticism, 1531–1555.* (University of Illinois Studies in Language and Literature, XXXII, no. 1. Urbana, 1946).

La Drière, Craig. "Horace and the Theory of Imitation." *American Journal of Philology* LX (1939), 288–300.

Rudd, Niall. "The Poet's Defense." *Classical Quarterly,* XLIX (1955), 142–56.

Smith, W. K. "The Date of the *Ars Poetica.*" *Classical Philology,* XXXI (1936), 163–66.

Solmsen, Friedrich. "Propertius and Horace." *Classical Philology,* XLIII (1948), 105–09.

DIONYSIUS OF HALICARNASSUS

Atkins, J. W. H. *Literary Criticism in Antiquity,* vol. II, pp. 104–36. See under Plato bibliography.

Bonner, S. F. *The Literary Treatises of Dionysius of Halicarnassus.* Cambridge: Cambridge University Press, 1939.

Grube, G. M. A. "Dionysius of Halicarnassus on Thucydides." *Phoenix,* IV (1950), 95–110.

———. *The Greek and Roman Critics,* pp. 207–30. See under Plato bibliography.

———. "Thrasymachus, Theophrastus and Dionysius of Halicarnassus." *American Journal of Philology,* LXXIII (1952), 251–67.

Roberts, W. Rhys, ed. Dionysius of Halicarnassus: *On Literary Composition.* London: Macmillan, 1910. This is the standard scholarly edition of Dionysius' work.

Wilkinson, L. P. *Golden Latin Artistry.* Cambridge: Cambridge University Press, 1962, *passim.*

QUINTILIAN

Atkins, J. W. H. *Literary Criticism in Antiquity,* vol. II, pp. 254–98. See under Plato bibliography.

Carver, P. L. "Quintilian's Approach to Literature." *University of Toronto Quarterly,* VII (1937), 77–94.

Clark, Donald L. *Rhetoric in Greco-Roman Education.* New York: Columbia University Press, 1957.

Cousin, Jean. *Etudes sur Quintilien.* 2 vols. Paris: Boivin, 1936 and "Quintilien 1935–1959." *Lustrum,* VII (1962), 289–331.

Grube, G. M. A. *The Greek and Roman Critics,* pp. 284–307. See under Plato bibliography.

Gwynn, Aubrey. *Roman Education from Cicero to Quintilian.* Oxford: Oxford University Press, 1926.

Kennedy, George A. "An Estimate of Quintilian." *American Journal of Philology,* LXXXIII (1962), 130–46, and *Quintilian.* New York: Twayne, 1969.

Laing, Gordon J. "Quintilian, the Schoolmaster." *Classical Journal* XV (1920), 513–34.

Leddy, J. F. "Tradition and Change in Quintilian." *Phoenix,* VII (1953), 47–56.

Marrou, H. I. *A History of Education in Antiquity,* tr. by George Lamb. New York: Sheed and Ward, 1956.

Odgers, Merle M. "Quintilian's Use of Earlier Literature." *Classical Philology,* XXVIII (1933), 182–88.

''LONGINUS''

Atkins, J. W. H. *Literary Criticism in Antiquity,* vol. II, pp. 210–53. See under Plato bibliography.

Boyd, M. J. "Longinus, the Philological Discourses and the Essay on the Sublime." *Classical Quarterly,* n.s. VII (1957), 39ff.

Brody, Jules. *Longinus and Boileau.* Geneva: Droz, 1958.

Grube, G. M. A. *The Greek and Roman Critics,* pp. 340–53. See under Plato bibliography.

———. "Notes on the *peri hypsous.*" *American Journal of Philology,* LXXIII (1952), 251–67.

Henn, T. R. *Longinus and English Criticism.* Cambridge: Cambridge University Press, 1934. A useful study of the influence of "Longinus" on English literary criticism which illustrates "Longinus'" major concepts with passages taken from English literature.

Monk, Samuel H. *The Sublime: A Study of Critical Theories in Eighteenth-Century England.* New York: Modern Language Association of America, 1935.

Olson, Elder. "The Argument of Longinus' *On the Sublime.*" *Critics and Criticism: Ancient and Modern,* ed. R. S. Crane. Chicago: University of Chicago Press, pp. 232–59.

Roberts, W. Rhys. "Longinus on the Sublime." *Philological Quarterly,* VII (1928), 209ff.

Russell, Donald A. *"Longinus" On the Sublime.* Oxford: Oxford University Press, 1964. A recent scholarly edition of the Greek text with useful introduction and notes.

Segal, Charles P. "*Hypsos* and the Problem of Cultural Decline in the *De sublimate.*" *Harvard Studies in Classical Philology,* LXIV (1959), 121ff.

Swanson, Roy Arthur. "'Longinus': Noesis and Pathos." *Classical Bulletin,* XLVI (1969), 1–5.

Tate, Allen. "Longinus and the 'New Criticism'." *Collected Essays.* Denver: Swallow Press, 1959.

Trowbridge, Hoyt. " 'Leda and the Swan': A Longinian Analysis." *Modern Philology,* LI (1953), 118–29; cf. rebuttal by Leo Spitzer in *Modern Philology,* LI (1953), 271–76.

P L O T I N U S

Aubin, P. "L'Image dans l'oeuvre de Plotin." *Recherches de Science Religieuse,* XLI (1953), 348–79.

Bréhier, Emile. *The Philosophy of Plotinus,* tr. by Joseph Thomas. Chicago: University of Chicago Press, 1958. This authoritative study of the thought of Plotinus is a standard reference work on the subject.

Grube, G. M. A. *The Greek and Roman Critics,* pp. 354–55. See under Plato bibliography.

Inge, W. R. *The Philosophy of Plotinus.* 3rd ed. 2 vols. London and New York: Longmans, Green, 1929. This work, containing some controversial judgments, makes an important contribution to the interpretation of Plotinus.

Keyser, Eugénie de. *La Signification de l'art dans les Ennéades de Plotin.* Louvain: Bibliothèque de l'Université, 1955.

Merlan, Philip. *From Platonism to Neoplatonism,* 2nd ed. The Hague: Nijhoff, 1963.

Rich, A. N. M. "Plotinus and the Theory of Artistic Imitation." *Mnemosyne,* XIII (1960), 233–39.

Rist, John M. *Plotinus: The Road to Reality.* Cambridge: Cambridge University Press, 1967. An important study, on an advanced level, of specialized problems in the philosophy of Plotinus.

Trouillard, Jean. *La Purification plotinienne.* Paris: Universitaires de France, 1955.

Whittaker, Thomas. *The Neo-Platonists: A Study in the History of Hellenism.* 2nd ed. Cambridge: Cambridge University Press, 1918.

GLOSSARY AND INDEX
OF PROPER NAMES

HEGEMON OF THASOS (a Greek writer of
parodies, mentioned by Aristotle in the
Poetics. His dates are uncertain), 109

HEGESIAS OF MAGNESIA (3rd-century B.C.
rhetorician, representative of the florid and
emotional style known as Asianism. He is
untrustworthy as a historiographer), 194

HELEN (in classical mythology, daughter of Zeus
and Leda, qq.v. In Homer, she is the
beautiful wife of Menelaus, and her
abduction by Paris starts the Trojan war),
233

HELICON (mountain range in Boeotia, about 50
miles N.W. of Athens, the home of the
Muses, q.v.), 165

HEPHAESTUS (in Greek mythology, the god of
fire and metallurgy; lame and plain, he was
married to the beauteous Aphrodite, q.v.),
53

HERA (in Greek mythology, the wife of Zeus
and protector of women and marriage), 52

HERCULES (or Heracles, mythological hero
celebrated for his courage and superhuman
strength), 116, 194, 221

HERMES (in Greek mythology, the messenger of
the gods; also, the guide of souls), 194

HERODOTUS (490/80–430/25 B.C., Greek
historian. His *History of the Persian Wars* is
a major historical and literary
achievement), 116, 142, 143, 146, 152,
172, 176, 195, 203, 210, 211, 213, 214,
219–20, 222–23

HESIOD (8th century B.C., early Greek didactic
poet), 14, 17, 23, 29, 39, 40, 70, 81, 197,
203, 237 fn. 28, 248 fn. 38

HOMER (8th century B.C.? In antiquity the
authorship of the *Iliad* and the *Odyssey* was
attributed to him. Nothing certain is
known of his life and career), 14, 17,
23–24, 29, 35, 176, 241 fn. 48; Demetrius
on, 144–45, 147–48, 151–52; Horace on,
155, 156, 160, 167; in Aristotle's *Poetics*,
108–11, 116, 123, 127, 132–34; in Plato's
Ion, 38–46, 48; in Plato's *Republic*, Book
III, 49–53, 55, 58, Book X, 65, 68–70,
75–77, 81, 237 fn. 1; "Longinus" on,
188–90, 196, 201, 203–204, 208, 211,

216–18, 224; Quintilian on, 178–81

HORACE (Quintus Horatius Flaccus, 65–8 B.C.,
Latin poet and critic), 106, 155–58, 178;
Ars Poetica, 105, 107, 155–58, 190

HYPERIDES (389–332 B.C., Athenian orator with
an occasional Demosthenes-like fervor),
205, 217

ICARIUS (in Homer's *Odyssey*, the father of
Penelope, the wife of Odysseus), 137, 241
fn. 48

IDA (mountain in Phrygia [central and
northwestern Asia Minor], where,
according to tradition, the shepherd Paris
chose Aphrodite over the other two
goddesses Hera and Athena—all of whom
claimed the golden apple inscribed "to the
Fairest"), 54, 148

INO (in Greek mythology, a daughter of
Cadmus, q.v., and Harmonia. When she
took care of the infant Dionysus, q.v., the
son of Zeus and Semele, Hera, Zeus' wife,
afflicted her with madness), 161

Io (mythological priestess of Argos with whom
Zeus fell in love. Afraid of being found out
by his wife Hera, he changed Io into a
heifer. Hera asked for the heifer and set the
monster Argos to watch her. When
Hermes, q.v., killed Argos, Hera tormented
Io with a gadfly, which finally drove her to
Egypt. There Zeus transformed her back
into a woman), 161

ION OF CHIOS (about 490–before 421 B.C., Greek
tragic, lyric, and elegaic poet), 24, 38–48,
217

IONIA (ancient Greek district on the western
coast of Asia Minor), 210

IPHIGENIA (in classical mythology, Agamemnon's
daughter who is sacrificed by her father for
the benefit of the Greek army. Her story is
treated by both Aeschylus and Euripides),
119, 124

ISOCRATES (436–338 B.C., important Athenian
orator and creator of a new prose style),
146, 194, 209, 219

IXION (in classical mythology, king of the
Lapiths, in Thessaly, who murdered one of

GENERAL INDEX

legislators, Plato on, 36, 91–92, 95. *See also* laws

letter, 128, 130, 227

lexis, 98

life, 20, 218; Aristotle on, 98, 104, 110, 114, 116, 130; best, 30, 92–93, 96

literature, 14–20, 22, 23, 25, 170; Christian, 103; criticism of, "Longinus" and, 188, 190, 191, 193, 194, 195, 196, 197–201, 202–204, 205, 206–207, 208, 210, 211, 212–13, 214–18, 219, 221, 223; decline of, "Longinus" on, 224–25; Greek, 14–20, 178–79, 180, 181, 184, 185; Latin 178–79, 182, 184, 185; oratorical training, and, 178–80, 184, 185. *See also* comedy, criticism, critics, drama, poetry, style, tragedy

love, 30, 231; Plato on, 25–30

lying. *See* falsehood

lyric, 41, 89, 107, *See also* dithyramb, ode, paean

lysis. See resolution (lysis)

madness, poetic. *See furor poeticus*, inspiration

magnitude, Aristotle on, 98, 106, 111, 113, 115, 116, 126, 133, 139; beauty, and, 232, 233

maker, 67, 70, 71, 100, 135. *See also* artist(s), poet(s)

man, 162, 190, 192, 218; Aristotle on, 110, 111, 114, 122; "common," as tragic hero, 104–105; Plato on, 26, 27, 31, 33, 35, 39, 91, 92, 93

mask, 112, 164

matter, Plotinus on, 227, 228, 229, 230, 231, 232, 233

meaning, 137. *See also* allegory

melodrama, 104

melody, Aristotle on, 97, 98, 101, 113, 115; as *katharsis*, 101, Dionysius of Halicarnassus on, 171, 172, 173, 174, 175, 176; Plato on, 36–37, 60, 61, 62, 91–92; poetry, and, 36–37; tragedy, and, 97, 101

memory, 28, 32–33, 34, 35, 93, 115, 124

metabole, 249 fn. 62

metaphor(s), Aristotle on, 129, 130, 131, 132, 134, 135, 136, 137; Demetrius on, 141, 148–49, 152, 153, 243 fn. 30, 32, 37;

Dionysius of Halicarnassus on, 171, 175; "Longinus" on, 196, 214–16

meter, 221, 242 fn. 4; anapaestic, 237 fn. 42; Aristotle on, 108, 109; 111, 112, 113, 117, 133–34, 138; dactylic, 112, 237 fn. 4, 42, 242, fn. 4; dactylic hexameter, 242, fn. 4; Demetrius on, 141, 143, 153; heroic, 62, 242 fn. 4, 244 fn. 57; Horace on, 156, 160, 164; iambic, 42, 62, 111, 112, 117, 131, 132, 134, 143, 160, 164, 237 fn. 42; paeon, 140, 142, 143, 236 fn. 6, 237 fn. 42, 242 fn. 4; Plato on, 26, 37, 41, 62, 70, 93; pyrrhic, 238 fn. 9; trimeter, 93, 108, 164; trochaic, 62, 134, 237 fn. 42. *See also* rhythm

mimes, 59, 108

mimesis, 157; Plato and Aristotle contrasted, 100; poets, and, 56; Quintilian on, 179; sublime, and, 189. *See also* imitation

mind (*nous*), Aristotle on, 103, 134; Plato on, 31, 62, 72

minstrels, 90

misfortune, 104, 105, 120

morality, 54, 62, 98, 102, 103, 104–105, 114, 122, 188, 229, 231; art, and, 22, 23, 102, 103; orator, and, 178, 180. *See also hamartia*

motions, 94, 95, 134, 138. *See also* dance

music, 138; as *katharsis*, 101–102; attacked by Plato, 22, 89, 90, 91; Dionysius of Halicarnassus on, 171, 174; in education, 23, 63, 64, 91; Plato on, 22, 23, 26, 37, 38, 41, 59, 60, 63, 64, 89, 90, 91, 95; Plotinus on, 227, 230, 232; poetry, and, 26, 41; soul, and, 63; speech, and, 171, 173, 174; words, and, 60

mysticism, 24, 226

mythology, 136, Plato on, 24, 55, 56. *See also* allegory

mythos. See plot(s) (*mythos*)

narration, 156, 211, 212; Aristotle on, 112, 116, 117, 132, 133, 134; Plato on, 49, 54, 55–56, 58, 59

nature, Aristotle on, 110, 111, 112, 113, 134; art, and, 34–35; education, and, 63; human, 27, 57, 59; Plato on, 27, 34–35, 57, 59, 63; Plotinus on, 232, 233, versus